W9-BAJ-753

The Four-Blocks™
Literacy Model

Guided Reading
The Four-Blocks™ Way
(With Building Blocks and Big Blocks Variations)

by
Patricia M. Cunningham
Dorothy P. Hall
and
James W. Cunningham

Emerg. 770-623-4966 1-3 SDR

Editors	Cover Artists
Tracy Soles	Mike Duggins
Joey Bland	Jeff Thrower

Cover photos taken at Westchester Academy in High Point, North Carolina

ISBN 0-88724-579-X

TABLE OF CONTENTS

PART ONE

GUIDED READING
THE FOUR-BLOCKS™ WAY

Chapter 1   **A Peek into Classrooms Doing Guided Reading the Four-Blocks™ Way**

In this first chapter, take an imaginary visit with Claire Leider to Fourblox Elementary. This chapter will give you a vision of the many ways you can tailor Guided Reading to the needs of your particular class, grade, and teaching style.

Chapter 2   **The Four-Blocks™ Framework**

In the second chapter, an overview of the Guided Reading Block is provided with instructions on how you can use this block—along with the Self-Selected Reading Block, the Writing Block, and the Working with Words Block—to accomplish all the goals of a balanced reading program.

Chapter 3   **Materials for Guided Reading**

Chapter 4   **Comprehension Skills and Strategies**

The third and fourth chapters describe the variety of materials you might include in your Guided Reading program, and the comprehension skills and strategies students need to use to "think their way through" those materials.

CHAPTER 1

A PEEK INTO CLASSROOMS DOING GUIDED READING THE FOUR-BLOCKS™ WAY

Guided Reading in Four-Blocks classrooms is difficult to characterize because it looks very different from grade to grade, class to class, school to school, and day to day. The purpose of this book is to share this variety with you and to help you see why teachers make the decisions they do about which materials to use, in which formats children will read, and which comprehension strategies to stress with particular selections and groups of children. This block is rich with possibilities, as proven by the clever teachers in hundreds of classrooms who put their creativity to work to make the Guided Reading Block a successful and enjoyable experience for students and teachers.

This book begins with an imaginary visit to Fourblox Elementary in the town of Fourblox, USA. Claire Leider is a reading resource teacher from another school, Tryon Elementary, that has just begun to implement the Four-Blocks™ Model. Claire is visiting her sister, Melodie, the music teacher at Fourblox. Claire has been helping the teachers at Tryon to implement the Four-Blocks and, like many schools in the first year of implementation, the teachers are having the most trouble with the Guided Reading Block. When Claire told Melodie that the Four-Blocks program was going well at Tryon, except for Guided Reading, Melodie arranged for Claire to spend a Wednesday during Tryon's spring break visiting in Fourblox classrooms during the Guided Reading Block. "I don't know any of the details, but all our teachers seem happy with however they are doing it. And, they love to show off their success," Melodie explained. We join Melodie and Claire as they arrive at Fourblox Elementary at 7:45 a.m. on a chilly spring Wednesday morning.

"Have a terrific day," said Melodie as she handed Claire a school map and a schedule. "I'll catch up with you at lunch." Claire smiled and waved at Melodie as she headed down the hall to find the first-grade classroom that was first on her schedule. She had been surprised to see that different classrooms did Guided Reading at different times—including in the afternoon. Melodie had assured Claire that this was the normal schedule and that the teachers must have some good reasons for scheduling the way they did. At Claire's school, scheduling was a big problem because all the teachers seemed to think that all of the language arts instruction needed to happen before lunch. Claire hoped she could find some convincing reasons for opening up the schedules at her school.

Here is the schedule that Melodie gave Claire to follow:

Time	Teacher	Grade Level	Room No.
8:20–9:00	Happy Kamper	Grade 1	Room 33
9:00- 9:30	Bea Ginning	Kindergarten	Room 22
9:30-10:00	Gay Smiley	Grade 1	Room 32
10:00-10:30	Deb Webb	Grade 2	Room 36
10:30-11:00	Laura Reading	Grade 2	Room 38
11:00-11:45	Faith Goode	Grade 4	Room 3
11:45-12:15	Lunch—Meet you in the cafeteria!		
12:15-12:45	Diane Duright	Grade 3	Room 17
12:45-1:30	Denise Lerner	Grade 3	Room 15
1:30-2:15	Will Teachum	Grade 5	Room 11

8:20–9:00   Happy Kamper   Grade 1   Room 33

Claire arrived early for her first observation. They had not yet begun their Guided Reading Block. The children were all busy doing things in the various centers around the room. Miss Kamper was sitting at a small table with five children reading a very easy version of *The Gingerbread Man* by Eric A. Kimmel*. After talking about the pictures on each page, Miss Kamper said, "Now, read the page to find out what is happening to our gingerbread man. Read it to yourself first, and then I will choose someone to read it aloud."

The children read the page to themselves, pointing to each word and whispering it as first-graders will. Three of the children read more slowly than the others and got stumped on a few words which they skipped over and continued reading. Two of the children read quite fluently. When the children had finished reading to themselves, Miss Kamper called on Paul to read the page aloud. She reminded everyone that one of the purposes of this group was for them to learn how to be a word coach, and said that she hoped Paul would have at least one word with which he needed coaching. Paul read the page and did indeed come to a word with which he needed help. Miss Kamper coached Paul to figure out the word, and the whole group cheered! Miss Kamper led the group in a quick retelling of what they had read, and then had the students read the page chorally before going on to the next page.

*Please refer to pages 220-222 for publication information on all children's books cited.

At 8:15, the timer on Miss Kamper's table rang. Miss Kamper pushed the "play" button on a small tape recorder, and a bouncy song blared forth. The children immediately began to clean up their centers while singing along with the tape. Miss Kamper had the children in the group with her put bookmarks in their books to show where they would start the next day. The students noticed that they had only three more pages to read in *The Gingerbread Man*. One child observed that they would probably finish it tomorrow, and then read the whole book again on Friday. Another child asked Miss Kamper what the new book would be on Monday, and if he could be in her "Reading for Fun" club again for the next book.

Miss Kamper smiled and told him that the next book was a surprise, but that it was an unusually fun book and she would consider his request to be included again. She reminded him that everyone wanted to be in the "Reading for Fun" club, and that he couldn't be there for every book! "Are these *Gingerbread Man* books going in the reading crates on Monday?" a third child asked. Miss Kamper assured her that she would put one copy of the book in each of the crates. "Good," said the student, "because I am going to read it all by myself!"

At 8:20, the music ended and the children sat down on the rug facing the board. Miss Kamper complimented them on how well they had come in that morning, as well as on how nicely they had worked in and cleaned up the centers. One child commented that cleaning up was a lot more fun now that they had the music to sing and dance to while they did it, and that it was fun to try to see if they could get their centers clean before the music stopped. Miss Kamper said, "Yes, the idea of using music for center clean-up is just another one of those great ideas I got from my 'virtual' friends on my favorite fourblocks mailring." One student asked, "Do you have any more good ideas from your Web friends?" "Not yet," said Miss Kamper, "but I'm sure I will get another one soon, and we will try it out!"

"Now," said Miss Kamper, "we need to start our Guided Reading for today because we have a fun activity to finish up our reading of *Are You My Mother?* by P. D. Eastman. On Monday, remember, after we looked at all the pictures and made some predictions of what would happen in the story, we read it in partners to see which predictions actually happened. Then, yesterday, you read it again in your playschool groups to answer the Beach Ball questions, and we did the Beach Ball. Today, we are going to act it out!" The children cheered and clapped as Miss Kamper pulled out the laminated, yarned character cards that she used to designate characters when they acted out stories—a very popular activity with all the children.

Miss Kamper directed the students to chorally read each page of the story with her. As they finished reading each page, she asked if this page had any new characters. As the children told her the name of each character, she wrote the name with a marker on one of the character cards. When the story had been reread, 11 character cards were lined up along the markerboard ledge.

"Now," said Miss Kamper, "we have 11 characters and 21 of you, so we will act out the story twice so everyone has a chance to be one of the characters." As she said this, she shuffled some index cards labeled with the children's names. She then pulled the card with

Roger's name and asked him to go to the markerboard and choose a character card. Roger, looking amazed to be the first student picked, went up and put the "snort" card around his neck. In less than a minute, Miss Kamper had pulled 11 names and 11 children were standing in front of the markerboard with character cards around their necks.

"Now," said Miss Kamper, "Our characters will act out the story while the rest of us will be the readers and read the pages aloud." The children who were not characters read the pages chorally along with Miss Kamper, while the characters came to the front and "did" their part.

Hurriedly, Miss Kamper collected the character cards, then pulled the rest of the students' names from her index cards to determine the second cast of characters. Once again, the audience chorally read with Miss Kamper while the characters acted out the story.

Claire, who had been entranced through her entire visit in Miss Kamper's class, hurried to the door when she noticed it was a few minutes after nine. As she left, she heard Miss Kamper remind the children that she was putting the character cards in the dramatic play center the next day so that they could "do the book" again if they chose that center.

9:00-9:30   Bea Ginning   Kindergarten   Room 22

At 9:04, Claire entered Miss Ginning's kindergarten classroom. Melodie had told Claire that Bea was a new teacher, having taken over this kindergarten class at the beginning of the new year after the holidays. Bea had been the student teacher in the classroom in the fall. She graduated from college after the first semester and was now the "real" teacher, since the previous teacher had decided to stay home with her new baby.

As Claire entered, the children were sitting on the carpet in front of a noticeably young teacher and looking at the big book *Is Your Mama a Llama?* by Deborah Guarino. The children were looking at the cover of the book and talking about llamas. The teacher pointed first to the title of the book and then to the author's name. "The illustrator of this book is Steven Kellogg," she said as she pointed to his name on the cover. "What did Steven Kellogg do?" she asked. One little girl quickly answered, "He makes cereal!" (Claire thought to herself how wonderful young students are and how smart they feel when they make a connection—and they want everyone to know they know! If only she had saved all their comments over the years!) Bea chuckled and said, "There are cereals by that name, but it says on the cover that Steven Kellogg is the illustrator. What does an illustrator do?" Several children chimed in that an illustrator draws or paints the pictures.

Next, the teacher opened the big book and asked the children to take a picture walk through the book with her, talking about the pictures on each page. They discussed the animals (bat, swan, cow, seal, and kangaroo) as the teacher turned the pages of the big book. "Can you tell what this story is going to be about?" the teacher asked. The children answered, "A llama and lots of other animals."

Miss Ginning pointed to one of the pages and asked, "What do you notice on this page?" Seth answered, "There is only one word on the page, and it is written in big, bold letters. I can read it! It's 'b-at'—and there is a picture of a bat." The teacher and the class continued the picture walk, but each time they came to a page with one word and a picture of an animal, some children looked at the beginning letter and the picture clue and then read the word aloud.

After the picture walk, the teacher read the story to the class and asked them to count how many animals there were to whom the llama asked the question, "Is your Mama a llama?" After reading the story to the students, having them answer the focus question ("How many animals . . ."), and talking about what happened in the story, Miss Ginning asked the children to "share" the reading of the book by reading it along with her. Some students read in loud voices—proud they could do it! Other children chimed in when they could—those big, bold words, one on a page, being the easiest to read! Everyone could see the teacher point from left to right, do a return sweep to the left, and read from the top of the page to the bottom.

After the shared reading of this big book, the teacher said, "I heard some rhyming words in this book, did you? Let's read the book again and listen for rhyming words." She then read the book to the children again and asked them to listen for rhyming words. The children identified the rhyming words, which Bea wrote on a piece of chart paper.

9:30-10:00   Gay Smiley   Grade 1   Room 32

The Guided Reading Block was already in progress when Claire entered Room 32. Miss Smiley was seated in front of the markerboard with six children, five pairs of partners were working together, and five children were reading by themselves. They were all reading *Caterpillar Diary* by David Drew. Claire knew from this arrangement that they were doing a Three-Ring Circus.

Claire went over first to observe the teacher's group. As Miss Smiley turned each page, she asked the students to remember what they had just talked about when the whole class had done a picture walk. The children told her what they saw in each picture, and she repeated their responses and prompted them for things they didn't mention. In addition to identifying the items in the pictures, she had them say and then stretch out one word, decide what letters they would expect to see in the word, and then find that word on the page before reading it. The students echo read each page. The teacher read each sentence, and then cupped her hand to her ear as she listened for the students to read it back just the way she had read it. As they finished each page, they talked about what they learned on that page about caterpillars and where that information would go on the "caterpillar" web they were making. Claire watched them read several pages, each time using the same procedure of continuing the picture walk, identifying one difficult word, echo reading each page, and deciding what could be added to the web. She noticed two children who attempted to echo read the pages and listened, but who didn't contribute to the discussion, and she wondered if these two were just learning to speak English.

Next, Claire walked around and watched the partners read. It was clear that these children had been taught how to partner read. They took turns with each page, one child reading and the other pointing to the words. At the end of each page, the reader asked the "pointer" what could be added to the web and where. Their eyes turned to the web, which had been started on the board, and they were quite engaged while coming up with suggestions. As the partners took turns, it was clear that struggling readers were partnered with someone who could help them. Claire was amazed to notice, however, that the partners didn't tell each other the words, but coached each other to figure them out. In one partnership, the child who was the better reader couldn't figure out a word, and her partner said, "Keep your finger on the word and finish the sentence. Then, we will go back and pretend it's Guess the Covered Word, and we have the beginning letters." It was clear that the helping partner didn't know the word either, but he did know some strategies that would help them to figure it out!

At 9:55, just a few minutes before the teacher signaled all the children to gather at the web, several sets of partners and almost all the individual children had finished reading. They all got index cards and began writing down some things they thought should be added to the web. The teacher and her group went up to the web, and as Claire once again hurried to her next observation, she noticed all the children—including those with whom the teacher had echo read—eager to contribute to the web.

10:00-10:30   Deb Webb   Grade 2   Room 36

Claire was on schedule as she entered Deb Webb's second-grade classroom. The children were seated on the carpet in front of Deb's rocking chair. The day before, the class finished reading a story about the cartoon character Arthur in their reading series. Today, Mrs. Webb was giving her class four *Arthur* books from which to choose for "Book Club groups." Using the story map they had filled in for the *Arthur* story they had read as a class, Mrs. Webb explained, "Arthur is the main character in all his books. But, just like in *Arthur's Pet Business* by Marc Brown, there are other characters in his stories. For the setting, the places are sometimes different, but in all *Arthur* stories the time is always the present. What really changes from story to story, and book to book, is what the problem is and how it is solved. So, as you choose a book and form Book Club groups, you need to think about what you believe Arthur's problem will be." Mrs. Webb explained to the students that their task for that day was to preview the four book choices and decide which would be their first, second, and third choices to read. She suggested that they look at the pictures and read a few sentences—not all the words on every page—to see if a book was one they could read and would enjoy.

Next, she sent five or six children to each of the four stacks of *Arthur* books placed in the four corners of the room. After the children had spent four minutes with a book, the timer rang and each group headed to the next set of books. There was a soft buzz in each group, but when Claire visited the groups, she was surprised that all children were "on task," reading or talking about Arthur and which book they liked best.

After all the students had previewed all four books, Mrs. Webb gathered them back on the carpet and asked them to think about the books and to write the titles of their first, second, and third choices on the index cards she passed around. Mrs. Webb overheard some children say that they couldn't decide—they liked all of the *Arthur* books. Mrs. Webb told them not to worry too much about their choices because all four books would be in the book baskets for Self-Selected Reading next week. This seemed to allay the students' anxiety, and they quickly made their choices.

10:30-11:00   Laura Reading   Grade 2   Room 38

Laura Reading was using the *Weekly Reader* for her Guided Reading lesson as Claire entered her room at 10:30. Although this weekly newspaper is written especially for second-grade students, some children find it difficult—especially when this week's issue is all about frogs, and they don't know much about frogs! (Even if they don't know much about them, children are interested in frogs and all the other topics covered in this weekly newspaper.) The *Weekly Reader* enabled Mrs. Reading to meet the goal of helping children learn to read informational text, and she used this student newspaper for Guided Reading one day each week. She was especially grateful she had these newspapers, since the reading series she used contained good stories but very little informational text. She told her students that "grown-ups read newspapers to learn about the world, and so do we!"

Next, Mrs. Reading told the children with whom they would work that day. As the names of two children were called, they sat together as partners on the floor and immediately began previewing the pictures and reading the captions under the pictures. Claire noted that this format must have been used before, for everyone seemed to know what to do without much direction from the teacher. When all partners were seated together, Mrs. Reading reminded them of their purpose, "Work together to read each page. Talk about what you learn, and think about what you can add to our Frog Facts list."

Mrs. Reading circulated from pair to pair as the students read and talked. Claire noted a happy buzz in this second-grade classroom as they found new and interesting facts about frogs. Soon a timer went off, and the children returned to the carpet in front of Mrs. Reading. They were eager to share their new information about frogs. Mrs. Reading called on someone in each pair to share something they had learned. As they did so, Mrs. Reading typed the "Frog Facts" list on the classroom computer. The children watched the monitor and read the sentences as Mrs. Reading wrote them. Each pair of partners seemed very pleased as their information was added to the list. One boy asked if they would all get copies of the information she was typing, and Mrs. Reading explained that she intended to include it in the parent newsletter going home next week.

11:00-11:45   Faith Goode   Grade 4   Room 3

As Claire settled herself into a rocking chair at the back of Room 3, she wondered if Melodie had the schedule mixed up or if Mrs. Goode had changed the schedule. The children all had their science books out and were reading and raising hands. Some children had two hands raised. "They must be really eager beavers," Claire thought.

"I am glad to see many of you with both hands raised," said Mrs. Goode, "because the purpose I gave you for this page was indeed a 'two-hander.' I asked you to read the page to find out the two different ways your body fights germs. Corinda, tell us one way." Corinda explained that a fever helps your body fight germs.

"Very good," responded Mrs. Goode. "Who can read aloud to us the sentences in the text that let Corinda figure out that fevers help you fight germs?" A boy sitting near Corinda quickly located the text and raised his hand. "Daniel, why don't you read those sentences for us," Mrs. Goode said. After Daniel finished reading, Mrs. Goode called on another student who said that white blood cells help fight germs, too, and then a fourth student was chosen to read the parts in the text that told how white blood cells fight germs.

As the lesson continued, Claire realized that she had indeed come in at the right time, and that Mrs. Goode was doing a Guided Reading lesson with a small portion of their science text. She was using the ERT format (Everyone Read To...), and most of her questions required students to connect text information with what they already knew and to make inferences. The class read several pages using this format, then Mrs. Goode asked the students to get out their science notebooks.

"There was a lot of new information here about germs," she said. "Let's write a summary together that you will all have in your notebooks, so that you can review the most important facts before our unit test."

As Claire was leaving, the teacher and the children were jointly constructing a summary. Mrs. Goode was writing on the overhead as the children wrote in their notebooks. Claire was amazed that this idea about integrating some of your Guided Reading and focused writing with content areas could look so easy and natural. She wondered why she and the other teachers at her school had talked about it, but never done it!

11:45-12:15   Lunch with Melodie

During lunch, Melodie told Claire that different teachers seemed to talk about different blocks, but that Diane Duright was always a champion for the Guided Reading Block. Diane always seemed to have the right answer for teachers when they asked about this block. Although the local school system had adopted a reading series, teachers were allowed and encouraged to use other materials—and Diane did. After their quick lunch in the cafeteria, Claire once again waved good-bye to her sister and hurried off to see Mrs. Duright.

12:15-12:45   Diane Duright   Grade 3   Room 17

At 12:15, Claire entered Diane's room. It was neat and orderly in spite of the fact that there were books everywhere—on book shelves, in plastic dish pans, and near every bulletin board and display! Claire could see from the mural on a large bulletin board in one corner of the room that these third-graders were studying the water cycle in science. The children's drawings illustrated the water cycle, and the parts of the cycle were neatly numbered and labeled in the children's best handwriting. Mrs. Duright told the class that today they were going on an imaginary field trip with a famous teacher named Ms. Frizzle. Several of the students now had big smiles on their faces—they knew Ms. Frizzle from the television show *The Magic School Bus*®. Diane explained that this field trip was imaginary because they were going with their eyes and minds as they read a book. She told the students that knowing what they did about the water cycle would help them to read the book.

Mrs. Duright then asked the students what they knew about water from their science lessons. "Water is a liquid," said one boy. Someone else added, "It is also a solid when it freezes and becomes ice." To which another student added, "Remember, though, if you heat it, water can become a gas." Mrs. Duright began a column on a large piece of chart paper and listed all the things the students knew about water. Next, she told them that this book had more facts that they would learn about water.

Mrs. Duright gathered the children around her and together they read a big book version of *The Magic School Bus at the Waterworks* by Joanna Cole. They talked about the different kinds of information on each page—pictures or illustrations, text in bubbles which showed what people were saying and thinking, boxed text which gave facts about water, "quicktext" under pictures and in diagrams, and the "regular text." They decided on an order to look at and read these different kinds of information—visuals (pictures or illustrations) and quicktext first; then regular text; bubbled text after that; and the boxed informational text last. The teacher then lead them though the reading of the book following the order upon which they had agreed. She invited the students to join in the reading with her, and she let volunteers read the dialogue in the thinking and speech bubbles.

The children discussed what they were learning and connected new knowledge to what they already knew about the water cycle. After they had finished, Mrs. Duright asked the children to take out their reading response logs and write something new they learned from this book about the water cycle. She ended her lesson by having several children read their sentences aloud.

"I learned that clouds are made of water."

"I learned that people store water in reservoirs."

"You have to purify water before you can drink it."

"Most of the water on the earth is saltwater in the oceans."

"Clear water is not always clean water. We can't see germs."

"Water pressure forces water through the pipes in our homes and at school."

12:45-1:30   Denise Lerner   Grade 3   Room 15

When Claire entered Room 15, the children were all seated at their desks with their reading textbooks open to a biography of Eleanor Roosevelt. Mrs. Lerner was reading aloud to them, and she stopped every few sentences, pointed to her brain, stared off into the distance and said things like:

"That reminds me of when I was little. I had to go into the basement to get things from our freezer and, if it was late at night, I was always afraid there was going to be someone down there."

"I can't imagine how she felt when she was only eight and her mother died. She must have been very lonely. I feel like crying myself when I think about it."

"It says she was a sad and lonely child. I wonder how she married the president and became such a wonderful first lady. I can't wait to see how she changed so much as she grew up."

The children were amazingly quiet and thoughtful as their teacher read a little aloud and then looked away, pointed to her brain, and told them "what her brain was saying to her." When Mrs. Lerner finished reading and "thinking aloud" the first three pages, she closed the book, opened and closed her eyes, and looked amazed to see the children. They laughed in delight and had clearly been anticipating her doing this, although it was quite a surprise to Claire! Mrs. Lerner congratulated the students on remaining so invisible that she forgot they were there. She then asked the students to recall what she had been thinking as she read the first few pages of the biography. The children told her that she connected things to her own life when she remembered going into the basement to get things out of the freezer, that she felt so sorry for Eleanor when her mother died that she almost cried, and that she was dying to read some more and find out how Eleanor became the great first lady she was!

The teacher told them that they had been so quiet while she was reading and thinking aloud that they almost became invisible, but it was clear that they were still there, listening to every word. She then told them that they were going to read the next six pages of Eleanor Roosevelt's biography in playschool groups. As they read, they should think about what their brains were telling them. She reminded the students that the first few times they did Think-Alouds, they were only trying to make connections. Then, they had added predictions, and finally, images. "Who can explain what connections, predictions, and images are?" she asked. The children told her about how you connect what you are reading to yourself, or to things you know about the world, or to other books you have read. They also told how you predict when you think you know what will happen, or when you don't know but you wonder about how something happened. Finally, the children explained that when you "image," it's like you're really there. You can see how something looks, and hear the sounds, and maybe even smell and taste and feel things.

Claire was amazed at how much these third-graders understood about how their brains thought when they read. She imagined that the teacher must have done lots of Think-Alouds and gradually introduced the three different thinking strategies. As Claire was trying to make sense of this, the teacher was having the children get into playschool groups. Each group had a "teacher" who was given three laminated index cards: a blue card which said "Connect;" a yellow card which said "Predict;" and a green card which said "Image." Mrs. Lerner said that they were to echo read the sentences and that they should stop after each paragraph and see if anyone's brain was "talking" to them—telling them any connections, predictions, or images.

The children quickly got into their appointed groups of four or five. The echo reading began with the "teacher" in each group reading each sentence and then having the rest of the group echo the sentence back to him. The "teacher" stopped at the end of each paragraph and asked what anyone was thinking. The children in the group, including the "teacher," pointed to their brains, gazed off into the distance, and told their thoughts.

When the groups finished reading the six pages, they began talking about their most interesting thoughts and negotiated the one Think-Aloud they would share with the whole class.

The Guided Reading time ended with each group sharing its most interesting Think-Aloud. Everyone in the group read aloud the sentences that preceded the Think-Aloud, and then one child stared off into the distance, pointed to her brain, and told what her brain was saying. The children all enjoyed this, and each group tried to "out-ham" the others. Claire walked out, shaking her head in amazement at the level of thinking and involvement she had observed in this classroom.

1:30-2:15   Will Teachum   Grade 5   Room 11

Claire was exhausted when she arrived for her last observation of the day. "I don't know how I can be so tired from just sitting all day," she thought. "My brain is on overload. I am going to need a vacation to get over my vacation."

She found Mr. Teachum's students in animated discussion in small groups. They all had copies of a *Harry Potter* book by J. K. Rowling in their hands and were clearly engaged in talking about it. As she approached the various groups, she noticed that the children had bookmarks on which they had written some questions. These questions seemed to be guiding their discussion, and Claire noticed that all the questions began with "How" or "Why."

At 1:45, the timer went off and Mr. Teachum told the groups they had exactly one minute to pick their best "How" or "Why" question to ask the rest of the class. The groups argued amongst themselves, and then quickly voted if they couldn't decide which question to include. Claire was amazed, as she had been all day, that the students knew just what to do. She realized that small-group discussions are often unfocused and a waste of time, and that a lot of time and modeling must have gone into teaching the students the procedures and what was expected.

When exactly one minute had passed, Mr. Teachum asked the first group for their best question. One member of the group read the question and called on three people from three different groups for responses. This procedure was followed as each of the five groups asked one question, and then called on three responders across the other groups.

Next, Mr. Teachum told the students that they would have the rest of the Guided Reading time that day to read the next chapter in *Harry Potter*. Just as before, their task was to come up with two good "How" and "Why" questions for their small-group discussions tomorrow. Mr. Teachum also told the students that today's reading would be a "You'se Choose" format—they could read by themselves, with a friend, or join his group. "Remember," he warned, "With choices come responsibility! If you choose to read by yourself or with a friend, you must be able to make up two good questions for your group tomorrow. If you make a bad choice today, you will lose the privilege of making a choice tomorrow."

The children scrambled around and in less than two minutes, they were all settled and reading. Six children chose to read by themselves. There were five pairs of partners reading together. Ten children joined Mr. Teachum. Claire circulated around and noticed that the children all seemed quite involved with their reading. Several of the children reading with partners stumbled over some of the words, but their partners coached them to figure out the words.

All the children had bookmarks and stopped periodically to write down a "How" or "Why" question. Claire noticed that Mr. Teachum was stopping the children every few pages and asking, "Has anyone got a good question?" He wrote their suggested questions on the board and asked them to wait until they were finished reading before choosing the best ones. Once they finished reading, they could pick the two they liked best and write them on their bookmarks. The group that read with Mr. Teachum had some struggling readers in it, as well as some very able readers. "Some children are there because they know they need the help," Claire concluded, "and other children would just rather read with the teacher than by themselves or with a friend."

As 2:15 approached, some children had finished reading and returned to their seats. Most began working on their math homework, but a few had to be reminded that "begin your math homework if you finish reading before the time is up" was the rule—and had been all year. Mr. Teachum's group ran about five minutes over, but by 2:20, the children were all in their seats and preparing for the 2:25 dismissal bell. Claire noticed that all the children had bookmarks in their *Harry Potter* books with two "How" or "Why" questions on them. Some of the questions intrigued her and, for just a moment, she was tempted to return the next day. But, she quickly changed her mind when she remembered that Melodie was taking a personal day and they were going shopping! "I've devoted enough of my vacation to work," Claire decided. "I deserve a shopping trip!"

Hopefully, after "tagging along" on Claire Leider's visit to Fourblox Elementary, you are intrigued by what you saw and have lots of "How" and "Why" questions to which you'd like answers. If your brain, like Claire's, is on overload, take a little break, and then continue to the next chapter to begin exploring answers to those questions.

CHAPTER 2

THE FOUR-BLOCKS™ FRAMEWORK

In the previous chapter, as you visited Fourblox Elementary with Claire Leider, you observed classrooms at all different grade levels during their Guided Reading Block. Guided Reading is one of the four blocks of instructional time which—along with the Self-Selected Reading, Writing, and Working with Words blocks—make up the Four-Blocks™ framework. This chapter includes:

- An overview of the Four-Blocks™ framework.
- An overview of the "Building Blocks" framework for kindergarten and the "Big Blocks" framework for upper grades.
- An overview of the other three blocks, Self-Selected Reading, Writing, and Working with Words, including the goals for each block and how each block is multilevel.
- An overview of Guided Reading.
- Some connections between the blocks and to other curriculum areas.

How and Why the Four-Blocks Framework Was Developed

The Four-Blocks™ framework was developed by teachers who believed that to be successful in teaching ALL children to read and write, we were going to have to do it ALL! "Doing it all" means incorporating on a daily basis the different approaches to reading. The four different blocks—Guided Reading, Self-Selected Reading, Writing, and Working with Words—represent four different approaches to teaching children to read. Daily instruction in all four blocks provides numerous and varied opportunities for all children to learn to read and write. Doing all four blocks acknowledges that children do not all learn in the same way, and provides substantial instruction to support whatever learning personality a child has. The other big difference between children—their different literacy levels—is acknowledged by using a variety of during-reading formats and before-and-after reading activities to make each block as multilevel as possible, thus providing additional support for children who struggle and additional challenges for children who catch on quickly.

The Four-Blocks™ framework began in 1989-90 in one first-grade classroom (Cunningham, Hall & Defee, 1991; Cunningham, Hall & Defee, 1998). In the 1990-91 school year, 16 first-grade teachers in four schools used the framework, making modifications to suit a variety of different school populations including a Title I school (Hall, Prevatte & Cunningham, 1995). Since 1991, the framework has been used in numerous first-, second-, and third-grade classrooms where many children still struggle with reading and writing.

(For more information about the Four-Blocks™ framework, see *The Teacher's Guide to the Four-Blocks™* by Cunningham, Hall, & Sigmon, 1999; *The Four Blocks: A Framework for Reading and Writing in Classrooms That Work*, a videotape by Cunningham and Hall, 1999; the "Four Blocks Column" by Cheryl Sigmon at *www.teachers.net* and the fourblocks mailrings at *teachers.net* and *www.readinglady.com*)

The Four-Blocks™ framework has many variations, but there are two basic principles which must be followed if reading and writing instruction can truly be called Four-Blocks. First, because it is believed (and research supports the idea) that children learn to read in different ways, each block gets 30-40 minutes of instruction each and every day. Providing enough and equal time to each block assures that children are given the same opportunity to become literate, regardless of which approach is most compatible with their individual learning personalities. The second basic principle is that while children are not put in fixed ability groups, the instruction is made as multilevel as possible so that average, struggling, and excelling students all learn to read and write at the highest possible level. Doing the four blocks every day and giving them approximately equal time is a simple matter of making a schedule and sticking to it. Making the instruction in each block as multilevel as possible is more complex, but it can be done. You will see many examples of this throughout this book.

Because 30-40 minutes each day for each block is a basic principle, Four-Blocks is not an appropriate organizational framework for kindergarten or for most intermediate grades. Children in every grade level should receive instruction in guided reading, self-selected reading, writing, and words, but for kindergarten and intermediate grades, the schedule would look quite different.

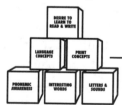

Building Blocks

The kindergarten program is called "Building Blocks," and it integrates guided reading, self-selected reading, writing, and words with the themes and units that are part of every kindergarten day. The blocks don't have a set time slot—and certainly don't each get 30-40 minutes every day. Four-Blocks is a primary grades framework that is consistent with how primary teachers teach and schedule their day. Building Blocks is a kindergarten framework which is consistent with how kindergarten teachers teach and how they structure their day.

(For more about Building Blocks, see *Month-by-Month Reading and Writing for Kindergarten* by Hall & Cunningham, 1998; *The Teacher's Guide to the Building Blocks* by Hall & Williams, 2000; and the video, *Building Blocks: A Framework for Reading and Writing in Kindergartens That Work* by Cunningham & Hall, 1996.)

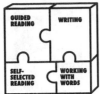

Big Blocks

Time allocation is also where the Four-Blocks™ framework changes for upper grades. Because each block is viewed as an approach to reading, and because there are children in every Four-Blocks classroom for whom each block is their best road to literacy, beginning readers are taken down all four roads every day. However, by the time children have achieved a fluent third-grade reading and writing level, they read and write well enough that the time allocations can be changed. Once children can read and write fluently at third-grade level, they have well-developed phonics and spelling skills, so Working with Words no longer needs one-quarter of your literacy instructional time. The Working with Words instruction can now focus on big words, most of which will come from science, health, and social studies units. Self-Selected Reading still needs a scheduled 30-40 minutes each day, but Guided Reading and Writing get longer blocks, and much of Guided Reading and the focused-writing component of the Writing Block are integrated with the content subjects of science, health, and social studies. Because this intermediate framework focuses on big ideas and big words from subject areas, and includes big blocks of time for content integration, it is called "Big Blocks." (The best example of the Big Blocks framework can be found in the fourth-grade chapter of *Teachers in Action* by Cunningham, Moore, Cunningham & Moore, 2000 and in Chapter 10 of *Classrooms That Work* by Cunningham & Allington, 1999.)

Now imagine an upper-grades classroom in which many children do not read and write fluently at the third-grade level. Perhaps they have not gotten appropriate instruction, or have moved from school to school, or are just learning English. For these classrooms, the Four-Blocks, with its roughly equal instructional time allocated to each of the approaches, would still be the most appropriate and effective organizational framework. The issue is not the grade level of the students, but their reading levels. Until children read and write fluently at third-grade level, they need a minimum of two hours of literacy instruction each day and equal attention to each of the four major approaches.

The Four-Blocks

Self-Selected Reading

Historically called "individualized reading" or "personalized reading" (Veatch, 1959), many teachers now label their self-selected reading time "Reader's Workshop" (Routman, 1995). Regardless of what it is called, self-selected reading is that part of a balanced literacy program in which children get to choose what they want to read and decide to what parts of their reading they want to respond. Opportunities are provided for children to share and respond to what is read. Teachers hold conferences with children about their books.

The goals of the Self-Selected Reading Block are:

- To introduce children to all types of literature through the teacher read-aloud.
- To encourage children's reading interests.
- To provide instructional-level reading.
- To build intrinsic motivation for reading.

In Four-Blocks classrooms, the Self-Selected Reading Block includes teacher read-alouds. The teacher reads to the children from a wide range of literature. Next, children read on their own level from a variety of materials, including the widest possible range of topics, genres, and levels. While the children read, the teacher conferences with approximately one-fifth of the class each day. The block usually ends with one or two children sharing their books with the class in a "Reader's Chair" format.

Self-selected reading is, by definition, multilevel. The component of self-selected reading that makes it multilevel is the fact that children choose what they want to read. In Four-Blocks classrooms, teachers read aloud all different types and levels of materials on all different topics, and then make the whole range of reading materials available. During the weekly conferences, they support children's choices and help children choose books for the next week that they can read and will enjoy.

Writing

The Writing Block includes both self-selected writing, in which children choose their topics, and focused writing in which children learn how to write particular forms and on particular topics. Children are taught to use process writing to improve their first drafts, so they don't have to think of everything at one time. Process writing is carried out in "Writers' Workshop" fashion (Graves, 1995; Routman, 1995; Calkins, 1994). The Writing Block begins with a 10-minute mini-lesson, during which the teacher writes and models all the things writers do. Next, the children go to their own writing. They are at all different stages of the writing process—finishing a story, starting a new story, editing, illustrating, etc. While the children write, the teacher conferences with individuals who are getting ready to publish. This block ends with "Author's Chair" in which several students each day share work in progress or their published work. The goals of the Writing Block are:

- To have students view writing as a way of telling about things.
- To develop fluent writing for all children.
- To teach students to use grammar and mechanics in their own writing.
- To teach particular writing forms.
- To allow students to learn to read through writing.
- To maintain the motivation and self-confidence of struggling writers.

Writing is the most multilevel block because it is not limited by the availability or acceptability of appropriate books. Because children are allowed to choose their own topics, whatever level of first-draft writing each child can accomplish is accepted, and students are allowed to work on their pieces as many days as needed, all children can succeed in writing. As teachers help children publish the pieces they have chosen, they have the opportunity to truly "individualize" their teaching. Looking at the writing of the child usually reveals both what the child needs in order to move forward, and what the child is ready to understand. The writing conference provides the "teachable moment," in which both advanced and struggling writers can be nudged forward in their literacy development.

Working with Words
In the Working with Words Block, children learn to read and spell high-frequency words and learn the patterns which allow them to decode and spell lots of words. The first ten minutes of this block are usually given to reviewing the Word Wall words. Students practice new and old words daily by looking at them, saying them, chanting the letters, writing the words, and self-correcting the words with the teacher.

The remaining 15-25 minutes of words time is given to an activity which helps children learn to decode and spell. A variety of different activities are used on different days. Some of the most popular activities are Rounding Up the Rhymes, Making Words, Reading/Writing Rhymes, Using Words You Know, Word Sorting and Hunting, and Guess the Covered Word. (For grade-level specific descriptions of Working with Words activities, see *Month-by-Month Phonics for First Grade* (Cunningham & Hall, 1997), *Month-by-Month Phonics for Second Grade* (Hall & Cunningham, 1998) and *Month-by-Month Phonics for Third Grade* (Cunningham & Hall, 1998).

The goals of the Working With Words Block are:

- To teach children how to read and spell high-frequency words.
- To teach children how to decode and spell lots of other words using patterns from known words.
- To have students automatically and fluently use phonics and spelling patterns while reading and writing.

Activities in the Working with Words Block are multilevel in a variety of ways. During the daily Word Wall practice, the children who have learned to read the words being practiced are learning to spell them. Other children who require lots of practice with words are learning to read the words.

Making Words, Rounding Up the Rhymes, Reading/Writing Rhymes, Using Words You Know, and other Working with Words Block activities are also multilevel. Most lessons begin with short, easy words and progress to longer, more complex words. Children who still need to develop phonemic awareness can do this as they decide which words rhyme and stretch out words. Each lesson includes some sorting of words into patterns, and then using those patterns to read and spell some new words. Children whose word knowledge is at all different levels see how they can use the patterns they see in words to read and spell other words. They also learn that rhyming words usually—but not always—have the same spelling pattern. All lessons provide review for beginning letter sounds for those who still need it.

Guided Reading

Guided Reading lessons usually have a before-reading phase, a during-reading phase, and an after-reading phase. Depending on the text being read, the comprehension strategies being taught, and the reading levels of the children, a great variety of before-, during-, and after-reading variations are used. Before children read, help them build and access prior knowledge, make connections to personal experiences, develop vocabulary essential for comprehension, make predictions, and set purposes for their reading. After reading, help children connect new knowledge to what they knew before, follow up predictions, and discuss what they learned and how they are becoming better readers by using these reading strategies. The variety of activities used in the before-and-after reading phases will be described in Part Two of this book.

In Four-Blocks classrooms, children read the selections in all different kinds of formats. On some days, the whole class reads together and the teacher uses shared reading, choral reading, echo reading, or Everyone Read To... (ERT) to encourage everyone's active participation. On other days, the children may read the selection in partners, playschool groups, Book Club groups, or Think-Aloud groups. Sometimes, teachers pull small coaching groups and read a selection with them while the other children read the selection in partners or individually. Depending on the comprehension purpose and the selection, you will see children doing Musical Riddles, Pick a Page, or You'se Choose. These and the many other activities used in the during-reading phase will be described in Part Three of this book.

The goals of the Guided Reading Block are:

- To teach comprehension skills and strategies.
- To develop background knowledge, meaning vocabulary, and oral language.
- To teach children how to read all types of literature.
- To provide as much instructional-level reading as possible.
- To maintain the motivation and self-confidence of struggling readers.

Guided Reading is the hardest block to make multilevel. Any selection is going to be too hard for some children and too easy for others. Our main reason for writing this book is to share with you some of the clever ways teachers have devised for making Guided Reading more multilevel. Throughout the book, you will see how various before-and-after reading activities and during-reading formats help to realize this goal. Here are some of the more common multilevel tactics:

- Guided Reading time is not spent only in grade-level material. Rather, teachers alternate selections—one at the average reading level of the class and one easier.

- In Book Club groups, select four books tied together in some way. In selecting these books, include one that is a little easier than average and one that is a little harder.

- Reread each selection—or parts of longer selections—several times, each time for a different purpose in a different format. Rereading enables children who couldn't read it fluently the first time to achieve fluent reading by the last reading.

- Children who need help are not left to read by themselves, but are supported in a variety of ways. Most teachers use reading partners and playschool groups, and teach children how to coach each other.

- On some days, some children read the selection by themselves and others read with partners while the teacher meets with a small group. These small coaching groups change regularly, and do not include only the low readers.

- Some teachers schedule their Guided Reading time when they have "help" coming. Guided Reading can be more multilevel if you have more adults working with coaching groups, or circulating and providing support to partners or groups.

- Provide some extra easy-reading time for children whose reading level is well below even the easier selections read. Some teachers meet children individually or in small groups while the rest of the children are engaged in center or other activities. Include some good reading models in your "Fun Reading Club" or "After Lunch Bunch." The most struggling readers are included more often.

- When available, coordinate with early intervention teachers and/or tutors to provide guided reading instruction on appropriate levels.

- Spread out your struggling readers across the days for Self-Selected Reading conferences. Conference first with them each day, giving them a little extra time and making sure they select books they will enjoy and can read.

One way or another, we try to make sure that children are getting the support they need, including some coaching each week, as they read materials at their instructional level.

Connecting the Blocks to Each Other and the Rest of the Curriculum

Each block has its scheduled time in every classroom, but Four-Blocks teachers also make many links among the four different blocks and to other areas of the curriculum. In Parts Two and Three of this book, you will find boxes which suggest links you might make from the suggested Guided Reading activity to the other blocks and other curriculum areas. Some of the links most commonly made include:

- Selecting high-frequency words which were included many times in one of the Guided Reading selections to add to the Word Wall.
- Doing a Guess the Covered Word activity with a paragraph that will soon be read as part of the Guided Reading selection.
- Rounding Up the Rhymes from a book or poem read during Guided Reading.
- Teaching a Making Words lesson with an important word from Guided Reading as the secret word.
- Reading aloud to children, during the first part of Self-Selected Reading, a selection which "sets them up" for an author, genre, or topic they will soon be reading during Guided Reading.
- Making books read during the Guided Reading Book Club groups available for children to choose during Self-Selected Reading.
- Choosing a topic for the writing minilesson which relates to something read during Guided Reading.
- Doing some focused writing lessons in which children learn to write a genre they have read during Guided Reading.
- Choosing materials for Guided Reading that fit the theme or relate to a science, health, or social studies topic.

You are probably thinking right now that the reading materials are a crucial part of the Guided Reading Block and wondering about what to use, how to choose materials, and where to get them. In the next chapter, you will learn about materials and how to use everything you have, not to mention what you can beg, borrow, and contrive!

CHAPTER 3

MATERIALS FOR GUIDED READING

Teachers who are the happiest and most successful with their Guided Reading Block use the widest variety of materials possible. In fact, meeting all the goals of the Guided Reading Block is impossible if you are stuck with just one or two things for everyone to read. In the last chapter, we listed the goals for each block. Again, the goals for the Guided Reading Block are:

- To teach comprehension skills and strategies.
- To develop background knowledge, meaning vocabulary, and oral language.
- To teach children how to read all types of literature.
- To provide as much instructional-level reading as possible.
- To maintain the motivation and self-confidence of struggling readers.

It is obvious that, if we are going to teach children how to read all different types of literature, we must include instruction with all different types. Why? Because different types of literature require different comprehension skills and strategies. When you read stories, you have to follow the story structure and think about the characters, settings, events, and conclusions. Your comprehension will be greater if you imagine yourself in the same situations as the characters, predict what they will do, and evaluate the choices they make based on what you think they should do. You also will comprehend the story better when you think about why things happen and why characters behave in the way they do.

Even within fiction, there are differences in specific comprehension strategies required. When reading mysteries, you need to watch for clues and draw conclusions if you want the experience of solving the mystery before the author solves it for you. When reading fantasy, you have to imagine a different world and infer the rules by which the characters in that world live.

Informational reading requires different comprehension skills and strategies from story reading. Even more so than in stories, in order to remember and learn from informational selections, you have to figure out and remember the sequence in which specific events occurred. Events which follow one another often cause each other, and you need to think about what causes what to happen. Often, several things—animals, people, events, places, etc.—are compared and contrasted, and you have to summarize and draw conclusions about their similarities and differences. Informational text contains special features, such as headings, bold print, maps, charts, and glossaries. These special features are there to help comprehension, but they only help if you know how to read and interpret them.

Poetry, plays, and directions each have their own structure. To comprehend these, students need to use different comprehension skills and strategies from those they use with stories and information.

To meet the two goals of teaching all the comprehension skills and strategies needed to read, enjoy, and learn from all the different kinds of texts, we need to provide students with instruction and practice in reading all these different kinds of text. A variety of materials is also essential to meet the goal of developing students' background knowledge, meaning vocabulary, and oral language. Since children require lots of different encounters with particular words and concepts to really begin to use them, we do as much integration as possible between the Guided Reading Block and our science and social studies themes and topics. We read both informational and story selections which relate to these themes and topics, and keep charts and lists of the new things and words our students are learning.

Finally, having a variety of materials is critical for the last two goals of Guided Reading—providing as much instructional material as possible and maintaining the confidence and motivation of struggling readers. The previous chapter described some of the ways in which to make your Guided Reading Block as multilevel as possible. We read both grade-level and easier material. When we do Book Club groups, we choose four books and make sure that one is easier and one is harder than the others. Many teachers form a "Fun Reading Club" or an "After Lunch Bunch" and read short, very easy selections with a small group that includes the most struggling readers several times a week. We provide many opportunities for struggling readers to get instruction in materials at their instructional level. Because a wide variety of materials and such a range of grouping patterns are used, none of the children will ever suspect that they are in "the dumb group" or reading "the baby books!" The best Four-Blocks teachers are very clever (Not to say conniving!) at getting everyone what they need and making everyone feel terrific!

To achieve all the goals of the Guided Reading Block, we must collect and use the widest range of materials possible. You may be thinking, "Easy for you to say! I don't have much to work with. I'm stuck with what I've got." In this chapter, you will become convinced that you have—and can get—more than you think, and that using more than just the reading text, or just the text sets, or just the book packs, etc., is crucial if children are to learn how to comprehend the universe of what we read. Let's begin by remembering all the different genres of literature for children. (You may want to search your brain or your basement for your old "kiddie lit" files!)

Fiction, Nonfiction, Plays, Poetry and Directions

Fiction is made up—it didn't happen! For some kinds of fiction—realistic fiction, historical fiction, mysteries—it could have happened, but it didn't. Other types of fiction, including folk and fairy tales, science fiction, and fantasy, are made up and probably couldn't have happened. Animals don't talk; fairy godmothers don't turn pumpkins into chariots; and there is no technology (as of now) for beaming people to faraway places. Fiction is almost always some kind of story and has the elements of story. There is a setting and some characters. The characters interact and do something. They have goals or solve problems. There is action and plot and drama!

Nonfiction could and did happen. Nonfiction includes informational books about animals, sports, places, art, cooking, gardening, health, and a host of other topics we can learn about through reading. Nonfiction also includes biography and autobiography.

According to a national survey, bookstores sell 80% of their fiction titles to women and 80% of their nonfiction titles to men! Considering that some women buy an occasional informational book along with their "novels," some men read stories, and that women buy books as gifts for men and vice versa, that is an astonishing statistic! There seems to be a clear preference for females toward fiction and for males toward nonfiction in the adult American reading population.

Now, consider the type of reading material that elementary teachers—who are overwhelmingly female—provide for their students and the generally less-positive attitudes of boys toward reading and ask yourselves if there might be a connection here. Could it be due to the fact that most of what students are given to read is fiction—a story of some sort that could or could not have happened—when boys may actually prefer nonfiction—books about people, places, and things that really exist or did happen?

Regardless of gender, people have different preferences about what they read. Adult readers tend to favor one or two types of books and do most of their reading in those books. In the Guided Reading Block, try to have your children read from "all the different sections of the bookstore." That way, you know that every child will have the opportunity to discover the type of book that grabs him or her.

In addition to story and informational text, there are three other specific types of text included in Guided Reading. These are plays, poetry, and directions. Each has its own form, and each requires some particular reading strategies. In addition, children enjoy the "change of pace" these three types of text provide and the special activities we do with these. We read plays aloud, do choral and echo reading of poetry, and draw and make things from directions.

Your Materials

Now, look at the materials you are using for Guided Reading and try to classify them into categories. If you use a reading text, look at the table of contents and try to fit each of the selections into the chart shown below. If you use text sets or book packs, try to classify them. Draw your own conclusions about how balanced your Guided Reading is from a text-type point of view and imagine how the different children you teach will view reading, given how much time is spent with which types.

Text Type	2 Examples Found	Total # of Type
Realistic Fiction		
Historical Fiction		
Mystery		
Fairy/Folk Tales		
Modern Fantasy		
Science Fiction		
Information–Science		
Information–Social Studies		
Information–Other		
Biography		
Plays		
Poetry		
Directions		
None of the Above		

What did you discover? When this chart was completed in one teacher's classroom with the typical materials used for Guided Reading, a huge amount of realistic fiction, folk/fairy tales and fantasy, some poetry and informational science (mostly about animals), and very little or none of the other types were found. The teacher then began "begging, borrowing and contriving" so that the Guided Reading Block provided a more balanced reading diet.

Begging, Borrowing and Contriving Materials for Guided Reading

When the Four-Blocks began, a very limited amount of materials were used in the Guided Reading Block. Some schools had basals or literature anthologies and relied primarily on them. Other schools had text sets and relied primarily on them. Now, a dozen years later, there is a wide variety of materials—some of which have been bought, but much of which has been begged, borrowed, or contrived. Here are some of the materials you may want to use and suggestions for how you might get them.

Reading Textbooks

Most elementary schools have reading texts, sometimes called "basal readers" or "literature anthologies." In some schools the adopted reading text is the core text for the Guided Reading Block. In these schools, teachers use most of the selections in the textbook and supplement as needed to get the necessary variety and easier reading. In other schools, the use of the reading text is optional, and teachers pick and choose what they want to use and the order in which they will read selections.

Most teachers have strong feelings about the adopted reading textbooks. Some teachers feel "hemmed in" by them and can't get their Guided Reading Block to work very well because they are giving equal time to each selection and trying to do everything suggested in the accompanying manual. Other teachers hardly ever use the adopted text and are constantly scrounging for appropriate things for Guided Reading—even though many of the selections contained in their reading text might be very useful if used in an appropriate way. The most successful Four-Blocks teachers use everything they can for Guided Reading, including the reading textbook if they have one. They look at the adopted text—and older texts from previous adoptions—as a wonderful source of multiple copies of things to read that they use to their best advantage. Here are some tips for using and obtaining reading textbooks:

1. **Evaluate the selections.** Go through your textbook and rank each selection. Use the categories in the chart from page 28 to determine what type of text it is. Decide how hard or easy each selection will be for most of your children and rate each as "easy," "hard," or "just right." Next, consider the "delight" factor. How much will your children love the selection? Finally, think about the rest of your curriculum. Does the selection have any link to what you will be teaching in math, science, or social studies? If you are the organized type, you may want to construct a chart like the one shown on page 30 to record your opinions.

Title, Pages	Type	Hard/Easy/Just Right	♥ /OK/ YUK!	Curriculum Link

2. **Decide which selections you will use, and when and how you will use them.**
   Once you have evaluated all the selections in your reading textbook, you can begin to use it instead of letting it use you! How much control you have will depend on the flexibility (or rigidity) of your school/district rules, but most teachers have more freedom than they think. Perhaps a selection that is much too hard, would hold no interest for your students, or doesn't link to anything only deserves a day of your precious Guided Reading time—not a week! If a selection would be of interest but is hard, could you skip it and do it in May when your children will be much better readers than they are in November? If you find selections to link to other parts of your curriculum, could you wait to read them when you got to the unit, or if you have to go in order, change when you do that unit?

Reading textbooks vary in how useful they will be to you. Some are harder than others. Some have a better balance of text types. They all have some wonderful and useful selections, some pretty good selections, and some "clunkers." Deciding what your adopted text can do for you will put you in control and tell you what else you need to hunt.

Old Textbooks
If you are in a school that uses reading textbooks, there are probably old books stored somewhere. They may be in your cupboards, or in the cupboards of the grade-level chair or the reading teacher. Perhaps they are located in the storeroom or on back shelves of the library. Sometimes they are stored at the "central office" or in a no-longer-used school/warehouse. Schools that adopt reading textbooks rarely discard them. They put them somewhere. You need to find out where and retrieve them.

In many school systems, you can cut these old texts apart and make "skinny" books with the selections you deem worthy. (This is a wonderful project for a parent volunteer who wants to be helpful but can't commit to a big project, or for someone who wants to help but is homebound.) If you can cut the books apart, be selective and take only those selections which will help you meet your goals. Think about when you could use them, and pair some of them with selections from your adopted text so that you will have a grade-level and easier text for one of your weeks. If you can't cut them apart, still decide upon which ones you will use and when you will use them. Make a master book for yourself with paper clips and sticky notes marking the selections you will use and when or where they will best fit. When looking at old basals, be even more picky about which selections you will use. Make the selections you choose earn the days you and the children will spend reading them. Selections which are easy, delightful, of a text type not well represented in your current textbook, or uniquely able to link to some other part of your curriculum get a perfect "10"! Hard, boring, same type as the others, and not linked to anything selections get a "goose egg." (If you are cutting books apart, put these out with the recycling!)

Reading Textbooks from Earlier Grades

When looking for easier selections, the reading textbooks from previous grades are a good place to start. Early in the year, first- and second-grade teachers are using the early-grade materials and are usually willing to loan their later books to a responsible second- or third-grade teacher who promises to return them in mint condition. But, how can you get the children to read these easier books without undermining their confidence and motivation? Here is what one enterprising (and desperate!) second-grade teacher did.

After realizing that almost all the selections in her reading textbook were too hard for almost all her children at the beginning of the year, the teacher borrowed the mid-first-grade book from the first-grade teacher. She then typed up a table of contents that listed the title and page numbers of all the full-length selections. She copied this for the children and distributed it to them, telling them that she had heard that there were lots of great things to read in the book they had read last year. She made a big deal about how she borrowed one of the books from her first-grade teacher friend, took it home the previous night, and discovered some really funny stories and selections with really interesting information. As she said this, the teacher pointed to a couple of titles on the table of contents and invited the children to share their remembrances.

Next, she explained that after a long summer of not reading too much, everyone needed to get warmed up again and ready to move ahead. She thought rereading some of their favorite selections might be a good warm-up. "But," the teacher explained, "I need your help!" (Children are always more cooperative when they think their help is needed!) "I don't know what your favorites are, and we don't have time to reread them all."

Next, the teacher went on to explain that she was going to give them each a book and 20 minutes to look through their books and get ready to vote on the best selections. She explained that each child could vote for four selections and that the selections that got the most votes would be the ones they would read. She also told the students that they had to make up their own minds, but that they could look at the books with a friend if they liked.

Without further ado, she handed each child a book and set the timer for 20 minutes. The children quickly settled down with the books and their typed table of contents. Most children were huddled with a friend and went through the book remembering favorites, enjoying the pictures, rereading a little, and lobbying each other to vote the way they intended to vote.

When the timer sounded, the children voted. The teacher tallied the votes and then ranked the selections from favorite to least favorite. There were six selections that got quite a lot of votes, and the teacher decided that those would be the ones they would reread, beginning with the one that got the most votes and working their way down the list.

They spent 18 days, 3 days on each selection, reading and rereading the selections. During this time the teacher used several of the before-and-after reading activities (KWL, beach ball, picture walks, etc.) to which she wanted them to become accustomed. She also taught them some of the during-reading formats she wanted them to learn how to do, such as partner reading, playschool groups, Sticky Notes, Three-Ring Circus, and You'se Choose.

At the end of the first month of school, these second-graders were becoming better readers. Reading and rereading easy selections in a variety of formats will get most classes back up to speed. They had also become comfortable with some of the before-and-after reading activities and during-reading formats they would use throughout the year.

At the suggestion of one of the children, echoed by all the rest, she borrowed from this same first-grade teacher the late-first-grade book and used the same procedure to have the children select the "Best Six" from it. By the time the second month of school ended, many of the children were able to read most of the selections in the grade-level text and, by combining it with some easier selections from a variety of sources and using the Book Club and other formats, the Guided Reading Block was off to a very successful start!

Of course, there are other possibilities for using reading texts from an earlier grade. If your school has a new adoption and your children haven't read the earlier books yet, you can use the choice procedure, but have students decide which selections they would have liked best last year and then read the top choices. You might institute a "community service" reading project and appoint all your children as reading tutors. They will then need to practice reading easier materials so that they can teach them to children at a younger grade level. When making skinny books, you can include "worthy" selections from easier texts and don't even have to make an excuse for them.

Sometimes in teaching children, as in cooking meals, it's all in the presentation! When clever teachers present easier reading in ways that whet children's appetites and then let them make some choices, they read and reread very happily.

Leveled Book Sets

Ten years ago, it was nearly impossible to find leveled books—books that get just a little bit harder as you move through the levels. Now, they are everywhere! Leveled books are controlled in a variety of ways. Some move from very predictable to less predictable text. Some books provide sight word practice with high-frequency words. Other books are controlled by phonics elements and provide practice in applying decoding to the actual reading of text. These leveled books are often sold in sets of six and provide lots of materials for coaching groups, After Lunch Bunches, and Fun Reading Clubs. Some teachers use them to provide easier selections for Guided Reading. If you share with another teacher on your grade level, you can probably create sets of 12, enough for partner reading in most primary classrooms.

Many leveled books give levels based on the Reading Recovery leveling system. Reading Recovery levels go from 1-20. Those books leveled 1-16 are first-grade selections. Levels 17-20 are early second grade. Later, additional levels were added to include books through third grade. *Matching Books to Readers* by Irene Fountas and Gay Su Pinnell (Heinemann, 1999) includes 7,500 titles from kindergarten to third-grade level. These grade levels are indicated by letters, with level A being kindergarten and level P being third-grade.

Science and Social Studies Textbooks

Science and social studies textbooks are a source of materials for Guided Reading, but again, you have to be "choosy." Often, the reading level of these books is higher than the grade level you are teaching. Because they have to cover so much information, they sometimes just include the "bare bones" and not the fascinating facts and examples which make non-textbook informational text so intriguing to young children.

In spite of these readability and motivational concerns, there is something in every science and social studies text that your children can read and will enjoy reading—the pictures and other graphics and the "quick-read" text that accompanies them. Look through your science and social studies textbooks and ignore everything but the visuals. Imagine how you could guide your children's comprehension as you teach them the skills of picture interpretation and graph, chart, and map reading. In Part Two of this book, you will learn about some Before-and-After reading activities, including KWLs and graphic organizers, which you can use to organize and summarize the information you and the children learn from the visuals.

As you are looking at the visuals, you might find some text to include in Guided Reading. Many science texts contain experiments with step-by-step directions. Social studies texts often contain directions for doing an interview or simulation activity. Sometimes, you may even find a poem or two from which to read, learn, and enjoy.

Many teachers avoid science and social studies textbooks because they are hard to read and often boring. But, the visuals—pictures, charts, graphs, maps, accompanying labels, and quicktext—are actually easier to read. Children, particularly struggling readers, enjoy the success they experience as they are able to read the visuals and explain what they are learning. The directions and informational poetry often found in these textbooks is a bonus. Look with a fresh eye at your science and social studies texts, and you may find they will be a major help to you in meeting all the goals of the Guided Reading Block. You can teach the specific skills needed to interpret pictures, graphs, charts, and maps. You will be helping students increase their background knowledge, meaning vocabulary, and oral language. The informational text broadens the variety of materials students are learning how to read. The reading is more apt to be at the instructional level of your struggling readers, and the experience will enhance their motivation and self-confidence. Not bad for something you probably already have!

Don't forget to go looking for old textbooks, and remember that the units on which you are working may be found in the old textbooks for earlier—or later—grade levels. If you can cut up the old textbooks, you may want to write some simple text and have children make their own books by cutting and pasting some of the visuals from the books and adding them to the text you provide.

Class Sets of Real Books

Some schools have a central store of class sets of popular books for each grade level. Teachers can come and check out the pack of *Frog and Toad Together* by Arnold Lobel, *Danny and the Dinosaur* by Syd Hoff, or *Cats* by Gail Gibbons. Many teachers use the points they get when children order books to accumulate class sets of books. Regardless of what you use "mostly" for Guided Reading, it is important that you try to "be conniving" in some way to get some class sets of popular books, so that you can guide students' reading through whole books. Many teachers worry because their children can't sustain their reading during the Self-Selected Reading Block long enough to read entire books, and yet the teachers never guide the students through entire books during Guided Reading! Learning how to read a whole book across several days is a comprehension strategy that can only be learned with whole books! Everyone needs to include some whole books in the Guided Reading Block.

So, what do you do if "you ain't got none?" First, consider how many books you need. Enough for everyone would be nice, but you can get by with half as many as you have children. Children can share a book during an ERT... lesson, and they can share books when they read in partners or playschool groups. (For some reason, who will hold the book seems to be the biggest issue for the students, so specify who will have the first turn and alternate on different days or halfway through the reading!)

Next, consider popular books that you may already have a few copies of in your room, and of which the school and public libraries have copies. In many schools, there are enough copies spread throughout the school to put together class sets, particularly if you are planning to have children share books. List the books you want to use and circulate it to other teachers, including special teachers and reading teachers. If you have some parents that buy books for their children, or if your children order from book clubs, you may want to suggest to parents that they buy the books, and then their children will get to keep them. What about the children you taught in past years? If you are choosing popular books, they may have some in their home libraries that they would be willing to loan you for a few weeks.

Gathering up the class sets of a few books for the Guided Reading Block is a hassle, but the payoff in terms of children's delight in reading "real books," their sense of community in enjoying the same book, and their increased ability to read longer texts makes it worth all the trouble.

If you plan ahead—and particularly if your grade level or school plans together—it should be less of a hassle in future years. Teachers only need each class set for a few weeks, and they don't need too many, because the more variety of materials used in Guided Reading Block, the better. Most schools can and will purchase a few class sets for each grade level if the teachers get together and take a solid and united stand!

> **Be sure to include both fiction and informational books in your class sets. Some teachers read a fiction and informational book on the same topic. Steck Vaughn (www.steckvaughn.com) makes this easy by providing Pair It Books, two books on the same level and topic—one fiction and one informational. For example, *A Look at Spiders* by Jerald Halpern is paired with *How Spiders Got Eight Legs* by Katherine Mead and *My Prairie Summer* by Sarah Glasscock is paired with a biography of *Laura Ingalls Wilder*, also by Sarah Glasscock.**

Book Club Sets

One of the most popular and multilevel formats for Guided Reading is Book Club Groups. To do Book Club Groups, you need to find four books tied together by author, text type, theme, or topic. In choosing the books, try to find one that is a little easier than the others and one that is a little harder. It is actually not hard to gather books for Book Club Groups because you only need 6-8 copies of each book (depending on how many students you have). If necessary, it is possible for two children in a group to share a book, so you could get away with as few as three or four of each title.

When considering which book is a little harder and which a little easier, depend on what you know about reading comprehension and about your students. Prior knowledge is the biggest determinant of comprehension. If you know a lot about a topic, you will understand text about it quite easily. You will also have lots of the words in your listening vocabulary, and thus, be able to more easily identify them when you see them in the book. Topics you know little about are harder to understand, and you are apt to have fewer words related to this topic in your listening vocabulary. Other factors that make books harder or easier relate to the amount of text on each page and the size of the print.

Even books by the same author can vary somewhat in difficulty. Gail Gibbons writes wonderful informational books about animals. Topic familiarity makes her *Dogs* and *Cats* much easier than most of her other books, and her *Sea Turtles* is a little more difficult than most. Looking at the amount of text and the complexity of the text on different pages will help you see that some of the *Magic School Bus* books by Joanna Cole are a little easier or a little harder than the others.

Several publishers list reading levels for their books, which makes it easier to select books for Book Club groups and include one book that is a little harder and one that is a little easier. Rigby (*www.rigby.com*) has animal fact books at different levels. Grolier (*http://publishing.grolier.com*) has sets of Pebble Books which connect by theme and contain books at different levels. For example, in the four-book Weather series written by Gail Saunders-Smith, *Clouds* is easier and *Sunshine* is harder than the two other books, *Lightning* and *Rain*. Dominie Press (*www.dominie.com*) has a collection of fables retold by Alan Trussell-Cullen in which *The Miller Who Tried to Please Everyone* is harder and *The Very Greedy Dog* is easier than *The Lion and the Mouse* and *The Boy Who Cried Wolf*. Do compare the levels given by the publisher with what you know about your children, particularly their prior knowledge of the topics.

Big Books

Big books are not just for little kids! Big books can be incredibly helpful in teaching comprehension strategies to big kids. The major advantage of big books is that you can gather your class around and focus their attention on whatever you want them to pay attention to. When you do shared reading using big books with beginning readers, you can point to the words, periods, first words, and other print features. Shared reading with big books helps beginners learn how to track print, along with other important print concepts.

As children get older, less shared reading with big books is done and more guided reading in which children are looking at their own copies of normal-sized books takes place. But, there continues to be a place for big books—even with children in intermediate grades. Big books are particularly helpful when you want to focus on a particular strategy. Predicting and anticipating, for example, is a strategy all good readers use to think about what they are reading. When children are reading in their own books, and you are trying to get them to predict and anticipate, there is always the temptation on the part of some children to look ahead so that they can make the "brilliant" prediction. This ruins the strategy lesson for everyone! If you are using a big book, you get to turn the pages, and everyone must use their brains and prior knowledge to predict and anticipate. The big book keeps them honest!

Perhaps the place where big books help us most with older children is in helping them learn to read informational text. Informational text has many features not found in story text. It often has a table of contents, an index, and a glossary. The glossary often contains the phonetic pronunciation of difficult words. Informational text has captioned illustrations and photographs, maps with symbols and a symbol key, graphs, and all different kinds of charts. To understand informational text, you need to understand how the headings work and what boldface print and bullets signify. Reading their science and social studies texts is a challenge for many children, including children who read stories quite well. Students need to be taught the specific comprehension strategies required by informational text. Big books allow you to focus your students' attention on the unique features of informational text.

Most primary teachers have lots of big books from which to choose. Teachers of older children may need to look to their content areas for these books. Many publishers produce big books to accompany their science and social studies textbooks. Even if these are not in your room, they may already be in your school. Many schools buy one set of the "supplementary" materials, and they sit in the closet of the science coordinator, or the grade-level chair, or the assistant principal, etc. Check to see if your current textbooks have big books available, and then start hunting. If they are available, but not in your school, perhaps one set could be purchased for your grade level. Once again, if every teacher needs everything to keep in his or her own room, you are going to have very limited materials, but each big book is probably going to be used for a week or less. There is never enough money or enough storage space for every teacher to keep in one classroom all the materials needed to provide the very best guided reading instruction. Once teachers begin pooling resources and sharing materials, the question becomes not, "What can I use for Guided Reading?" but "How can I use all the different materials my kids need and deserve?"

> **There are lots of sources for informational big books. Begin by looking for some that accompany your science or social studies textbooks, or the textbooks from a previous adoption. In addition, many companies have content-area big books available. Rand McNally (*www.k12online.com*) produces big books that contain content connected to the geography, social studies, and science standards. Shortland publishes big books for life, physical and earth science in their Science Alive Series.**

Weekly Magazines

Magazines such as *Weekly Reader* and *Scholastic News* can be a wonderful source of material to include in your Guided Reading Block one day each week. The selections included are usually informational, along with an occasional play or poem. Often, they also include directions for making something or doing some kind of experiment. Adding these weekly magazines can take you a long way toward meeting all the goals of the Guided Reading Block as you teach the comprehension skills and strategies needed for these text types. The reading, accompanied by lots of visuals, is usually easier, and being able to read and comprehend this highly-motivating material enhances the self-confidence of your struggling readers. Because each issue has a topic, reading these selections helps your students increase their prior knowledge, meaning vocabularies, and oral language.

But, what if your school has very limited funds, and your children can't afford the cost per child per year of most subscriptions? First, consider if this is really true! Does your school have a business partner who might want to sponsor these weekly subscriptions for your class? Do you have a few parents who might organize a fund-raiser so that everyone could have some weekly material to call their own? Could you collect something and get money for recycling it? Sometimes, when the need is apparent, the benefits are very obvious, and the cost is not absolutely outrageous, there are ways to get the needed funds.

It would be best if all your children could have a weekly magazine to learn how to read during Guided Reading one day, and then to take it home and "show off" to everyone what they know and can do. But, even when you think creatively, that may not be possible. So, consider this possibility. What if you could partner up with three or four other teachers and order 10-12 copies of the weekly magazine you decided best fit your curriculum, reading levels, and text needs? Each teacher would have the magazines for one day's Guided Reading. Children could share the magazines in partner reading, playschool groups, Everyone Read To...(ERT), or whatever format you decide to use. (If possible, laminate the copies. If not, be "strict" about their care and handling.) At the end of each week, each teacher would get two or three copies to keep in the room. These could go in a special place and be some of the many materials available for Self-Selected Reading. As the weeks go on, your supply of interesting informational reading for Self-Selected Reading will grow rapidly. Children's fluency will grow as they choose some of their favorite pieces for rereading.

> Both *Weekly Reader* (*www.weeklyreader.com*) and *Scholastic News* (*www.scholastic.com*) cost about $4.00 per child per year if you order at least 10 copies. You also get a desk copy free!

Local Newspaper's Kid's Section
Many local newspapers have a Kid's Page or Mini-Page supplement one day a week. Does your paper have one? If so, you may have found another accessible source for Guided Reading material. Most mini-pages include a good variety of text types, with a preponderance of short informational pieces, visuals—including maps, charts, graphs, and some puzzle and riddle-like activities. If you can get enough copies for each child, let the students take them home and share with their parents. If you need to share the copies in class, alternate the weeks and let each child take a copy home every other week.

Many teachers ask children who receive the paper at home to bring in the mini-page the next day. They also ask everyone they know (friends, neighbors, teachers of upper grades and special subjects, custodians, secretaries, etc.) to save the mini-page supplement for them. Some newspapers print extra copies of the mini-page each week and will give them to you for use in your classroom. Just ask, and you shall receive!

In addition to the obvious ways using the mini-page helps you meet your Guided Reading goals, there are some fringe benefits. Many children will begin to read other parts of the paper which will increase the amount of at-home reading they do and broaden the type of text they can read. This reading is often done along with parents or older siblings, and there is talk and interaction going on among family members around a reading stimulus. Children who look forward to the daily newspaper begin to see themselves as readers and see reading as a "real-world" source of entertainment and information.

Poetry

If you find the right kind of poetry, children love it! Poems are usually short and "unintimidating." They "speak" to all five senses. They appeal to and stimulate your imagination. Most poems have rhythm or rhyme and are sometimes silly, sometimes informational. There are poems to fit all your themes and topics. There are poems with which your older, struggling readers or your children just learning English can experience success and enjoyment. You can build concepts with poems, and help your children understand figurative language. You can do echo and choral reading to improve students' reading fluency. Poetry should be a part of every teacher's Guided Reading Block.

If you have been "thinking along" with the previous sections, you have probably got in mind lots of sources of poetry. You have probably found poetry in your reading textbooks (old and new), along with your science and social studies textbooks. Poetry is often found in the weekly magazines and on the newspaper mini-pages. In addition, you can find poetry in anthologies and at various web sites, and use it with your class by writing it on a chart. Some teachers have their children create poetry notebooks in which they put favorite poems.

The biggest problem with poetry, once you start to look for it and use it, is that you can overdo it. Remember that Guided Reading has as a major goal that children learn the skills and strategies needed to read all different kinds of text. Including poetry often—but not too often—will help you achieve that goal.

Some of the most popular poets for children are:		
Gwendolyn Brooks	Eleanor Farjeon	Aileen Fisher
Eloise Greenfield	Karla Kuskin	Myra Cohn Livingston
David McCord	Eve Merriam	Jack Prelutsky
Shel Silverstein	Judith Viorst	

Plays

Plays are another type of reading material children enjoy enormously. Plays have a particular style, and as children learn to read them, they practice reading their lines several times until they can read them expressively. (Don't memorize plays; it would take a very long time, and it would not help increase the children's reading fluency which is one of the many reasons to use plays with children.) There are usually some plays in the textbooks and magazines previously mentioned, but plays are perhaps the most difficult material to find. Many teachers resort to writing simple plays for their children or letting the children help them turn stories into scripts for plays. Older children enjoy doing "Reader's Theatre." They write the scripts during the writing block as a focused-writing activity, and then practice reading and performing them one day during the Guided Reading Block.

Rigby (*www.rigby.com*) publishes some wonderful books in their PM Traditional Tales and Plays series. The first part of each book tells the tale, and the last part of the book has the script for a play based on the tale. These would be perfect for Book Club Groups because Rigby produces them at all different reading levels. *Robin Hood and the Silver Trophy* by Jenny Giles is harder and *Town Mouse and Country Mouse* by Annette Smith is easier than *Beauty and the Beast* by Annette Smith and *The Foolish Fisherman* by Beverley Randell. By reading the tale in the front and then rereading the play in the back, you give children experience with two text types—folk tales and plays! There are many books of reproducible plays, including *25 Just Right Plays for Emergent Readers* and *Easy-to-Read Folk and Fairy Tale Plays* by Carol Pugliano-Martin, and *Multicultural Plays* by Judy Truesdell Mecca.

Directions

You have probably already found some directions in the books, magazines, and newspaper mini-pages you have scrounged. There are also some truly wonderful books just full of directions. In addition to Ed Emberley's wonderful *Drawing Book of Animals*, there are other books which help children draw a variety of objects by following the step-by-step directions given in words and pictures. There are books which give directions for making things, for science experiments and for recipes children can cook.

Learning how to read and follow directions requires some specific comprehension skills and strategies not required by any other kind of reading. Including some direction reading in your Guided Reading Block will allow you to teach these strategies, and will motivate some of your struggling readers who don't particularly like to read, but do like to "do things" and "make things."

Blackline Masters

Many companies produce blackline masters of little books which you can duplicate and use occasionally for Guided Reading. Many reading series provide these masters which can be used to create "take home" books connected in some way to the selection read in class. Often, these are easier to read than the selections in the reading text and may be used as "the easier" selection you try to include every week in the Guided Reading Block. Some companies, such as Creative Teaching Press, produce blackline masters that are little versions of their books. One advantage of the blackline masters is that they are economical, and children can take them home and have something with which they can "show off."

Creative Teaching Press, Scholastic, Frank Schaffer and many reading textbook publishers have reproducible pages from which children can construct minibooks. If your children don't have many books of their own at home, you might use these one day a week during Guided Reading and then suggest that children take them home and put them in a special place so they will have their own reading library.

Another advantage to using this type of material is that you can "contrive" some. You can write out or type some simple text—fiction or informational, poetry, plays, directions, etc.—and copy it for all your children to use during Guided Reading and to take home. When you are the one writing it, you are in control and can make it as hard or easy, or as predictable or unpredictable as you like.

Some teachers are intimidated by the idea of writing something for their children to read, but perhaps you are not giving yourself enough credit or are trying to be too literary. You should force yourself to write simple text, particularly if you are trying to get some easier text to provide fluency practice for everyone and instructional-level reading for your struggling readers. Many teachers take something they have read to the children or a selection which everyone has read during Guided Reading, and write a similar improvised text. For example, imagine that you have read *The Little Red Hen* by Paul Galdone. You could write a nice improvisation, perhaps making yourself the little red hen and including all your children in the story as in the following example:

> **Once upon a time, there was a teacher named Mrs. Cunningham. She was the first-grade teacher at Brown School. She wanted to make some cookies. She wanted some help. She asked the children for help. "Who will help me sift the flour?" "Not I," said Brandon and Joshua. "Not I," said Cerise and Rasheed. "Not I," said Pablo and Jasmine. "Then I will do it myself," said Mrs. Cunningham, and she did.**

The improvised story continues and includes all the children. At the end, the students help the teacher eat the cookies after promising to help her make the cookies next time. You can also write some simple text summarizing what you have learned from reading an informational book. Here is a written summary about sharks:

> **Some sharks are short. Some sharks are long.**
>
> **Some sharks are thin. Some sharks are fat.**
>
> **Some sharks are as big as an 18-wheeler truck.**
>
> **Some sharks are as little as your hand.**
>
> **Sharks eat clams, crabs, turtles, fish, and other sharks.**
>
> **Sharks don't usually eat people, but they might if they think you are a fish!**
>
> **Sharks have many teeth. When one tooth falls out, another one grows in.**
>
> **Most sharks live in deep, warm water.**
>
> **Most sharks can swim 20 to 30 miles per hour, and they live for 20 to 30 years.**

These two samples of teacher-created text were included to show you that you can create easy text for children (probably much better than these examples)!

Teachers in Four Blocks classrooms typically don't use a lot of copying paper, so don't feel guilty about copying some blackline masters—either commercially-produced or teacher-created—to provide children with the variety of types and levels of materials they need and deserve during Guided Reading.

Hopefully, you are feeling empowered by this chapter, and have decided that you have more materials than you thought you did and know how to beg, borrow, and contrive what you still need. There is just one more piece to this puzzle, and you will be ready to sample all the different before-and-after reading activities and during-reading formats that you can mix and match for an endless variety of Guided Reading lessons. The next chapter will help you understand what the important comprehension skills and strategies are, and how you decide what to teach, when, with which materials, and to whom. Read on!

CHAPTER 4

COMPREHENSION SKILLS AND STRATEGIES

When you read, you do two things simultaneously—you say the words, and you "think about" what you are reading. Saying the words aloud (or to yourself if you are reading silently) is the word identification part of reading. Understanding the meaning the words convey is the comprehension part. Word identification is necessary for comprehension, but word identification does not guarantee comprehension. How do you comprehend the meanings of the many and varied sentences in which you identify the words? Comprehension—understanding what you read—is accomplished in your brain as it processes the word meanings and language structures of the text. In simplest terms, your brain thinks about what you are reading and have read. But what is **thinking**, and how does it occur? What do you mean when you say, "Think about this"?

For more than a century, psychologists have tried to determine the exact nature of thinking, and there are many lists of the possible components of thinking. Because thinking is a complex process, it is difficult to describe. Nevertheless, because thinking is how your brain allows you to comprehend what you are reading, it is important to have some understanding of what some of the components of thinking might be. This chapter will describe six strategies which seem to play a large part in how your brain thinks as you read. Using a magazine article about Mia Hamm, a professional female soccer player, this text will help to demonstrate how your brain might be connecting, predicting/anticipating, summarizing/concluding, questioning/monitoring, imaging/inferring, and evaluating/applying information as you read.

The Thinking Strategies

Connecting

As soon as you see the title of the magazine article, before you actually start reading the article, you begin to connect some of the things you already know about soccer, the Olympics, and women athletes. You may think,

> "I never played soccer but my kids did."

> "Mia is my sister-in-law's name."

You begin to read and learn that Mia was born in Florence, Italy, and you may think,

> "Soccer is really big in Italy."

You read that Mia went to the University of North Carolina at Chapel Hill, where they already had a championship soccer team and you may think,

> "I knew they were a powerhouse in men's basketball, but I didn't know about women's soccer."

You read about the USA soccer victory in the 1996 Olympics in Atlanta and may think,

> "I remember the bombing and how tragic it was. I was recovering from surgery and watched a lot of the events. I don't remember watching any soccer, though."

Connecting is probably the most pervasive thinking strategy one uses while reading. You connect what you are reading to your own life, to what you know about the world, and to other things you have read. Connecting is so integral to reading comprehension that it is sometimes forgotten that fledgling readers need some "prompting" to make the personal, world, and intertextual connections that are critical to comprehending.

Predicting/Anticipating
Another thinking strategy you use while you read is predicting and anticipating. This, too, begins when you see the title and accompanying pictures.

"I think she is a soccer player."

"She was probably on the Olympics team."

As you read, your mind thinks ahead about where the text is going and what it may tell you. Sometimes you have a specific guess or prediction about what is going to happen. You read about UNC's outstanding women's soccer team and before the text tells you what happens, you may think,

"I bet that's where she will go to college."

You read about the injuries to the World Cup team in 1995 and think,

"They probably won't win this time."

Sometimes, you don't have a specific prediction about what will happen, but you anticipate the direction the text will take. Often your anticipating includes a voice in your brain starting sentences with "I wonder...."

"I wonder what she will do next."

"I wonder what she is doing today."

Connecting and predicting/anticipating are strategies your brain uses to make sense of, enjoy, and learn from whatever you are reading. In addition, prediction/anticipation has a motivating effect. Once it occurs to you that something may happen, you read to see if it does indeed happen. When you wonder what will happen, you read to find out what does happen. Sometimes your ideas about what will happen are confirmed, and sometimes you may be surprised by the text. Regardless of how accurate your predictions and anticipations are, they keep you reading and actively engaged in that reading.

Summarizing/Concluding
As you read, your brain synthesizes information from the words to comprehend the sentences, information from the sentences to comprehend the paragraphs, information from paragraphs to synthesize sections, and so on, as you move through the text. You read about Mia's early years in Italy, her playing soccer with her older brother, and her childhood soccer leagues and you conclude,

"She had many early experiences and the perfect personality to become a great soccer player."

The text did not say this. You read about those early experiences and about Mia's personality, and you concluded that she had "what it takes" to make it in soccer. Later, you read about her leaving school for a year to compete in China and about the hours of practice she puts in, and you conclude that,

> "Mia Hamm is a hardworking, focused, and determined competitor, and she would have to be in order to become a world champion."

Again, the text told you some things about her, and you drew conclusions that pulled together information you had read and what you knew from your own life experiences. As you read, you constantly accumulate information, and you keep this information in mind by subsuming smaller facts into larger generalizations. You summarize, conclude, infer, and generalize, and then you read some more, incorporate the new information, and draw even bigger conclusions.

Questioning/Monitoring

As you read, your brain monitors your comprehension. When something does not make sense, you ask yourself questions. "What does that word mean?" "How can that happen?" "What are they talking about here?" The more complex the topic, the more monitoring and questioning your brain has to do. Even in familiar text, you may sometimes misread a word, and then have to go back and reread when you realize something is not right. In reading about Mia, if you are not very athletically savvy, you may ask yourself,

> "What's a shutout?"

You may be able to make a guess at what a shutout is when you see that the final score was 2-0. Later, you may learn that Mia's brother suffered from aplastic anemia and ask yourself,

> "How is that different from regular anemia?"

You won't find a definitive answer to this question in the text, but you might conclude that aplastic anemia is probably a more serious disease when you learn that her brother died from it.

As you read, your brain is constantly monitoring whether or not what you are reading makes sense. As long as it seems to make sense, you are not aware of this monitoring function but when something—an unknown word, a misread word, an apparent contradiction—disrupts the meaning making, your brain sends up a red flag with a big question mark on it. Once you realize that something is not working, you try some fix-up strategies—rereading, continuing to read while looking for clarification, or asking someone. Sometimes, you may decide that the confusion is not worth the trouble, and you "forget about it" and read on. If your brain raises too many red flags and you have too many questions to try to resolve, you may decide you didn't really want to read this anyway and quit reading.

The brain's self-monitoring function works best when you encounter some—but not too many—comprehension red flags. This is one of the major reasons that children need to spend some time reading materials at just the right instructional level and be given appropriate support when reading material that is too hard for them to read and comprehend on their own.

Imaging/Inferring

When you read, you use all your senses. You see things in your "mind's eye" and hear the sounds you connect to that about which you are reading. When you really get into what you are reading, you can sometimes almost taste, smell, and feel the physical sensations you would actually have if you were in that situation. You get "lost" in the book and may sometimes be startled if someone interrupts your reading. While reading about Mia's Olympic victory in Atlanta, you might see the soccer field and hear the roars of the USA fans in the crowd. You might feel the heat of a summer day in Atlanta. As you read about the victory celebration, your mouth might water as you imagine them sipping champagne and eating pralines.

As you read, you imagine the situation about which you are reading, and you infer things the author has not told you in the text. You infer why things happen, why characters behave the way they do, and how characters are feeling. You enter the world created by the author, and you create images and inferences based on what the author tells you and your own knowledge and beliefs about that world.

The imaging and inferring thinking process is the perfect complement to the summarizing and concluding thinking process. In order to summarize and conclude, you usually read part-to-whole—synthesizing word meanings into sentence meanings, sentence meanings into paragraph meanings, and so forth. In order to image and infer, however, you do the opposite—you usually read whole-to-part. You use your background knowledge and your understanding of the whole text, so far, to image and infer the situations in the text. You use your background knowledge and understanding of the sections and paragraphs to image and infer events or features not stated in sentences. You use your background knowledge and understanding of the sentences to image or infer details not given in those sentences.

Evaluating/Applying

Perhaps the most lasting traces you have of the multitude of things you have read across the years are the opinions you form and the actions you take based on what you read. As you are reading about Mia and her soccer and life successes, you might think:

"That's the kind of woman I hope my daughter will grow up to be—not necessarily that she will be an Olympic champion, but that she will believe she can do whatever she sets her mind to and will work hard toward her goal and reach out to other young women."

That kind of thought is indeed a conclusion, but it is more—it is your personal opinion. Reading about Mia has helped shape the way you look at the world, and this opinion of Mia and of the role you want your "soon-to-be-a-woman" daughter to play in the world will become a part of you.

Not all your opinions or evaluations will be this momentous. You also form smaller opinions as you read.

"She made exactly the right decision."

"Soccer is really a much more interesting sport than I thought."

Sometimes you act on your evaluations, and sometimes you don't. If after reading the article about Mia, you suggest that your daughter read it, or tell her about it, or initiate some kind of discussion based on it, you have applied something of your reading to your life. If you get an opportunity to go to a soccer match and you go (when you never would have considered going before reading about Mia), then you have applied something from the reading experience to your life.

How much you evaluate and apply of what you read depends on all kinds of factors—what you are reading, why you are reading it, the mood you are in while reading it, the particular life challenges and opportunities facing you at the moment you read it, etc. Evaluating and applying is a strategy your brain uses while you read to understand, enjoy, and learn. Most of you can name a book or two you absolutely love or that has helped you in some way. These books are proof that you evaluate and apply some of what you read.

Thinking is something you do all the time. You daydream, plan, worry, scheme, and ponder. As you think, you use a variety of thinking strategies. To comprehend what you read, you think as you are reading. The six strategies described above are some of the components of thinking that seem to be the most useful while reading. To help you think about "thinking," each one has been described separately, but in reality, your brain often employs several strategies simultaneously. You make a connection which leads you to anticipate something. You conclude and then form an opinion or decide to use this information in some way. You use your senses to imagine yourself in the world about which you are reading. Questions occur to keep you on track and help you monitor your comprehension.

The Text Strategies

The six thinking strategies—connecting, predicting/anticipating, summarizing/concluding, questioning/monitoring, imaging/inferring, and evaluating/applying—are used to help you comprehend, enjoy, and remember what you read regardless of what you are reading. In fact, these strategies are also used in "real life" when you are not reading. While some texts challenge your mind more than your daily activities do, you also engage in these six thinking strategies as you do your grocery shopping, watch a movie, and have a conversation with a friend.

In addition to thinking, there are some specific text-related things you need to do to make sense of reading. Fluency is important to comprehension because you have to identify the words quickly enough so that you can put words together in phrases and clauses, which are the building blocks of meaning. Expressive reading both indicates and promotes comprehension. For all text, you need to be able to understand meaning at the sentence and paragraph level. If what you are reading is some kind of fiction, you need to follow the story structure. Informational text requires you to understand a variety of different text structures and to read and interpret special informational text features, including pictures, maps, charts, and graphs.

Fluency

The best way to understand fluency is to think about its opposite—word by word, labored, non-expressive reading, which might sound like this:

> Once   up—on a time   there   was   a lit——tle house   in a val——ley.

Fluent reading would sound more like this:

> Once upon a time   there was a little house   in a valley.

Fluency is important to comprehension because you get meaning at the phrase level, and because fluent reading is also expressive reading. Because reading with expression requires comprehension, children who try to read expressively must also try to comprehend.

Fluency is best developed with easy material—material in which almost all the words are automatically identified. Another important activity for developing fluency is rereading. Even good adult readers read more fluently and with better expression when they practice the reading a few times, so that difficult words, including names, are quickly and correctly pronounced and the phrases are clearly articulated. If you have ever done the readings for a religious service or read the narration for a play, you know that several practices will make your final reading a pleasurable and informative event for all. (If you have ever sat through some halting, word-by-word readings, you can also appreciate the importance of fluency!)

Developing fluent reading cannot be accomplished in the Guided Reading Block alone. One of the goals of the Working with Words Block is that all children should be able to quickly, accurately, and automatically read and spell all the high-frequency words included on the Word Wall. In Self-Selected Reading, children are reading materials at their instructional level or easier and are encouraged to reread favorite books. But, because fluency is so important to comprehension, we also see it as a comprehension strategy and include some easy reading and rereading activities in the Guided Reading Block. In addition, choral and echo reading of rhymes and poems and oral reading of plays are included throughout the grades. Fluency is both an indicator and a facilitator of comprehension and deserves regular attention.

Following Sentence and Paragraph Structure

You construct meaning as you read by identifying and understanding words and then using the words to make sense of the sentences and the sentences to comprehend the paragraphs. Sentences and paragraphs are the basic meaning units, and yet very little attention is given to helping children make sense of them. Think about how meaning accumulates in the following first paragraph of a familiar tale:

> Once upon a time, there were three pigs who lived with their mother in a little house in the woods. One day, their mother told them that they needed to go out and build their own houses. They headed out, and the first little pig met a man with some sticks. The pig asked the man for some sticks so he could build a house for himself. He got the sticks and stopped right there and began building it.

In order to understand this paragraph, you have to follow the sequence of words in each sentence and think about how they are related, and you have to see how the sentences relate to each other. You have to notice where sentences begin and end. If you ignored the ending punctuation and beginning capitals, this paragraph would look like this and be much harder to follow:

> once upon a time, there were three pigs who lived with their mother in a little house in the woods one day, their mother told them that they needed to go out and build their own houses they headed out and the first little pig met a man with some sticks the pig asked the man for some sticks so that he could build a house for himself he got the sticks and stopped right there and began building it

You also have to realize to whom or what the pronouns refer. When you read "their mother" and "their own houses" you have to realize that "their" refers to the pigs (the *pigs'* mother and the *pigs'* houses). You have to realize that in the last sentence the "he" who got the sticks was the first little pig and the "it" that he began building was his house.

In addition to paying attention to sentence boundaries and understanding the pronouns, you have to follow the logic and the sequence and keep one idea in mind as you read the next. In chapter 13, you will find four before-reading activities you can do with children before they read a passage that introduces some of the words in that selection and helps them begin to focus on sentence and paragraph structure.

Following Story Structure

Pick up the newest John Grisham novel, and you have certain expectations of what you will find there. You know that there will be characters—main characters who will probably be present throughout the book and other characters who will come and go. You expect that the story will take place somewhere and in a particular time period. You also know that the setting—both time and place—may change and that you need to keep up with when and where the action is happening. Speaking of action, you are expecting some! Things will happen and problems will arise which need to be resolved. You don't know the "plot" but you know good novels have them.

In addition to the normal expectations you would have for any novel—characters, settings, plot, resolution—you probably have some more specific expectations if you are a John Grisham fan. Some of the characters are apt to be lawyers, and courtrooms and jails are apt to be some of the many settings. The plot will require some crime to be solved and will have some twists and turns that may keep you reading late into the night to see how it "turns out."

Good readers have expectations in their minds about what stories include. If they are readers of particular authors or types of stories—mysteries, science fiction, fantasy, etc.—they have more specific expectations. Following story structure is a comprehension strategy which helps children learn what to expect, and increases their understanding of and enjoyment in story reading.

Following Informational Structure

Imagine now that you are reading a magazine, and the first article you read is about Africa. You would not be expecting characters, settings, plots, and resolution, but you would still have some expectations. You would expect to learn some facts about Africa—its geography, history, economy, people and animals, politics, etc. You would also expect to find some things in the text other than just lots of words. You would expect illustrations and photos with some accompanying "quicktext" labels or captions. You may also expect to find a map or two and perhaps some charts.

As you begin to read, you connect what you are reading to what you already know about Africa and its geography, people, and other subtopics. If there is a lot of new information, you might begin to construct in your mind a web of Africa facts and place the information you found interesting on the appropriate spokes of the web. When you finish reading, you will have lots of information in your Africa "brain site" and it will probably be organized in some fashion with the interesting facts (details) connected to the main ideas.

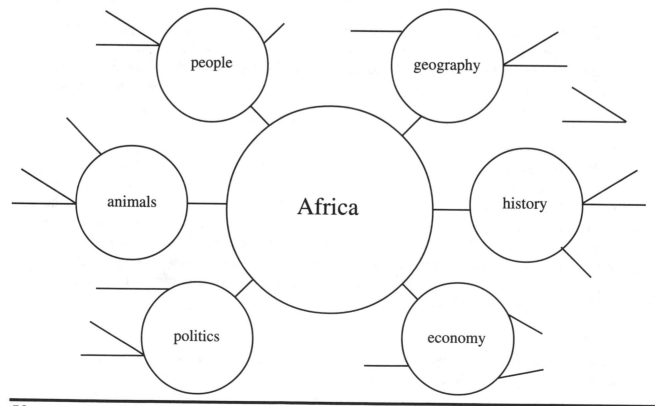

Guided Reading The Four-Blocks™ Way

Imagine that the next piece you read in the magazine is an article about spiders. In this text, you also find lots of captioned illustrations, along with some diagrams showing various body parts and a chart that shows a spider web being spun in various stages. Different kinds of spiders are described, and you learn that while spiders share certain features—eight legs, two pinchers, spinnerets, etc.—other features are specific to each particular spider. When you realize that these spiders are being compared and contrasted, you begin to construct in your mind a chart with features going down the side and spider types across the top. As you read about the different kinds of spiders, you put their contrasting features in the appropriate categories:

	Tarantulas	Crab Spiders	Jumping Spiders
How They Look	Large and hairy	Short, wide, crab-like bodies	Most colorful, w/ brightly colored hair on their legs
Where They Live	Burrow into the ground		
How They Move	Crawl	Sideways, like a crab	Jump more than 40 times their body length

Next, you read the article about Mia Hamm mentioned earlier in this chapter and, realizing that sequence is important to biography, you begin to construct an internal timeline for Mia:

1972	1977	1986	1989
Born in Florence, Italy	Played soccer with brother in Texas	Star soccer player in high school	UNC freshman 21 goals in 23 games

Finally, you read an article about the effects of inflation on the stock and bond markets and your brain starts constructing a causal chain of events:

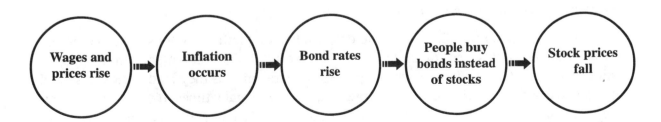

Wages and prices rise ⇒ Inflation occurs ⇒ Bond rates rise ⇒ People buy bonds instead of stocks ⇒ Stock prices fall

The previous examples were included to illustrate for you the most common expository text structures—main idea/details; compare/contrast; sequence; and cause/effect. Many informational pieces include two or more of these structures. We hope that the graphic organizers—which some people call "mind maps"—helped you to understand these different structures. Because different informational pieces are structured in these different ways, and because your brain stores information in intricately networked and interconnected ways rather than in lists, it is believed that graphic organizers are excellent devices to help children learn to follow the structures in informational text. Chapter 9 provides lots of graphic organizers and suggestions for using them with children in before-and-after reading activities.

Helping Children Use Comprehension Strategies Independently

It is much easier to teach strategies than it is to actually get children to use strategies when they need them. Many children can pick out the main idea from a list of four possible choices, but don't sort out the main ideas from the details when reading on their own. Many children can put story events in order if you give them the events, but cannot retell a story and include the important events in the right order. Many children can fill in the details on the spokes of a web if you tell them to, but they don't construct internal webs when they read to help them follow the informational text structure and organize important details under their topics.

In Part Two of this book, some powerful before-and-after reading activities which help children learn to use thinking strategies—connecting, predicting/anticipating, summarizing/concluding, questioning/monitoring, imaging/inferring and evaluating/applying—and develop text strategies—fluency, following sentence and paragraph structure, following story structure, and following informational structure—which will help them learn to independently comprehend all kinds of texts, will be presented. Each of the before-and-after reading activities helps develop one or more of the strategies. The Guided Reading Block always includes a before-reading activity and children read every day. Some days, we finish the Guided Reading time with an after-reading activity. Other days, we do the after-reading activity at the beginning of the Guided Reading Block, and then on the next day, we do a before-reading activity and read.

We read every day in the Guided Reading Block. On some days, we reread a selection for a different purpose, in a different format, and work on a different comprehension strategy. Longer selections may take several days to read, but we include before-and-after activities with each segment of these longer pieces.

Assuming you jump right into some Guided Reading on the first day of school and have a wonderful selection saved for the last day, you have 180 before-and-after reading opportunities to teach children how to use comprehension strategies as they read. Across a school year, you can do all the before-and-after reading activities many times. If you organize your instruction within the Four-Blocks framework for first, second, and third grades, you have over 500 before-and-after opportunities! As children participate day-in and day-out in these varied before-and-after reading activities chosen to fit with the selections to be read, they learn to use the comprehension strategies independently.

PART 2
TEACHING COMPREHENSION WITH "BEFORE-AND-AFTER" READING ACTIVITIES

There are many good lesson frames for teaching comprehension skills and strategies with a variety of materials. What all these comprehension lesson frames share is that the teacher guides the children in some way before, during, and after reading. In this part of *Guided Reading The Four-Blocks™ Way*, some of the lesson frames which Four-Blocks teachers use to teach comprehension before and after students read will be described. You will see how previewing, predicting, Think-Alouds, KWLs, graphic organizers, story maps, Beach Ball, "doing the book," small-group discussions, sentence and paragraph detectives, drawing and writing, and even "souvenirs" can help students become better comprehenders of all kinds of text, and build their prior knowledge, meaning vocabulary, and oral language.

CHAPTER 5

PREVIEWING

You learned in Chapter 4 that comprehension requires thinking, and that there are specific thinking strategies readers use to make sense of, enjoy, and learn from what they are reading. You are teaching comprehension strategies when you help children think about what they are reading. Two thinking strategies that all good readers use before they actually begin to read the text are connecting and predicting/anticipating. In this chapter, you will see how teachers use picture walks and "What's For Reading?" to help children learn how to preview before they read.

Picture Walks *Make this quick*

If the text the children are about to read has lots of pictures, begin your Guided Reading Block with a picture walk. Page through the book, looking at and talking about the pictures. (If the story has a surprise ending, either don't do a picture walk or "walk" only partway through the book.) The questions to ask are quite simple and predictable—the kinds of questions you want children to get in the habit of asking themselves as they preview a selection before reading it:

- What do you see in these pictures?
- What is the boy (girl, lady, man, shark, cat, etc.) doing?
- Where is this happening?
- Where are they now?
- What do you think this is?

In addition to getting children talking about what they see and what they think is happening, these questions get them to name items in the pictures—particularly the items for which some children probably don't know the names. You could also ask the students to stretch out a few words that name things, to identify the letters in the words, and then to point to the words in the text.

Picture Walk with a Story
Here is an example of a picture walk using the popular book *There's An Alligator Under My Bed* by Mercer Mayer. (The bold-faced type indicates the teacher's words.)

"Let's look at the cover of our book. What do you see here?" The children talk about the boy and the alligator.

"Where is the boy?" "In bed," reply the children.

"Where is the alligator?" The children respond, "Under the bed."

"Now, let's see if we can read the title." The children read the title aloud, *"There's An Alligator Under My Bed."*

The teacher then leads the students to talk about the next several pages. She helps them to understand that the Mom and Dad can't see the alligator, who only appears when the boy is alone in his bedroom.

"Now, look at this page. What is the boy doing?" "Getting something out of the refrigerator," respond the children.

"The boy isn't in his bedroom anymore. What room do you think he is in?" "The kitchen," the children reply.

"Let's stretch out the word 'kitchen' and decide what letters 'kitchen' probably has." The children stretch out "kitchen" and decide that they hear a *k*, a *ch,* and an *n*.

"Now, look at the sentence here and see if you can find and put your finger on the word 'kitchen.'" The children all point to the word "kitchen," and the picture walk continues.

A few pages later, the teacher asks:

"What room do you think the boy is in now?" "In the garage," the children say.

"Yes, the car is parked here, so this is probably the garage. Let's stretch out the word 'garage.' We hear a *g* and an *r* and a *j* sound. See if you can find and point to a word in this sentence that is probably 'garage.'" The children all point to the word "garage."

"Yes, that is the word 'garage.' We don't see a *j,* but what letter do you think has the *j* sound in 'garage'?" The children decide that "garage" has two g's and the last g has the j sound like it does in "gerbil."

The teacher leads the students to talk about the rest of the pages, having them stretch out and identify a few more key words, such as *stairs*, *crawled*, and *note*.

Link to Working With Words Block: Making Words	
Make:	rat, rot, got, goat, gate, late, grit, girl, gill, grill, trail, trial, troll, gorilla, alligator
Sort:	animals; gr, tr words; rhyming words
Transfer:	spill, skate, plot, chill

Picture Walks with Informational Text

Picture walks are also an effective way of helping older children begin to connect and predict/anticipate, particularly when they are about to read some informational text. Here is an example using the first third of one of the Eyewitness books, *Amazing Fish* by Mary Ling.

The book has bold-faced captions next to each of the pictures, and labels to go with some of the pictures. As you do the picture walk with informational text, read the "quicktext" (labels, captions, etc.), but move fast enough so that the children have to wait to read the rest of the text. You want to whet their appetites for the feast of amazing facts they will get when they read.

> **"These two pages are called 'What Is a Fish?' Let's look at the pictures and their labels, and see what we think they might tell us about how we can decide if an animal is a fish or not."**
>
> **"What do you see next to the label, 'Our Wet Home?' Yes, it is a picture of Earth."**
>
> **"Now, look at the diagram next to the label about how fish breathe underwater. Who can explain what we see in the diagram? Yes, the water goes in through the gills and then out. From the water, the fish get oxygen. Say 'oxygen,' and then see if you can find the word 'oxygen' in the text and point to it."**
>
> **"In the next diagram, you see their fins, with labels naming each fin. Point to the dorsal fin, the tail fin, and the pectoral fin."**

The teacher continues to help the children preview the pictures and labels that accompany the text they will read that day. Each two-page spread is discussed quickly, but not every picture and label is discussed. The teacher introduces a few words that will probably cause difficulty in the students' reading by using the labels and pictures to build meaning, and then having the children point to the word as they locate it in the text.

> **"Look at the two pictures of this fish. In the first one, the fish is relaxed, but in the second picture, it is disturbed. What animal does the disturbed fish resemble? It looks kind of like a porcupine, doesn't it? It is actually called a porcupine fish. Say 'porcupine,' and see if you can find the word 'porcupine' in the text."**
>
> **"The stripes on this fish help it blend in with the coral reef. What do we call it when an animal can hide because it is the same color as its surroundings? Yes, we call it 'camouflage.' Stretch out the word 'camouflage.' What letters do you hear? See if you can find the word 'camouflage' in the text and point to it."**

After the picture walk, the children will read the first third of the text for some purpose. They might be asked to read for information they could add to a fish web or data chart, or to list some questions they still have about fish to which they would like to find the answers. After reading the first third of the text, the students would do whatever task the teacher had set. Then, on the second day, the teacher and class would do a picture walk on the middle third of the text, read that section, and add information to whatever web or chart they were compiling. On the third day, they would do a final picture walk through the last third of the book, finish reading the book, and add their facts or questions to the list.

Link to Working With Words: Making Words

Make:	am, emu, elf, flag, flea, leaf, loaf, foal, coal,
	glue, clue, clam, camel, camouflage
Sort:	animals; cl, fl words; rhyming words
Transfer:	true, slam, goal, due

Link to Writing—Minilesson

In your minilessons, try to write about the widest variety of topics you can. Once in a while, model how something you read during Guided Reading inspired a writing topic. Fish are a high-interest topic to children. Some children like to fish. Others have goldfish as pets. Some children have watched fish at an aquarium, in ponds, or at the beach. Other children just like to eat different kinds of fish. You might write about fish in your writing minilesson—your experiences with fish, a pet fish you had, fish you like to catch and eat, or some other fishy topic. Some of your children may be inspired to write about fish, too. If you get "inspired" by what was read during Guided Reading and share that inspiration, your children will begin to see the things being read during Guided Reading as possible topics for their own writing.

Pictures help us to recall prior knowledge and connect it to what we will read. They help us begin to build new concepts. Teachers can also develop vocabulary by using some new words and connecting these to the pictures. Children can be led to identify some words in the text that might be impossible for most of them to figure out if they encountered the words while reading. Pictures help us anticipate what the text will tell us. If your prior knowledge is great, you can actually predict where a story might go or what information you might learn. Even when you don't know exactly where the text will take you, the pictures get you to anticipate and wonder:

- I wonder what that is?
- I wonder why he looks so unhappy?
- I wonder how that happened?
- I wonder how they can do that?

Once children begin to predict and wonder, they are eager to read and find out if their predictions are true, and if their wonderings will be answered. Briskly-paced picture walks are great "teasers" for the reading to come. When you start considering how you will help your children access their prior knowledge, begin to make connections to the text, and get their little brains predicting and anticipating, try leading them on a walk through the pictures. See if you don't agree with the old adage, "A picture is worth a thousand words."

What's For Reading?

When it gets close to dinner time in most houses, people start to ask, "What's for dinner?" They peek into the kitchen to see what's cooking. The water boiling away in the large pot foretells some kind of pasta. Salad fixings are sitting on the counter waiting to be washed and chopped. Tantalizing aromas coming from the oven indicate something good for dessert. What's for dinner varies, but most people expect there will be dinner, and everyone likes to anticipate what it might be.

You want children in your classroom to know that they will read something every day during Guided Reading, and as Guided Reading time approaches, you want them to begin asking themselves, "What's for reading?" Then, you want them to know that they can take a quick peek into the text and see the kinds of reading they can anticipate. "What's For Reading?" is the name for a previewing activity in which children decide what kind of text they are going to read and what special features that text has. Here are some "What's For Reading?" examples:

Poetry
Poetry is included in your Guided Reading Block because children enjoy it. It is easy to find poems that are related to your topics and themes, and that are easy to read, yet don't look "babyish." Remember that two of your goals in the Guided Reading Block are to provide as much instructional-level reading as possible, and to maintain the self-confidence and motivation of your struggling readers. Poetry is easily found and three or four poems on a topic make a good Guided Reading day. Read and reread the poems several times—often using choral and echo reading formats. This rereading promotes reading fluency.

On the day that you have selected poetry for the "What's For Reading?" activity, don't say, "Today, we have some poems about animals to read." That takes away all the fun of letting the students figure out that they are going to read poems, and the poems are all about animals. Rather, say something like:

> "I am going to show you what we will read today, and I want you to try to figure out what kind of text it is and what it is all about. To do this, you need your eyes and your brains. I will show you the three things we will read, and you see if you can answer these two questions:
>
> What kind of text will we read?
>
> What are all the things we will read about?"

Next, signaling to the children that they are to "zip their lips" and just use their eyes and brains, show them—one at a time—the poems you have selected, but don't say anything. (This is hard, but if you mime and point and don't say a word, the children will follow your example.)

When the students have had 30 seconds to look at each poem, ask the first question:

"What kind of text will we read?"

The children should be able to tell you that all three are poems, but probe a little and have them explain how they know this. They will probably tell you about the verses, and the way the poems look, and a few students may have noticed some rhymes—if some of the poems rhyme. Congratulate them on what good "looking and thinking" they did, and then ask them the second question:

"What are these poems all about?"

Follow up their "Animals" answer with a "How do you know?" question. The children will probably respond by telling you what the titles are, assuming that the animals were in the title. They might also mention some animal words that they saw or some pictures, if there are any.

Following up students' answers to questions with a "How do you know?" question is important. It gives the children who couldn't figure out what kind of text the poems were or what they were all about a "window" into the minds of the children who could figure it out. Some children are just better at figuring things out than other children, but all children profit from hearing the "figuring out" strategies explained by their friends.

Plays or Directions

Use a similar procedure on a day when you are going to read a play or directions. Tell the children that you are going to give them one minute to look at the text they will be reading, and they need to try to answer the two questions:

"What kind of text will we read?"

"What will it be about?"

After a minute of complete silence—on their part and yours—ask the students what kind of text it is, and more importantly, how they know.

For a play, they should notice that the text lists the characters and that it may be divided into different scenes or acts. The students should also notice how the characters' names are listed and then their words. Sometimes, there are also directions listed in parentheses.

Directions usually have numbered steps and are often accompanied by little pictures or diagrams to try to make each direction clear. Depending on what the directions are, there is often a list of things you need and a picture of the finished product.

Once the students have explained that the text is a play or directions and how they know that, ask the second question,

"What do you think the play is about?"

Or

"What are these directions for?"

Be sure to follow up the students' answers with the "How do you know?" question, so that every child can get in on the secrets of previewing text to see what it will be about.

Story or Information

Text that is not poetry, a play, or directions is called prose—not a term that is used much with young children. Unfortunately, because the word "prose" isn't used frequently, children—and some teachers—call all ordinary-looking text "stories." This is confusing to children because when you are anticipating a story, your brain starts expecting characters, settings, problems, and solutions. Informational text has different structures, such as main-idea/details, sequence, cause/effect, and compare/contrast. In addition to illustrations, informational text often contains other visuals—photos, maps, charts, graphs, and diagrams. Informational text also uses headings and bold text in a different way from story text, and often includes a table of contents, index, and glossary. When you are going to have children preview text that is not a poem, play, or directions, change your first question a little. Instead of asking what kind of text, ask the students to decide:

"Is what we will read today probably a story or probably information?"

Keep the second question the same:

"What will it be about?

For your first several "story or information previews," choose some selections that are clearly one or the other. You can easily tell that *The Three Pigs* and *There's An Alligator Under My Bed* are stories. To make the contrast clear, you might choose an informational book about pigs or alligators for your next preview.

Once the children have the books, and know that they are trying to decide if the selection is story or information and what it is about, give them one minute exactly (This is more dramatic if you time it with the second hand of your watch or classroom clock!) and then ask:

"Story or information? What's your guess and why?"

For story texts, the children may respond by telling you that "pigs don't wear clothes" or that "there aren't really alligators under beds." For informational selections, they may tell you that they see real pigs, that the pigs are doing real things, and that the text shows the different kinds of pigs and how they live, etc.

Sometimes it is difficult to tell by previewing whether a selection is story or information—especially for children. Many stories contain lots of true facts, and some informational books have some fanciful-looking illustrations. You probably would not want to choose these as your first examples, but eventually you will be faced with selections where it is hard for the children to figure out what kind of text it will be before they read it. In your discussion with the children, if they are not in agreement, or if they all think it is information when it is a actually a story, or vice versa, you might say,

"Sometimes you can tell right away, and sometimes you can't. Let's read the selection first, and then let's try to decide if it is a story or information after we have read it."

Once the children have decided that a selection is probably information, there is another question for which you might ask children to preview:

"What special features do you see in this selection that you don't usually see in stories?"

This would be a good time for the students to notice the special features of the text, such as maps, charts, graphs, diagrams, bold-faced text, headings, table of contents, glossary, index, etc. Whatever special features the text has that your children notice should be briefly discussed. Later, as you read the text with the students, you can guide them to interpret these special features, but during the preview, they should just notice them and begin to expect to see them when they are reading informational text.

What's For Reading? is a simple and quick before-reading activity, but it is an important activity to do with children. When you begin to read something, you have in your mind what kind of text it is and what it is about. This helps you to think about how to read the text and to begin making connections and predictions/anticipations based on your prior knowledge of this kind of text as well as your prior knowledge of this topic. Children need to learn to do this so that when they read without you there to point out, "Here are some animal poems," etc., they can figure it out on their own. Remember that in the Guided Reading Block, you are trying to teach students to read all different kinds of texts, and to use specific comprehension strategies as they are needed.

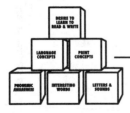

Building Blocks Variations

Picture walks are done with kindergartners, but they don't usually include the "stretching out a word and finding it in the text" step. We would not do What's For Reading? with kindergartners.

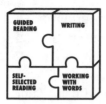

Big Blocks Variations

Most content-area text students read includes lots of new vocabulary. Often, there is a visual, such as a picture, map, chart, graph, etc., which could help sudents build key vocabulary. Picture walks, including introducing and finding new vocabulary words, is especially helpful to older children. What's For Reading? (with an added emphasis on the special features of informational text) is a before-reading activity you could use regularly with older children.

Previewing

The goal of comprehension instruction is for children to learn how to independently do the strategies as they read on their own. Previewing helps children make connections and anticipate/predict. If you begin your Guided Reading Block with a picture walk or What's For Reading? activity on a regular basis, children will get in the habit of previewing text before they read it. They will take their own picture walk, or page through the text to see what kind of text it is and what it is all about. This is how students become independent, strategic readers.

Picture Walks

1. **Walk students though the text, looking at some or all of the visuals.**

2. **Ask questions about the visuals, and let the children explain what they can learn from these to the other children.**

3. **Use the visuals to introduce key vocabulary. Ask questions that might elicit the word, and if students don't come up with the word, say something like, "We call this a …."**

4. **Have students say the key vocabulary word, and stretch it out to decide what letters they would expect to find in that word. Have students locate and point to that word in the text.**

What's For Reading?

1. **Give students one minute to preview the text and decide what kind of text it is and what it is all about.**

2. **Have students explain what kind of text it is, what it is all about, and how they know.**

3. **If the text is story or informational, have students try to decide which it is and justify their answers. Explain that sometimes this decision is easy, but other times you can't tell until you have read some of the text.**

4. **If the text is informational, have students identify any special features, such as bold-faced text, etc., and tell how these features can help them when they are reading.**

Guided Reading The Four-Blocks™ Way

CHAPTER 6

PREDICTING

A time-tested way to help children access prior knowledge, help them connect reading to their own experience, and engage them in what they are reading is to have students make predictions before reading. Many teachers read just the first page or two of a story aloud to children, and then stop and ask,

"What do you think is going to happen?"

All responses are accepted, and followed up with a question to evoke students' thinking, such as:

"What makes you think that?"

The teacher is very non-judgmental, and says things like:

"That's an interesting idea."
"I never thought of that. She could do that, couldn't she?"

Usually, teachers record children's predictions on a chart. With older children, you can appoint two recorders to write down the predictions.

Helping children make predictions before they read is a powerful strategy because instead of the teacher setting purposes and telling children what to read for, the children are learning to set their own purposes. This is what real readers do. You begin making predictions from the minute you see the title and cover of a book. As you read the first several pages, your brain thinks ahead about what may happen. Sometimes, you have a specific prediction:

"If Clifford goes in there, he'll get stuck!"

Other times, you may not have a specific prediction, but you anticipate the direction the text is likely to take:

"Clifford is going to get into trouble here!"

As you read, your predictions are sometimes proven true and other times you get surprised. When helping children make predictions, don't place emphasis on whether the predictions are right or wrong. Rather, put your emphasis on the predictions making sense and being something that could happen. Sometimes, you may tell a child that his prediction is wonderful, and that the author would probably have written a more interesting story if that prediction had actually happened. The important part about predictions is not whether they are right or wrong, but that they are made. Once you have made a prediction, your attention is engaged and comprehension is enhanced. Teachers produce motivated, active, engaged readers when they regularly help children to make predictions based on the cover, title, first few pages of text, illustrations, etc., and then follow-up the reading by discussing which predictions really happened and what surprises the author had in store for the readers. The remainder of this chapter will describe three prediction/anticipation activities: Prove It!, Anticipation Guides, and Rivet.

Prove It!

Prove It! can be used with story or informational text. Before reading, the teacher leads the students through the text, asking them to make predictions. Then, they read a section to see which predictions were accurate, make new predictions, read some more, and predict some more. Children are encouraged to use pictures, headings, graphs, charts, and other visuals to make these predictions, and they are asked to tell "why they think so" for each prediction. Here is an example of a Prove It! activity based on the book *Wagon Wheels* by Barbara Brenner.

Wagon Wheels is a fairly easy, four-chapter historical fiction novel. Do the reading across four days and do the Prove It! activity each day. Begin your Guided Reading Block and the Prove It! activity by having children look at the book cover and the title, and make predictions on what the book is going to be about, based on just these two factors. Number each prediction so you can talk about them more easily later. Here are some students' predictions, which were written down on a chart or overhead.

1. It's about a man and three boys.
2. The boys are his sons.
3. They are traveling west in a wagon.
4. It happened in the old days.

Then, look at the table of contents, read the titles of the four chapters, and make some more predictions based on them. Here are examples of these types of predictions:

5. There's going to be some Native Americans.
6. They will move somewhere.
7. They are going to get a letter.
8. There is a dugout—like in baseball.

These are vague predictions, but that is fine. Remember that the comprehension strategy you are working on is predicting/anticipating. The children would not know how the Indians, letter, and dugout actually fit into the story, but they are wondering—and that is anticipating, and anticipating helps comprehension.

Next, explain to the children that you are going to read the first chapter, "The Dugout," today, and that you want them to look only at the pictures in the first chapter and come up with some more predictions. Give them two minutes, and then ask them to close their books and give you their new predictions. If you give them too much time, or let them keep their books open while the predictions are being made, the fast readers will read all the text so that they can make the "right" predictions. This ruins the activity for everyone, and gives the fast readers an unfair advantage. So, have a "two-minute look, then books closed" rule! After looking at the pictures for two minutes (and with their books closed, although they were dying to open them), the children made the following predictions. These predictions should be labeled with the chapter title and numbered.

   Chapter 1: "The Dugout"
   9. They cross the river in the wagon.
   10. They meet another man.
   11. They dig a huge hole.
   12. They get down in the hole.
   13. The man can play the banjo.

Now, the children read the chapter. Their purpose is to decide which of the predictions is true, and to prepare to Prove It! by reading aloud the part that helped them figure out whether it was true or not. They read the chapter in whatever format (ERT, Partners, Three-Ring Circus, Pick A Page, etc.) the teacher has decided will provide the right amount of support for everyone.

After reading, the teacher asks, "Who has a prediction they think is either true or false, and can read a part of the text that proves it?" The children respond enthusiastically:

"Number 9 is true. It says, *We crossed the river, wagon and all.*"

"Number 10 is true. It says, *a man was waiting on the other side. 'I am Sam Hickman,' he said.*"

"Number 8 is not true. The dugout is not like in baseball. It is where they live. It says, *We got our shovels and we dug us a dugout.* And later it says, *Pretty soon the dugout felt like home.*"

The children continue to prove or disprove the predictions. The teacher puts a check next to those that are true, and either crosses out the untrue ones, or changes them to make them true if only a small change is necessary. So, the eighth prediction becomes:

   8. There is a dugout that they live in.

When the children have finished, all of the predictions for this chapter will have been marked with a check, crossed through, or changed into true statements. Some of the overall predictions have been checked or changed, but many are left for the remaining chapters.

Next, the teacher asks the students what important things they learned from the text that they hadn't been able to predict from the pictures. The children share some of the important events, including:

"Their mama died on the trip from Kentucky."

"They moved from Kentucky to someplace in Kansas."

The teacher then leads the students to find the name of that "someplace in Kansas" and pronounce "Nicodemus." The children continue to add what they found out from their reading, and the teacher leads them to the text to clarify as needed. The lesson ends with the teacher and the children pulling down the map and tracing the characters' probable route from Kentucky to Kansas. The children marvel that the family traveled all that way in a wagon, without any motels or restaurants!

The next three days of the lesson continue in much the same way. By the fourth chapter, the students are much faster at making predictions, and their predictions are more precise.

25. The letter was from the Daddy.
26. The three boys went out to be with their Daddy.
27. They slept outside at night and built a fire.
28. They saw wolves and snakes out there.
29. They found their Daddy.
30. They had a real house to live in, not a dugout.
31. They grew corn to eat.

Prove It! is a wonderful prediction activity that leads to active reading by the children. It is important to carry out the steps of Prove It! each time you do the activity, so that children will learn to anticipate the purpose for which they need to read.

Social Studies Link

Wagon Wheels is historical fiction. It is a story, with characters, a setting, and a plot. But, like most historical fiction, it could have happened, and there is much information to be learned. After the children finish reading it, you might have them "reread to decide what true things you learn about life on the prairie many years ago." Or, you could guide the students to specific pages you want them to reread, or put them in four "playschool groups," and have each group reread one chapter to come up with things to add to the chart.

Anticipation Guides

Anticipation Guides also require children to predict, but their predictions are based on statements prepared ahead of time by the teacher. Anticipation guides can be used with stories, but they are more commonly used when children are about to read an informational selection. As each statement is presented, the children talk about it and share their reasons why they think it is true or false.

When using an Anticipation Guide to teach anticipating/predicting, try to include the major vocabulary the children will need in order to read and make sense of the selection, and have the children read the statements with you as each is presented. Once all the statements have been read aloud, have students indicate in some way—by shaking or nodding their heads, signaling "thumbs up" or "thumbs down," etc.—which statements they believe are true and which are false before they actually read the selection. After reading the selection, return to the statements and decide which are true and which are false. Just as in Prove It!, have students read the sentences from the selection that let them know which statements in the Anticipation Guide are true and which are false. You might end the lesson by seeing if the students can help you turn the false statements into true statements. Here is a sample Anticipation Guide lesson given before the children read a selection about Japan.

> "Boys and girls, today we are going to read about a faraway country—Japan. To get ready for our reading, I am going to show you some sentences about Japan, and you have to decide whether you think each sentence is true or not true. Here is the first sentence:
>
> 1. Japan is in Europe.
>
> Let's read this sentence, and then talk about it."

The teacher and the children read the sentence and talk about it. One child says he went to Europe. He went to Italy and France, but he didn't go to Japan, so he doesn't think Japan is in Europe. Another child says there are lots of countries in Europe, and just because the other student didn't go there, doesn't mean Japan is not in Europe. The discussion continues, and the teacher tells the students that we call Europe a continent. She asks if anyone can name any of the other continents. With help from the teacher, the children name the continents. Then, the teacher helps the students to understand that they will have to decide if Japan is on the continent of Europe, along with Italy and France, or on one of the other continents—Asia, North America, South America, Africa, Australia, or Antarctica. One child suggests pulling down the map to look, but the teacher tells her that they will use the map and talk more about the continents after they read about Japan. They can figure out from their reading selection on which continent Japan is located.

Guided Reading The Four-Blocks™ Way

"Now, I am going to show you a second sentence. Read it with me, and think about what you know that will help you decide if it is true or false.

2. Japan is made up of many islands."

Again, the teacher and the children discuss this statement by questioning what an island is and if one country could be made up of many islands. The students do not have much knowledge about this particular subject, but their curiosity is definitely piqued. The next sentences are shown, one at a time. Each is read aloud by the teacher and children and then discussed.

3. Mt. Fuji is the highest mountain in Japan.
4. Many Japanese people eat rice.
5. Many Japanese people eat seaweed.
6. Most people in Japan live in large houses out in the country.
7. The capital of Japan is Tokyo.
8. There are many temples in Japan.
9. Japan's money is called dollars.
10. Japan is the home of Sumo wrestling.

Before the children read the selection, they reread all the sentences and indicate which ones they believe are true and which are not true. Then, they read the selection, using whatever format the teacher has chosen. They know that they are reading to determine which statements are true and which are false, and that they need to be able to read aloud some sentences from the selection to prove each statement. To make the purpose a bit more multilevel, ask children to try to think of a way to word any false statements so that they would be true.

When the lesson ends, the true statements will be left the same. but the false statements will be written to show that Japan is in Asia, that most Japanese people live in small apartments, and that Japanese money is called "yen."

Social Studies Link

Remember that one of the goals of Guided Reading is to build knowledge, meaning vocabulary, and oral language. Linking what students read in Guided Reading to your science and social studies topics helps to meet this knowledge building goal. This Guided Reading lesson on Japan would tie in to a unit on Japan or other countries. This activity is based on the book *Japan* by Henry Pluckrose. *Japan*, along with *Germany, India, France, Jamaica, China, Egypt,* and *Spain* (also by Henry Pluckrose) are part of the Picture a Country series. All the books have easy-to-read text, colorful photos, maps, an index, and a table of contents. They would be very good for helping children learn to read informational text and to use the special features of a social studies book. In addition to linking some of what you read for Guided Reading to social studies, use social studies content in some of your writing minilessons, focused writing lessons, and teacher read-alouds. You could also provide topic-related books for children to choose during Self-Selected Reading.

Link to Working With Words: Guess the Covered Word

Write a paragraph that links to your science or social studies topic and cover one word in each sentence. Use this in your Working with Words Block to help children practice cross-checking meaning and using beginning letters and word length as clues. For each covered word, have the students make four guesses with no letters showing, and then reveal all the letters up to the first vowel. Ask the students to make some additional guesses that make sense in the sentence and have the correct beginning letters. Here is a sample paragraph related to the reading on Japan. (The covered words are underlined)

Japan is made up of <u>four</u> main islands. There are also several <u>smaller</u> islands. Over 12 <u>million</u> people live in Tokyo. Many Japanese people work in <u>factories</u>. They also work on <u>farms</u> and in offices. Japanese people like to go to the <u>theater</u>. For dinner, they might eat rice, seaweed, noodles, fish, and <u>fruit</u>. They might eat their dinner with <u>chopsticks</u>. In Japan, people celebrate <u>special</u> days with festivals.

Rivet

Rivet is an activity that was created by one of the authors of this book after watching a student teacher try to introduce some vocabulary words to her students. The vocabulary she was introducing was important to the story, and many of the students needed to focus on these words and their meanings. The student teacher diligently wrote the words on the board, had students use the words in sentences, and tried to help the students access meanings and relate them to each other. Unfortunately, the students were not particularly interested in the words, and their attention was marginal at best. After the words had been introduced and the students began to read the selection, many of the struggling readers couldn't decode the words, much less associate meanings with them. Rivet was conceived that day and has since saved many a teacher from the dreaded experience of having taught some words that no one seemed to have learned!

Activating children's prior knowledge and getting them to make predictions before they read is one sure way to increase the involvement and comprehension of most children. Rivet is an activity designed to accomplish this critical goal. To prepare for a Rivet text introduction, read the selection and pick six to eight important vocabulary words, with a particular emphasis on big or difficult words. Include the names of characters if they are interesting or will be difficult for students to decode. An important two-word phrase can also be included, if necessary.

Rivet can be done with informational text to introduce vocabulary and help children make predictions, but is more fun to do with stories. The following Rivet activity is based on the book *Arturo's Baton* by Syd Hoff. Begin the activity by writing numbers and drawing lines on the board to indicate how many letters each word has. (Some teachers have the students draw the same number of lines on a piece of scratch paper and fill in letters as they are filled in on the board.) Your board at the beginning of this Rivet activity would look like this:

1. __ __ __ __ __ __ __ __ __ __

2. __ __ __ __ __ __ __ __ __ __

3. __ __ __ __ __ __ __ __ __ __

4. __ __ __ __ __ __

5. __ __ __ __ __

6. __ __ __ __ __   __ __ __ __

7. __ __ __ __ __ __ __

8. __ __ __ __ __ __

Fill in the letters of the first word, one at a time, as the students watch. Stop after each letter and see if anyone can guess the word. Students are not guessing letters, but are trying to guess each word as soon as they think they know what it is. Most students will not be able to guess the first word when the board looks like this:

1. c o n _ _ _ _ _ _

2. _ _ _ _ _ _ _ _

3. _ _ _ _ _ _ _ _

4. _ _ _ _ _ _

5. _ _ _ _ _

6. _ _ _ _ _   _ _ _ _

7. _ _ _ _ _ _ _

8. _ _ _ _ _ _

But many will guess with a few more letters:

1. c o n d u c _ _ _

2. _ _ _ _ _ _ _ _ _

3. _ _ _ _ _ _ _ _ _

4. _ _ _ _ _ _

5. _ _ _ _ _

6. _ _ _ _ _   _ _ _ _

7. _ _ _ _ _ _ _

8. _ _ _ _ _ _ _

Once someone has guessed the correct word, ask everyone to help you finish spelling it, and write the word on the board. Begin writing the letters of the second word, pausing for a second after writing each letter to see if anyone can guess the word.

1. c o n d u c t o r

2. o r c h _ _ _ _ _ _

3. _ _ _ _ _ _ _ _

4. _ _ _ _ _ _

5. _ _ _ _ _

6. _ _ _ _ _ _ _ _ _

7. _ _ _ _ _ _ _

8. _ _ _ _ _ _

The attention of all the students is generally riveted (thus the name Rivet) to each added letter, and with a few more letters, many students will guess the second word.

1. c o n d u c t o r

2. o r c h e s _ _ _ _

3. _ _ _ _ _ _ _ _

4. _ _ _ _ _ _

5. _ _ _ _ _

6. _ _ _ _ _ _ _ _ _

7. _ _ _ _ _ _ _

8. _ _ _ _ _ _

If they are right, have them help you finish spelling it. If they give you an incorrect guess, just continue writing letters until someone guesses the correct word. Continue in this fashion until all the word have been completely written and correctly guessed.

Here is what the board would look like when all words were introduced:

1. <u>c</u> <u>o</u> <u>n</u> <u>d</u> <u>u</u> <u>c</u> <u>t</u> <u>o</u> <u>r</u>

2. <u>o</u> <u>r</u> <u>c</u> <u>h</u> <u>e</u> <u>s</u> <u>t</u> <u>r</u> <u>a</u>

3. <u>T</u> <u>o</u> <u>s</u> <u>c</u> <u>a</u> <u>n</u> <u>i</u> <u>n</u> <u>i</u>

4. <u>A</u> <u>r</u> <u>t</u> <u>u</u> <u>r</u> <u>o</u>

5. <u>b</u> <u>a</u> <u>t</u> <u>o</u> <u>n</u>

6. <u>w</u> <u>o</u> <u>r</u> <u>l</u> <u>d</u>   <u>t</u> <u>o</u> <u>u</u> <u>r</u>

7. <u>p</u> <u>a</u> <u>j</u> <u>a</u> <u>m</u> <u>a</u> <u>s</u>

8. <u>c</u> <u>a</u> <u>n</u> <u>c</u> <u>e</u> <u>l</u>

So, far this looks like a word-identification activity, not a comprehension activity. But, the second step of Rivet is where comprehension and, specifically, predicting come into play. Once the students have figured out the big, important words you chose, have them use these words to predict some of the events in the story. Here are some of students' predictions based on these eight important words:

Arturo Toscanini was the conductor of the orchestra.

They had to cancel the concert because the orchestra members wore their pajamas.

Toscanini wore his pajamas when he took the orchestra on a world tour.

If children fail to use some of the words in their predictions, prompt them to think about how those words might fit into the story. After asking students how the baton fits into the story, you might get these predictions:

Toscanini needed the baton to conduct the orchestra.

Toscanini got mad and threw the baton at the orchestra, so they had to cancel the show.

Children generally enjoy trying to combine the important words and make predictions—some serious and some silly. The important thing is not how serious the predictions are, or even whether or not the predictions are right. What matters is that students are using the key vocabulary and anticipating how these words might come together to make a story.

When you have some predictions (6-8 is plenty), have students read the selection to see if any of their predictions were true. After the students have read the selection, ask them once again to use the key words to write some true things that happened in the story.

The students' sentences after reading might include:

Arturo wanted to cancel the concert because he lost his baton.

Toscanini was Arturo's dog, and he found the baton.

Arturo decided he didn't need a baton, and he went off on a world tour.

One teacher told on the *teachers.net fourblocks mailring* how her class enjoys playing "Rivet vs. The Class." She reported that they have a contest between "Rivet" and the class. The students try to guess the word. If they guess the word, they are given points for every letter remaining. Rivet gets points for letters she has to give them.

Link to Working With Words: Making Words

Make: act, art, cart, arch, cash, crash, roach, torch, actor, starch, arches, torches, roaches, orchestra

Sort: arch, arches; roach, roaches; torch, torches; act, actor; rhyming words

Transfer: smash, march, smart, trash

Building Blocks Variations

You do want kindergartners to make predictions, but the predicting you would do with them would be less formal and depend more on oral language than on writing down predictions.

Big Blocks Variations

Older children love to Prove It! They are also usually intrigued by Anticipation Guides and Rivet.

Predicting

Predicting/anticipating is one of the comprehension strategies children need to get in the habit of doing. The important thing is not whether the predictions are right or wrong, or how specific they are, but that once the predictions have been made, children are motivated to read and see whether or not their predictions actually happen. Children who predict and anticipate as they read are more active readers, and thus better "comprehenders." Prove it! can be used with a story or informational text. Anticipation Guides work better with informational selections. Rivet works for both, but is more fun for stories.

Prove It!

1. Ask students to make predictions based on the title, book cover, and table of contents (if there is one). Number their predictions.

2. Decide which section of the book will be read first, then have students make predictions for that section based on the pictures—including any labels, captions, charts, maps, and other visuals. Limit the time students can look at the chosen section to about two minutes, and have them close their books while making predictions.

3. Have students read the text in whatever format you choose.

4. After reading, have children tell which predictions are true or not, and have them read parts of the text aloud that "prove it."

5. Put a check next to any predictions that are true, and cross out or modify any untrue predictions.

6. Ask children what other important things they found out that couldn't be predicted based on the visuals. Discuss this information and refer students back to the text to clarify words or meanings as necessary.

7. If you are reading a longer piece, continue steps 2-6 for each section.

Anticipation Guides

1. Write some statements concerning the main topic about which students will be reading. Include some statements that are common misconceptions that many children will think are true, and some statements that are so silly and ridiculous the students will know they are not true. "Stack the deck" so that there are many more correct statements than incorrect ones.

2. Read each statement with students and talk about what it means. Emphasize names and key vocabulary.

3. Have students write "yes" or "no" for each statement. Encourage risk-taking and guessing by saying something like, "You have a 50-50 chance. Take a guess!"

4. After students read the selection, go through each statement and have students indicate whether or not it is true. When there is disagreement, refer students back to the text and let them explain their reasoning.

5. If possible, have students help you reword false statements to make them true.

Rivet

1. Choose six to eight important words, including important names and words likely to be difficult for your students to decode.

2. Draw lines on the board to indicate the number of letters in each word.

3. Write the letters in each word, one at a time, pausing for a second after you write each letter and encouraging students to guess the word. When a student guesses the word, finish writing it. (Unlike Hangman, students are not guessing letters. Their eyes are riveted to the board as you write the letters, and they are trying to guess the word based on the letters you have written and the number of remaining blanks.)

4. When all the words are written, have the students use as many of the words as possible to make predictions about what is going to happen in the story. Record these predictions.

5. Have students read the selection, and determine which of their predictions actually happened.

CHAPTER 7

THINK-ALOUDS

Think-alouds are a way of modeling, or "making public," the thinking that goes on inside your head as you read. To explain think-alouds to young children, tell them that there are really two voices speaking as you read. The voice you can usually hear is your actual voice, reading the words aloud, but there is also a voice inside your brain which is saying what it thinks about what you are reading. Use think-alouds to demonstrate for children how you think as you read.

Thinking is the most complex act humans do, and it is risky to try to define it. Chapter Four of this book described six thinking strategies that seem to play a large role in reading comprehension. It is these six thinking processes which you demonstrate in your think-alouds. Use words for these think-alouds that seem natural, and that the children will understand. Here are some examples of words that might be used to communicate each of the six thinking strategies:

Thinking Strategies for Think-Alouds

Connect

"This reminds me of . . ."

"I remember something like this that happened to me when . . ."

"I read another book where the character . . ."

"This is like what happens in our school when . . ."

"Our country doesn't have that holiday, but we have . . ."

Predict/Anticipate

"I wonder if . . ."

"I wonder who . . ."

"I think I know what is coming next . . ."

"He will be in trouble if . . ."

"I think we will learn how . . ."

Summarize/Conclude

"The most important thing I've learned so far is . . ."

"It didn't say why she did that, but I bet . . ."

"I know he must be feeling . . ."

"So far in our story . . ."

"So far, I have learned that . . ."

Question/Monitor

"I wonder what it means when . . ."

"I don't understand . . ."

"It didn't make sense when . . ."

"I'm going to reread that, because it didn't make sense that . . ."

Image/Infer

"Even though it isn't in the picture, I can see the . . ."

"Mmm, I can almost taste the . . ."

"It sent chills down my spine when it said . . ."

"For a minute, I thought I could smell . . ."

"I could hear the . . ."

"I can imagine what it is like to . . ."

"I can picture the . . ."

Evaluate/Apply

"My favorite part in this chapter was . . ."

"I really liked how the author . . ."

"What I don't like about this part is . . ."

"It was really interesting to learn that . . ."

"I am going to try this out when I . . ."

"I wish I could . . ."

"If I were her, I would . . ."

A Think-Aloud Example

Teachers use think-alouds in a variety of ways, but the most efficient and effective use of time is probably to read and think aloud the first quarter or third of the selection the children are about to read. In addition to hearing you "think your way" through the text, children get introduced to the selection, including characters, setting, type of writing, and important vocabulary. When the children finish reading the selection, their purpose is to become attuned to the thinking voice inside their brain. Here is an example of a think-aloud based on the first third of *Aunt Flossie's Hats (and Crab Cakes Later)* by Elizabeth Fitzgerald Howard. The bold-faced words indicate what the teacher is saying (thinking) aloud. The think-aloud begins with the cover of the book. The teacher reads aloud the title, *Aunt Flossie's Hats (and Crab Cakes Later)* and looks at the picture, saying something like:

"I bet the lady in the picture is Aunt Flossie. She is a pretty lady, and she has two hats—one on her head and one on her lap. I bet she likes hats, and is going to have a lot of them. The two girls have hats, too. I wonder if those are their hats? They don't really look like kid's hats. Maybe they belong to Aunt Flossie. I wonder what the girls' names are, and if they are sisters? I think I am going to like this book, because everyone looks happy...and because I love hats!"

The teacher turns the page and thinks-aloud about the picture on the title page:

"This is a nice, quiet street, and the houses are all joined together. I think they are called row houses. They remind me of the house my great-grandma lived in. The houses were all connected, and didn't have any yards. When I went to visit her, we played in the street."

The teacher turns the page, and thinks aloud about the pictures on pages 4-5 before she begins reading:

"Now, there are the two girls. I think they are the same girls we saw on the cover. I am going to look back and check. Yes, they are the same girls. It looks like they are knocking at the door. I wonder if this is Aunt Flossie's house, and if she is home?"

The teacher then reads the first sentence:

On Sunday afternoons, Sarah and I go to see Great-great Aunt Flossie.

"Oh, it's their great-great aunt. She must be really old. I had a great-aunt named Aunt Hester. I wonder which girl is Sarah?"

The teacher continues to read these two pages and then comments:

> **"My great-grandmother's house had lots of stuff, too. I used to love playing up in the attic. She didn't have a lot of hats, though."**

The teacher turns the page and again thinks aloud about the picture before reading the words:

> **"Mmm, those cookies look delicious. I bet she baked them. I can almost taste them."**

The teacher reads the page and comments:

> **"So, the other girl's name is Susan. I wonder which one is Susan and which one is Sarah? It doesn't say they are sisters, but she is their great-aunt, and they look alike, so I think they probably are. They are going to have tea and cookies, and later crab cakes. Now, that really makes my mouth water. Crab cakes are one of my favorite foods in the whole world!"**

The pictures on the next page elicit these comments:

> **"Yes, they are having tea and cookies, and the younger girl is trying on a hat. The older girl is opening a box. I bet it is a hat box, and she is going to try on that hat."**

She reads the words, and then says:

> **"I wonder why Aunt Flossie says that the hats are her memories? That doesn't really make sense to me. Maybe we will find out as we read the rest of the story."**

The next page shows hat boxes and hats everywhere:

> **"Now this lady has a lot of hats! On this page, she looks like she is telling Sarah and Susan something. I wonder if she is telling them about the hats?"**

She reads the text and comments:

> **"It says the green hat has a smoky smell. I wonder if you can really smell something on the hat? Sarah and Susan can't smell it."**

She turns the page and comments extensively on the pictures.

> **"Whoa, I wonder where we are now?! I think these people are all firefighters, but the fire truck is being pulled by horses. This must have happened a long time ago. There is a woman holding on to a child. They both look very frightened. I can almost feel how afraid they are. I wonder who they are, and if the fire is at their house? I wonder what this has to do with Aunt Flossie and her hats?"**

While reading the page, the teacher stops several times and thinks aloud:

"The book said it was a really big fire, and that everything smelled of smoke for days and days. I think I can smell the smoke now."

"Oh, now I get what it says."

Your great-grandma and I couldn't sleep. We grabbed our coats and hats and ran outside."

"The child must be Aunt Flossie, and the other woman must be her sister. Aunt Flossie is wearing the green hat. That's why she thinks she can still smell the smoke on it. It was the hat she was wearing when they had the big fire in Baltimore."

"She says the hats are her memories because they remind her of something. I wonder what the other hats remind her of?"

"I can't wait to read the rest of the book!"

The Think-Aloud ends here, and the teacher and children discuss what they know so far. Together, they summarize what has happened in the story, and the teacher asks the children what they think will happen in the rest of the story. The children then read the rest of the story (in whatever format the teacher has chosen). The teacher gives them each four sticky notes and asks them to mark places where they hear their brain's voice telling them things, so that when they gather again to read the story together, they can share their think-alouds.

You Can Do Think-Alouds

Many teachers, when they first hear about Think-Alouds, are afraid to do them because they don't know exactly what they are supposed to think! Hopefully, the previous example will show you that your brain is thinking as you read, and if you will tune into that thinking and how you can communicate that to your students, Think-Alouds are not difficult to do. It is important to read the selection and plan what you are going to say as you think aloud. Many teachers find it is helpful to attach sticky notes with reminders to the appropriate pages.

It is not necessary to include all six thinking strategies in every lesson. Some texts don't lend themselves to particular strategies, and you don't want to force it. Across several lessons, however, you will want to be sure to include examples for each thinking strategy. Try to use as many different ways of expressing your thinking as you can, and have it match as closely as you can the thinking actually engendered by the text.

While teachers normally invite participation while reading, it is important not to let the children "chime in" as you are demonstrating thinking-aloud for them. If you use the procedure of beginning the selection with your Think-Aloud, and then having the students finish the selection and share their think-alouds, they are usually willing to let you have your turn!

Some teachers tell the children that they are to pretend to be invisible while the teacher is reading and thinking. They get to hear her thinking, but they are invisible and shouldn't let her know they are there! You want to signal to the children when you are reading, and when you are thinking. Many teachers look at the book when they are reading, and then look away from the book—perhaps up toward the ceiling—to signal their thinking. Other teachers use a different voice to signal their thinking. They read in their "reading voice" and think in their "thinking voice." An excellent source of information and classroom examples of Think-Alouds is *Mosaic of Thought* by Ellin Oliver Keene and Susan Zimmermann (1997).

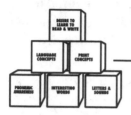

Building Blocks Variations

Many kindergarten teachers do Think-Alouds with children as they read books to them and as part of shared reading. It is very difficult to keep very young children from chiming in, however. You may need to stop and share your Think-Alouds, and let the students share theirs. You would then be doing a think-along Think-Aloud!

Big Blocks Variations

Think-alouds are particularly important for older children. As the text becomes more complex and less familiar, children need lots of modeling to see how you make sense of it. With younger children, you don't usually specify the six thinking strategies, but with older children, you might make this more explicit. You might even form some think-aloud groups with six people in a group. Model the think-aloud with the beginning of a selection and then have children draw cards to see what their thinking role would be that day. The cards have the thinking strategies—connect, anticipate/predict, conclude/summarize, monitor/question, infer/image, and apply/evaluate—written on them. As the group discusses the pictures and reads the pages of the selection, children share their thinking according to the card they have drawn. Do be sure that the children understand what each thinking strategy is and don't expect every child to respond to every page.

Think-Alouds

The goal of comprehension instruction is for children to learn how to think as they read on their own. Think-alouds help children see what good "comprehenders" do. If you do your think-aloud based on the first part of the selection the students are going to read, you give them a "jumpstart" into the selection. To do Think-Alouds:

1. Choose a selection that truly causes you to think.

2. Decide how much of that selection you will read aloud.

3. Look at the pictures and read the selection before you do the Think-Aloud. Look for places where you actually use the thinking strategies—connect, predict/anticipate, summarize/conclude, question/monitor, image/infer, and evaluate/apply. Think about how you will explain your thinking to your children. Mark these places with sticky notes and cryptic comments if this will help you remember.

4. Do the Think-Aloud as the "invisible" children watch and listen. Comment on all pictures first, and then read the text. Stop at appropriate places in the text and comment.

5. Don't try to "force" all the thinking processes into any one selection, but do try to include all six of them across your lessons.

6. Provide a structure for your children to "get in tune with," and have students share their thinking as they read the selection.

CHAPTER 8

KWL CHARTS

One of the most popular ways of helping children connect prior knowledge and make predictions for informational text is the KWL (Ogle, 1986). The letters stand for what you Know, what you Want to find out, and what you have Learned. Before reading, the teacher leads the class to brainstorm what they already know about the topic. Then, they talk about what they want to know, and brainstorm questions they think might be answered by the text they are about to read. After reading, the children share what they have learned. All this information is recorded in a three-column chart.

Here is an example of a KWL using *Bats* by Gail Gibbons. The lesson begins with the teacher holding up a copy of *Bats* and drawing students' attention to the pictures of bats flying at night on the cover. He lets the children discuss bats for a few minutes, telling whatever they know. The children respond that they have never seen a bat, but they have heard a lot about bats—and some of it is scary! On a large piece of chart paper, the teacher has labeled three columns K, W, and L. He writes what the children know under the K column. They know that bats can fly at night. They know that bats have large wings and small bodies. They know that bats live in caves. One students says that bats eat fruit—but others don't agree, so the teacher writes, "What do bats eat?" as the first question in the W column.

Next, the teacher tells the students that they are going to read this book about bats, and that there is a lot of information about bats in the book. "We are going to learn a lot about bats, but let's list in the Want, or W, column the questions about bats which we really want to be answered. One child says he wants to know if bats live near the school. The teacher writes a more general question, "Where do bats live?" Another child wants to know if bats bite people. Several other questions follow: "How do bats see at night?" "Are there different kinds of bats?" "Are bats a kind of bird?" "Can bats hurt you?" and "Are there really vampire bats?"

Bats		
K	W	L
Bats can fly at night.	What do bats eat?	
Bats have large wings and small bodies.	Where do bats live?	
Bats live in caves.	Do bats bite people?	
Bats eat fruit.	How do bats see at night?	
	Are there different kinds of bats?	
	Are bats a kind of bird?	
	Can bats hurt you?	
	Are there really vampire bats?	

Next, the teacher tells the class that they are going to read the book across two days of Guided Reading. He has put a large paper clip in each copy of the book to indicate how far the students should read, in order to keep them from "gaining an edge" by getting ahead of everyone else in the class. Their purpose for reading is to see which of their questions are answered in the text, and what new information from the text can be added to the L column of the KWL chart. If they finish reading before the time is up, the students are to write down information they want to add to the L column. The teacher reminds the class that they have learned how to read informational books and shows them a few pages, asking them what they will read and talk about first on each page. The students tell him that they will read and discuss the pictures, charts, diagrams, and the "quicktext" which goes with them first, and then read the text to see what else they can learn.

The students read the book in whatever format the teacher decides will provide the right amount of support for everyone. They have a limited amount of time, and they know what to do if they finish reading before that time is up. When the time is up, the teacher gathers the students together, and they begin the after-reading part of the lesson. (If children are not through reading, they can be asked to join the group anyway, or they can continue until they finish and then join the group.)

When the class is reconvened, they first look at the questions and decide if they have found answers to any of these. Answers are recorded in the L column. Then, the children tell other things they learned, and these are also recorded in the L column. This activity is done with the book closed, so that children have to summarize what they learned and not just tell back every fact from the book. If there is disagreement about what was learned, the teacher puts it in the form of a question in the W column, and tells students that they can try to resolve this when they read the next day.

Bats		
K	W	L
Bats can fly at night.	What do bats eat?	Bats eat insects, fruit, nectar, and
Bats have large wings and small	Where do bats live?	small animals.
bodies.	Do bats bite people?	Bats live together in caves, atttics,
Bats live in caves.	How do bats see at night?	barns, and tall trees.
Bats eat fruit.	Are there different kinds of bats?	Bats live almost everywhere, except
	Are bats a kind of bird?	Antarctica.
	Can bats hurt you?	Bats are shy, gentle animals.
	Are there really vampire bats?	Bats are nocturnal; they come out
		at night.

The next day, the teacher and class review the information in the W and L columns. A few more questions may have occurred to the students, and if so, these are added to the W column. They finish reading the book using the same format as the day before, and then complete the chart.

Bats		
K	W	L
Bats can fly at night. Bats have large wings and small bodies. Bats live in caves. Bats eat fruit.	What do bats eat? Where do bats live? Do bats bite people? How do bats see at night? Are there different kinds of bats? Are bats a kind of bird? Can bats hurt you? Are there really vampire bats?	Bats eat insects, fruit, nectar, and small animals. Bats live together in caves, atttics, barns, and tall trees. Bats live almost everywhere, except Antarctica. Bats are shy, gentle animals. Bats are nocturnal; they come out at night. Bats are mammals. Vampire bats like to sip blood from animals, but they do not live here! Bats are good hunters. Today, bats have trouble finding places to roost and are endangered.

Some of the children notice that all of their "want to learn" questions have been answered. This does not happen all the time. When the text does not answer all the students' questions it leads some children to read more about the topic or go to the Internet to find out more and answer the unanswered question(s)!

Link to Working With Words: Guess the Covered Word

Write several sentences that tell some fascinating bat facts that were not included in the book the children read. Use these sentences in your Working with Words Block to help children practice cross-checking meaning and using beginning letters and word length as clues. For each covered word, have the students make four guesses with no letters showing, and then reveal all the letters up to the first vowel. Ask students to make some additional guesses that make sense in the sentence and have the correct beginning letters. Here are some more bat facts. (The covered words are underlined)

Some bats eat <u>scorpions</u> and spiders.

Many bats eat <u>half</u> their weight in food each night.

At birth, most bats weigh only about a <u>fifth</u> as much as the mother.

Bats do not have <u>strong</u> legs.

The largest colony of bats lives in Bracken Cave in Texas and includes 20 <u>million</u> bats.

Many people in <u>China</u> think bats are a sign of good luck.

Guided Reading The Four-Blocks™ Way © Carson-Dellosa CD-2407

A second example for KWL uses the book *Tornado Alert* by Franklyn M. Branley. Again, the lesson begins with the teacher using the cover of *Tornado Alert* to spark the discussion. The picture on the cover shows a large, black, funnel-shaped cloud. The teacher encourages the children to tell about their experiences with tornadoes in an open-ended way before asking them to add specific things they know to the chart. Two children have actually experienced tornadoes. One child, whose house was in the path of a tornado, tells how he got in a closet and heard a strange noise as the storm passed by. He concluded, "Tornadoes are scary!" Two other children have relatives who experienced tornadoes. Other children talk about what they have heard at school, how they have practiced tornado drills in the spring of the year, and what they have seen and heard about tornadoes on news reports.

When the children have had a chance to talk about their tornado experiences, the teacher tells them that they obviously know a lot, and begins to record what they know under the K column of a KWL chart. The students know that tornadoes have powerful winds! They know that tornadoes can cause lots of damage. They know that tornadoes usually happen in the spring of the year because that is when they have tornado drills at school.

Next, the teacher asks the students what they want to learn about tornadoes. One child says he wants to know what causes tornadoes. Another child wants to know why some homes get hurt and others don't. Several other questions follow: "How do weather forecasters know that a tornado is coming?" "What should you do if you are not at school, but at home or outside, and you see a tornado or hear that one is coming?" "Do tornadoes happen everywhere?" and "What's the fastest the winds blow in a tornado?"

Tornadoes		
K	W	L
Tornadoes have powerful winds. Tornadoes can cause lots of damage. Tornadoes usually happen in spring. Schools have tornado drills in spring.	What causes tornadoes? Why do some homes get hurt and others do not? How do weather forecasters know tornadoes are coming? What should you do at home or outside if a tornado is coming? Do tornadoes happen everywhere? What is the fastest the winds blow in a tornado?	

The children read *Tornado Alert* in whatever format the teacher chooses. Before reading, the teacher reminds the students that they should read all the visuals and quicktext first, then read the text to see what else they can learn. She also asks students what it is that they should always do if they are working on a KWL chart and finish reading before the time is up. The children respond that they are to begin writing down things they think should be added to the "Learned" (or L) column. Here is the KWL chart the class completed together after reading:

| Tornadoes | | |
K	W	L
Tornadoes have powerful winds. Tornadoes can cause lots of damage. Tornadoes usually happen in spring. Schools have tornado drills in spring.	What causes tornadoes? Why do some homes get hurt and others do not? How do weather forecasters know tornadoes are coming? What should you do at home or outside if a tornado is coming? Do tornadoes happen everywhere? What is the fastest the winds blow in a tornado?	When warm air and cold air meet, tornadoes can start. Some tornadoes are big; they can wreck houses and kill people. Small tornadoes don't travel far or cause much damage. Weather forecasters watch closely for signs of tornadoes during tornado season. At home during a tornado, find a safe place away from windows, then crouch down and cover your head. If you are outside, find a ditch and lie in it. Tornadoes usually happen where there is a lot of flat land. Some people call tornadoes twisters and cyclones because they spin around and twist.

Some of the children are fascinated by tornadoes and want to add a lot more details to the chart. The teacher helps the class come up with sentences that tell about tornadoes but don't contain every detail, just the important facts. The class discusses their "Want to learn" questions and what they have learned from reading the book. In this KWL chart, as in most, there is a question that was not answered by the book they read. The teacher leads the students to think about the question (why one house gets hurt but the one right next to it doesn't), and the children decide that probably no one knows the answer. If the unanswered question(s) probably do have answers somewhere, the teacher may encourage the most interested children to do some additional research.

Link to Working With Words: Making Words

Make: at, art, rat, rot, not, nod, rod, road, toad,
         dart, odor, donor, tornado

Sort: rhyming words

Transfer: chart, prod, load, flat

Link to Self-Selected Reading

Many children are fascinated by animals and storms. Often, the teacher chooses another book about bats or tornadoes to read aloud to the children, and/or rounds up some more topic-related books to add to the Self-Selected Reading collection. Another link is the author link. Gail Gibbons has written many informational books about animals, including *Wolves*, *Gulls* and *Sea Turtles*. Franklyn Branley has also written books about earthquakes and volcanoes.

KWL is an excellent format for helping children connect and predict/anticipate what they will learn. *KWL Plus* (Carr and Ogle, 1987) is a variation which helps children learn to summarize. Teachers help children take the facts they have learned and write a summary. Depending on the age and levels of your children, you might model summary writing, and then have the students write a summary. You may also want to write a summary together in a shared-writing format, or give the children a simple, summary writing frame (like the example below) which they can use to organize important information.

Bats are very interesting animals. Bats have _____. Bats eat _____. Bats live in _____. The most fascinating thing about bats is _____.

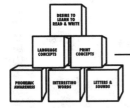

Building Blocks Variations

KWL is not a strategy we would use with kindergartners. We talk about what they know, what they would like to know, and what new things they learned, but we do not record all their responses in writing.

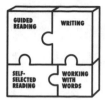

Big Blocks Variations

KWL is a popular strategy with older students. They enjoy telling what they know and they are always impressed with themselves when they see the amount of information in the Learned column.

KWL

KWL charts help children connect what they know to new information. They are particularly helpful to children as ways to guide their reading with science and social studies texts.

1. **Before beginning the chart, lead a general discussion about the children's experience with the topic. By letting a student tell about how her aunt was in a tornado, or how another student saw a bat at the zoo before beginning the chart, you avoid having the students want these "experiences" put in the Know column.**

2. **After the general discussion, ask students what they know about the topic. List the facts. (If a student tells you again that her aunt was in a tornado, accept that, but don't write it because it is not a fact about tornadoes!)**

3. **If children disagree, turn the fact into a question, and put it in the Want column. ("Bats eat fruit." "No, they don't!" is recorded as "What do bats eat?" on the chart.)**

4. **When you have recorded all the facts that the children know about the topic in the "Know" column, show the students what they will read, and ask them to come up with questions they think that text will answer. If their questions are too specific, help the students to make their questions broader. "We are trying to come up with questions that might be answered in this book. I doubt that this book will tell us if Gibsonville has ever had a tornado, but it might tell us where tornadoes happen. Let's make the question 'Where do tornadoes happen?'"**

5. **After reading, begin with the questions first, and add answers to the Learned column. Then, add other important facts.**

6. **If students are going to continue reading about the topic for another day, ask them if what they have read so far has helped them think of any other questions that might be answered in the remaining part of the text. Add these additional questions to the Want column.**

CHAPTER 9

GRAPHIC ORGANIZERS

Doing a KWL is a good ways of focusing children's attention on what they know, what they want to know, and what they have learned. They are always amazed to see how long the "Learned" column is when the chart is completed. What you don't get with KWLs is any sense of how the information is organized. In Chapter Four, we described 10 comprehension strategies, one of which was following informational text structures. Information is usually presented in a way that either highlights topics and subtopics, compares two or more things, or shows sequential or causal relationships. Graphic organizers help make these relationships concrete and visible to children. When students read to fill in the spokes of a web, they have to decide which details go with which subtopic. When they complete a data chart or a Venn Diagram, they compare some information. Time lines help children attend to sequence, and causal chains help them attend to cause/effect relationships. As children complete different graphic organizers, they learn how to follow different text structures.

Web and Data Chart

To decide which graphic organizer to use for a book, the teacher first reads the book and determines what the important information is, and how it can best be organized and displayed. Informational texts, like *Sarah Morton's Day* by Kate Walters, have lots of information. While looking through this book, the teacher notices important information about Sarah Morton and her life as a pilgrim girl. There are pages on what Sarah wears, her house, her chores, what she eats, the games she plays, and her lessons. The teacher can decide to display this information on a web, a chart drawn on a piece of large paper, an overhead projector transparency, or on the markerboard. To do a web, she writes the topic "Sarah Morton, pilgrim girl" in the large center circle, and spokes lead from this center circle to six smaller circles labeled with the words "clothes," "food," "chores," "home," "games," and "studies." The teacher will add spokes to these smaller circles with the information the children give her after they read the book. A web is a wonderful way to organize information so that young children can see what they are learning by reading. Graphic organizers, like a web, help children to become active readers who search for more information about the topics displayed on the web.

Another way to organize this information is with a chart that has two columns. The first column is labeled "Pilgrims." The second column is labeled "Us." The headings beneath the columns are: "clothes," "food," "chores," "home," "games," and "studies." Children read the book to find information about how the Pilgrims lived long ago, and then compare this information to their lives today. Since they have firsthand knowledge about themselves and their lives today, they can easily do this column.

	Pilgrims	Us
Clothes		
Food		
Chores		
Home		
Games		
Studies		

Link to Writing: Focused Writing Lesson

One of the goals of the writing block is for children to learn to write in a variety of forms, including letters, summaries, and reports. Once you have information organized in a graphic organizer, you can use that information in a focused writing lesson. Students could write a short report about pilgrims by writing a paragraph related to each of the smaller circles on the web. They could compare and contrast pilgrim children to themselves and write two paragraphs, one beginning with the sentence:

Pilgrim children were like us in many ways.

The next paragraph could begin with:

Pilgrim children were different from us in some ways.

Children's writing often lacks cohesion because they just put sentences down in the order they think of them. If you use some of the graphic organizers constructed during Guided Reading as topics for focused writing lessons, children will learn to write more organized summaries, reports, and letters.

Venn Diagrams

Venn Diagrams can help children to compare two characters, books, animals, events, etc. The teacher draws two large circles that intersect like this:

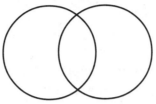

Things that are alike are put in the oval that intersects. The things that are different belong in the remainder of each circle. This way, it is easy to see what information is similar and what information is different.

After reading *Frog and Toad Together* by Arnold Lobel, many children wonder how frogs and toads are alike and how they are different. Frog and Toad in this book look a lot alike, except for height and color. This leads the teacher to two informational books: *Frogs* by Kevin J. Holmes, and the Eyewitness Juniors book *Amazing Frogs and Toads* by Barry Clarke.

The Venn Diagram is completed after any informational books are read. We have learned that frogs live near water, have smooth, slimy skin, and have webbed feet. This information is put in the circle labeled FROGS. We have also learned that toads: live on land; have dry, bumpy skin; and are more stout. This information goes inside the circle labeled TOADS. What is inside the intersecting circles is the information relating to both. Frogs and toads both have short, round bodies; and large heads with bulging eyes. They are amphibians, which means they live on land and in the water. Scientists also use the name "frog" for both frogs and toads. That's why you can find more books on frogs than toads! Children (and teachers) can learn new facts that they connect to information they already know by using Venn Diagrams after reading.

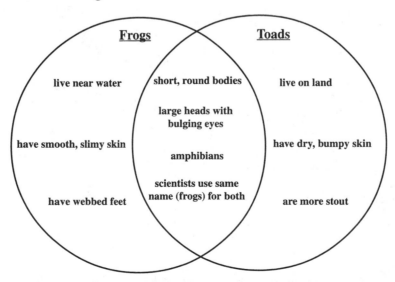

Bats and birds can be compared after reading *Stellaluna* by Janell Cannon. Using a Venn Diagram, any two books by the same author can be compared (For example, *Days with Frog and Toad* can be compared with *Frog and Toad Together*, both by Arnold Lobel), or any two topics (birds and bats).

Time Lines

Time lines help students understand what happened in the text and when it happened. The essential feature is that events are labeled and represented in sequence on a linear chart or time line. Using *Caterpillar Diary* by David Drew, your class can show what is happening to a caterpillar at the different times in its life.

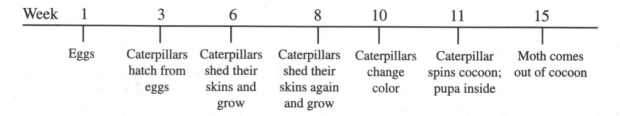

Week	1	3	6	8	10	11	15
	Eggs	Caterpillars hatch from eggs	Caterpillars shed their skins and grow	Caterpillars shed their skins again and grow	Caterpillars change color	Caterpillar spins cocoon; pupa inside	Moth comes out of cocoon

Causal Chains

A causal chain is a graphic organizer that help students "see" the relationship between cause and effect. They also see how there is often a "chain reaction," as one thing causes something to happen and that, in turn, causes something else to happen. Much of the text students read in science and social studies have cause-effect structures, and children can understand this kind of text better if they graphically depict these causes and effects. A book or informational article on environmental pollution may show how motor vehicles (cars and trucks) put out gases. These gases then combine to cause smog. Smog irritates people and causes harm to plants.

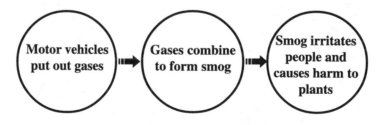

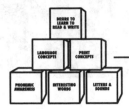

Building Blocks Variations

You can use simplified versions of these graphic organizers with your kindergartners to help organize information they are learning related to your themes.

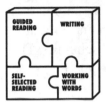

Big Blocks Variations

Older children need to learn how to construct their own graphic organizers. Introduce them gradually. Some teachers make laminated posters of the graphic organizers and let the students use these each time. When used often, the laminated posters help children internalize the structure of the graphic organizer, and thus, become independent in organizing information. When a student reads content-area or informational texts, her or she will begin thinking, "Which graphic organizer should I use to organize this information?" The ultimate goal is for students to preview the text, decide what kind of graphic organizer will best help them organize that information, and then create that graphic organizer.

Graphic Organizers

Graphic organizers help children organize and summarize information. They are often used as the pre-writing activity for focused writing lessons.

1. Look at the text and decide how the information can best be organized. If the text structure is topic/subtopic/details, you will probably want a web or data chart. If the text compares two or more things, a data chart or Venn Diagram works well. Time lines help children focus on sequence. Causal chains focus students on causal relationships.

2. Let the children see you construct the graphic organizer skeleton. Use this time to discuss the words you are putting in the organizer, since these are apt to be key vocabulary from the selection.

3. Have students read to find information to add to the organizer.

4. Complete the organizer together.

5. You may want to do a focused writing lesson in which you help children use the information from the organizer to write summaries or reports.

6. When children understand and can complete the various organizers, have them preview the text and decide what kind of graphic organizer would work best. Then, let them help you construct the organizer's skeleton.

CHAPTER 10

STORY MAPS AND BEACH BALLS

What comes immediately to mind when you hear the words,

"Once upon a time . . ."?

Most of you would expect to hear a story, and you also expect some characters, a setting, some kind of problem or goal, and a solution. You would expect there to be a beginning part in which the stage is set, a middle part in which some events occur, and an end in which things get resolved in some way. Psychologists say humans have a story "schema." The schema is a set of expectations, and these expectations allow us to anticipate and interpret. Children who have been lucky enough to have had someone read or tell stories to them have already begun to develop their story schema. All children need to develop this story schema. Story maps and "Beach Ball" are two ways of helping children develop their story schema.

Story Maps

Story maps are a type of graphic organizer that help students organize information from stories they read. Just as with other graphic organizers, the teacher and student talk about the information needed to complete the story map before reading. Then, working together, they fill in the information after reading. There are many different story maps. Here is one that works well for young children:

Story Map

Title: Author:

Setting:

Characters:

Beginning: Middle: End:

Conclusion:

Story maps can be used to set the purpose and help children organize information from a story or chapter book. If the chapters of the book have most of the elements listed on the story map, children might fill in the map together after reading each chapter. Here is an example based on the popular mystery character Cam Jansen. There are many mysteries in this series. This lesson is for *Cam Jansen and the Chocolate Fudge Mystery* by David A. Adler.

This mystery has eight chapters which are about six pages each. There are one or two pictures in each chapter. The teacher decides that he will read the first chapter to the class, and they will fill out the story map together. The class will then read the remaining six chapters and complete the story map together or in "playschool groups."

The teacher begins by showing the children the story map skeleton and explaining how they can help him complete the story map after listening to the first two chapters. He then leads the students to look at the two pictures in Chapter One and make some predictions:

"The girl is trying to give something to the boy."

"The boy and girl are following a suspicious-looking woman."

"The woman in the sunglasses has something stolen in the big bag."

The teacher listens to their predictions and makes noncommittal comments:

"Hmmm. Very interesting!"

"That's a possibility."

"What makes her look suspicious?"

The purpose of having children make predictions before reading is not so that their predictions will be "right," but rather that the students will be thinking about the text! Once they begin thinking about what's happening, the students want to read to find out more!

The teacher then tells the students that he will read the whole first chapter without stopping, and that they should listen for and think about what they can contribute to the story map for this first chapter. The children listen attentively, and their eyes dart back and forth to the story map. When the teacher finishes reading, he turns to the story map and asks questions to help the students formulate concise answers.

At the end of the first chapter, the story map looks like this:

Story Map

Title: *Cam Jansen and the Chocolate Fudge Mystery* (Chapter One)

Author: David A. Adler

Setting: A street in town

Characters: Cam Jansen, Cam's father, Eric Shelton, Mr. And Mrs. Miller, a man and a woman running, a "suspicious-looking" woman

---

Beginning: Cam and Eric are going to houses selling chocolate and rice cakes to raise money for Ride and Read.

Middle: A man and woman run past them and won't stop.

End: The suspicious woman rushes past, wearing a raincoat when it isn't raining and dark glasses when it isn't sunny.

Conclusion: Cam thinks the woman has something dangerous in the bag and decides to follow her.

The teacher reads the second chapter to the children and they complete a second story map for it. By now the children are all involved in the mystery. They know the characters and want to find out what the suspicious woman is up to. They complete the mystery, filling out a story map for each chapter.

Link to Self-Selected Reading

Read aloud to students a mystery or two from a different mystery series, and stock your room with mysteries from all these series. You will probably start a mystery-reading frenzy in your classroom!

The Beach Ball

The Beach Ball is not a story map, but using this format helps children develop the same important concepts, and can lead to the development of written story maps. The Beach Ball is a real beach ball that has a question written in black, permanent marker on each colored stripe of the ball. Here are the questions one teacher used:

What is the title and who is the author?

Who are the main characters?

What is the setting?

What happened in the story?

How did it end?

What was your favorite part?

Another teacher phrased the questions as sentence starters to use with her class:

My favorite part was . . .

The setting was . . .

The main characters were . . .

In the beginning . . .

In the middle . . .

At the end . . .

Just as with story maps, let children know before reading that your after-reading activity will be the Beach Ball! This sets their purpose for reading, and after a few times of doing this activity, you will notice that as the students read, they look over at the ball. They are noticing information from the story that they want to use to answer the questions. This is active, purposeful reading!

After reading, the teacher and the children form a large circle. The teacher begins by naming a student and tossing the ball to him or her. That student catches the ball and can answer any of the questions written on the ball. He or she then names another student (so the children know whose turn it is to catch the ball!) and tosses the ball to that student. This student can add to the answer given by the first student or answer another question. The ball continues to be thrown to different students until all the questions have been thoroughly answered. Some questions, such as *What happened in the story?* and *What was your favorite part?* have many different answers.

Fluency is one of the strategies that requires constant attention in the Guided Reading Block. Rereading selections for a different purpose is one of the major ways to build fluency. Each rereading of a text should always be done for a different purpose and in a different format. Often, your first reading is to confirm predictions in some way—Prove It!, Anticipation Guide, Rivet, etc. If the reading selection was a story, reread it and do the Beach Ball. Children love doing the Beach Ball, so they are usually eager to reread a selection if the Beach Ball is what they will do after rereading.

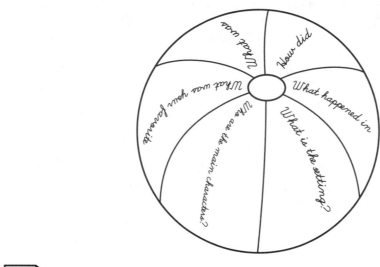

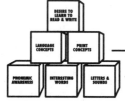

Building Blocks Variations

Kindergarten children love to retell stories using the Beach Ball.

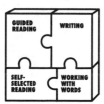

Big Blocks Variations

Story maps are commonly used in intermediate grades. Unfortunately, some older children dread reading because "you always have to write something!" Using the Beach Ball activity on some days, instead of a story map, can provide variety and accomplishes the same comprehension purpose. Older kids need to have some fun, too!

Story Maps and the Beach Ball

The goal of comprehension instruction is for children to learn how to independently do the strategies as they read on their own. Following story structure and summarizing stories are two important comprehension strategies. Both story maps and the Beach Ball help children develop story structure and learn to summarize/conclude.

Story Maps

1. Decide on a story map skeleton that will work best for your children.

2. Talk about the slots on the map, and make sure the students understand their purpose for reading.

3. Have students read (or read to them) the first part or chapter.

4. Have students complete the story map together or in small groups.

The Beach Ball

1. Decide on the questions and write them with permanent marker on a beach ball.

2. Talk about the questions on the stripes, and make sure students understand their purpose for reading.

3. Have the children read in whatever format you choose.

4. Toss the beach ball to a student to begin the activity, then let students continue tossing the ball to one another and answering the questions.

CHAPTER 11

"DOING THE BOOK"

Kids love to "do" things—and that includes reading! They love to pretend. When they pretend, they are imagining. When a child acts out a book or story by portraying a character, he feels like he is that character in that setting and in those circumstances. He moves like the character, talks like the character, and for a brief moment, becomes the character. Having children "do the book" is one of the best ways to work on the comprehension strategy of imaging and inferring. This chapter will describe three ways of "doing the book."

Plays

Children love plays, and in many classrooms, the whole year passes without students doing a single play. Why does this happen? Here are some of the reasons teachers give as to why they don't do more plays, and ways to combat each.

"Oh, no, it's our year to do the PTA program!"

When most teachers think of plays, they imagine productions with costumes, scenery, rehearsals, and lines to be memorized! Many teachers have lived through one or more of these, and don't ever want to live through one again! The plays you could do with children during Guided Reading are ones that help the stories they read come to life for them. Plays for Guided Reading are not productions! You don't do costumes or scenery. You never memorize any lines, because you always read your plays. Reading and rereading builds fluency; memorizing doesn't. When the children are going to do the play, it means that they are going to stand up, move around, gesture and make faces, and read their lines. They will practice a few times, and then they will do it for the rest of the class, but these plays are not productions—they are more like "happenings!"

"Plays don't have enough parts. What do I do with the other children?"

Many plays only require four or five characters, which makes them perfect for playschool groups or book club groups. When the whole class is doing the same play, put them into playschool groups—heterogeneous groups with a "teacher" in each group. Either assign the parts or let the children choose a part, and then each group reads and practices the play. Four groups are simultaneously reading and practicing the same play. The next day, combine the casts and "do the play" twice. Two groups are combined into one cast, with one group reading the first half of the play, and the other group reading the second half. When the first two groups read the play, the other two groups are the audience. Then, the remaining two groups combine and read the play while the first two groups become the audience.

For book club groups, you could have four plays—one that is a little easier, one that is a little harder, and two that are "just right." The children practice plays in their groups, but each group has a different play. When it is time to do the plays, each group reads its play for the rest of the class. If the number of group members doesn't work out quite right for the number of parts in a play, members from other groups can be "drafted" to read bit parts.

"I don't have time!"

Reading and doing the play are not extra "fit them in sometime" activities. They are the only activities used during the Guided Reading Block for the two or three days in a row you spend on them. Remember that Guided Reading is where students learn to read all different types of materials, along with learning comprehension strategies. When you include plays in your Guided Reading Block, the comprehension strategies you are focusing on are imaging/inferring and fluency—both underemphasized in most primary classrooms. To produce a whole class full of good comprehenders, you don't have time *not* to do some plays!

"I'd do some, but I don't have any!"

Are you sure you don't have any plays? Look back at Chapter Three and think about the suggestions for begging, borrowing, and contriving materials. There are a lot of plays out there. Most reading textbooks have one or two per grade. Most magazines include several plays over a year's time, and these often fit into holiday or seasonal themes. There are also plays in many of the sets of leveled books now flooding the market. Finally, you can write some plays of your own and duplicate them for the class. The advantage to this method is that after reading and doing them in class, you can give students the homework assignment of assembling some "characters" in their homes or neighborhoods and conducting a reading of the play there! If you still think you don't have any plays for your students, think about having the students create plays using a writing activity called Reader's Theater.

Reader's Theater

Reader's Theater is an activity where you turn something you read into a play script, and then read and act out the play. In Chapter 16, you will find an example of Reader's Theater when the class and teacher create a script for *The Doorbell Rang* by Pat Hutchins. In this example, the script is actually being written in a shared writing format where the children and teacher share the process of coming up with ideas, but the teacher does the writing. Children can also learn to write scripts, and this is an excellent activity to integrate reading and writing. Here is an example of Reader's Theater based on *Frog and Toad Are Friends* by Arnold Lobel.

This *Frog and Toad* book has five chapters. The teacher and class are going to work together to turn the first chapter into a play script. The children will then work in playschool groups to do the other four chapters. Each group will read and write the script for one chapter.

The teacher reminds the children of plays they have read and how these plays were written. She then tells them that they are going to help her write a play based on the first chapter of *Frog and Toad Are Friends*. She leads the children to talk about the pictures in this chapter before they read it. The students decide that Frog is going to visit Toad, and Toad doesn't want to get out of bed. At the end, Frog and Toad are outside. They don't see any other characters in the pictures, but there may be some. The teacher takes out some copying paper and three colorful markers. She explains that she is going to write the narrator's part in black, Frog's part in green, and Toad's part in red. "If there are other characters, we will choose some other colors," she explains.

The teacher then leads the children in an echo reading of the first two pages. After they have echo read it, the students decide what Frog says, what Toad says, and what the narrator needs to explain. The teacher tapes each page on the wall or the board in order. The play script after the first two pages looks like this. (Since these examples can't show the different colors of markers used, each part is indicated: N for Narrator, F for Frog, and T for Toad.)

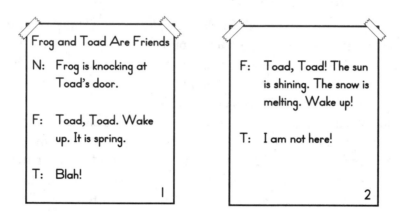

They echo read the next two pages and write the script, which looks like this:

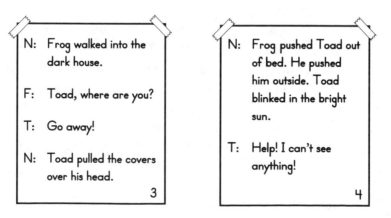

The teacher and children continue to echo read each two-page spread, and then write the lines and tape them to the board in order. They get about halfway through the chapter on the first day. Then, to finish that day's Guided Reading Block, they do a choral reading with a third of the class reading each character's part. The next day, they chorally read the first part of the script again, with each third of the class reading a different character's part than the day before. Then, they write the script for the last half of the chapter and chorally read it.

For the next several days, the children work in playschool groups to read one chapter and write the script. In each group there is a "teacher" who is the first voice in the echo reading, a child with a black marker who will write the narrator's lines, a child with a green marker who will write Frog's lines, and a child with a red marker who will write Toad's lines. The third chapter has a sparrow and a raccoon, so the teacher assigns six children to this group and gives blue and orange markers to the children who will write the sparrow's and the raccoon's lines. The fifth chapter has a snail, so that group has five people. The fourth chapter absorbs everyone else because it has a turtle, a snake, a field mouse, two dragonflies, and some lizards. Because the group for the fourth chapter is larger-than-usual, the teacher assumes the "teacher" role in this group and keeps everyone on track! (Knowing she was going to do this, the teacher has included the children who need the most help and structure in this group!)

As the groups are writing, they number the pages in the order in which people speak. When the script is finished, the students practice reading it with the person who was the teacher in the group assuming the role of director, and the others reading the lines they wrote. The groups read and act their parts for each other, and *Frog and Toad Are Friends* comes to life.

Writing and reading this Reader's Theater for *Frog and Toad Are Friends* takes six or seven days, but a lot is accomplished. As the children echo read and reread to determine lines, write lines, practice lines, and then do the Reader's Theater, they develop reading fluency. Determining exactly what Frog, Toad, and the other characters said and what the narrator needs to explain requires the students to pay attention to detail and to read each page carefully. As they read and act out their parts, the children have to imagine what the characters sound like and how they move and look. Turning a book into a script is not something you would do every day during Guided Reading—perhaps only two or three times a year—but it is a welcome change of pace and an enjoyable reading experience from which all levels of children can learn.

Pantomiming (With Just a Little Speaking)

Pantomiming is an "acting out" of the selection, with various children playing different parts as the rest of the class reads the story. You may sometimes do pantomiming in playschool groups or book club groups, but you can also do it with the whole class. If you are going to do it with the whole class, try to find selections in which there are enough characters for at least half the class to be actors while the other half of the class reads. Then, you switch the cast and audience. Unlike in plays and Reader's Theater, you won't have a script and the actors are not reading. They are pantomiming the action about which the readers are reading, and you prompt the actors to say an occasional ad-libbed line. Here is an example based on P. D Eastman's *Are You My Mother?*

The first reading of the book was done in some other format (echo reading, partners, ERT…, playschool group, etc.) for some other purpose (to make and check predictions, do a story map, do the Beach Ball, etc.). The second reading is done to determine who the characters are in the book and what they do. This second reading probably works best as a choral reading, with half the class reading chorally for several pages while the other half listens to decide if there are any new characters and if the new characters say or do anything. The designated half of the class reads the first page.

A mother bird sat on her egg.

Volunteers from the other half of the class report that there is one character so far, the mother bird, and she hasn't said anything—she's just sitting there. The teacher helps the students to realize that the egg is also a character—or soon will be.

The teacher writes "Mother bird" and "egg" on two laminated yarned index cards.

The reading half of the class continues to read the next several pages, and the listening half of the class determines that there aren't any new characters. The mother bird said her baby would soon be here, and she flew away to get food, saying she would be back. While the mother was away, the egg jumped and a baby bird came out. He looked for his mother and said:

"Where is my mother? I will go and look for her."

The teacher adds another character card, "Baby bird," and switches the roles of the readers and listeners. The other half, who had been listeners, does the choral reading for the next several pages, and the first half, who had been readers, listens for new characters and what those characters say and do. The teacher does not write down dialogue since this is going to be pantomiming while others read, but she does continue to write characters on the character cards, and have the children tell her what the characters are saying and doing. As they read, the students decide that the car, boat, plane, and snort are not really characters, but they need them to do the story, so they include cards for these, too.

When they finish reading the book, they have these cards:

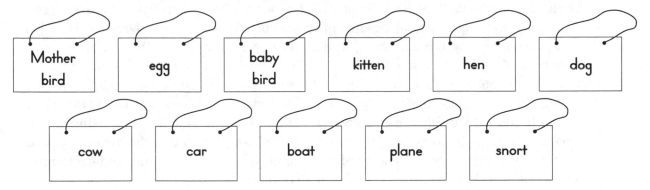

Next, the teacher shuffles some index cards containing the names of the children and begins calling out names. As each child's name is called, the child gets to select the part he wants to play. Each student comes up, gets the card to designate what character he is, and puts the card around his neck. Now, the reading of the play can begin. The teacher and the children who don't have parts read the play, while the children with parts come "onstage" when they are mentioned in the reading. They don't read any lines, but they are encouraged to say appropriate things after the class reads all the text. So, the class might read:

He could not fly, but he could walk. "Now I will go and find my mother," he said.

Then, the baby bird character would pantomime not being able to fly, but being able to walk and the character might say something like,

"I've got to go find my mother."

This is much harder to explain than it is to do. Basically, the teacher and the non-acting children read everything, including the dialogue, and the characters prance around and say things with the same meaning, but not necessarily the same words.

When the book is read, the teacher collects the character cards from the actors and goes through the shuffling of names and choosing parts with the part of the class that hasn't been actors yet. Some actors from the first cast fill in as needed in the second "playing," and the entire book is done again.

Pantomiming the story with some ad-libbed speech is the easiest way to do the book. No script or practice is required. Children become good at identifying characters and what these characters say and do. They imagine the actions of the character and then actually do them. The selection is generally read four times, the first time for the general story, the second time to determine the characters and their actions and speech, and then twice for the different casts. Children love this way of acting out stories, and this enthusiasm often spreads to the whole Guided Reading Block.

Building comprehension strategies is a major goal of the Guided Reading Block. When children "do" the book, they think about all the important story elements—characters, settings, actions, and sequence. The benefits of acting out the book as a regularly-used Guided Reading format become obvious when the children come to expect that they might act out a story or book. Children who know the book or story might be acted out think about things, such as which character they would like to be and what they would do if they were that character. This kind of thinking greatly increases students' comprehension. "Doing the book" is especially helpful for children who are not fluent in English. Watching and being part of the enactment helps build vocabulary, and gives ESL students a non-threatening way to practice reading and speaking. The regular use of plays, Reader's Theater, and pantomiming during Guided Reading produces more active, fluent readers.

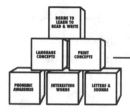

Building Blocks Variations

"Doing the Book" is very important to comprehension development for kindergartners. Do some choral reading and pantomiming to act out some of the big books read during shared reading.

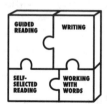

Big Blocks Variations

"Doing the book" is extremely rare in intermediate grades, in spite of the fact that older children have the reading and writing facility to write nice Reader's Theater scripts and become better comprehenders as they translate a story into a script. If you teach older children, try some plays and Reader's Theater activities and observe what happens to the motivation, engagement, and comprehension of your students, especially your struggling readers.

"Doing the Book"

Children who "do the book" become more active readers. Characters, setting, events, dialogue, conclusions, mood, and motivation become important, and the students pay more attention to them. Children who do plays, Reader's Theater, and pantomiming become better comprehenders.

Plays

1. Choose plays with lots of characters or several plays with fewer characters.

2. Have children read the plays first, then assign parts and have the students practice reading their parts until they can read them fluently.

3. If you have one play with lots of characters, have it read by two different casts, and alternate the cast/audience roles. If you have groups reading plays, let each group read its play for the class.

Reader's Theater

1. Choose stories in which there is a lot of dialogue.

2. Work together as a class to turn the first part or chapter into a script.

3. Have the children work in groups to write some of the script. Give the children in the groups specific roles, and determine how many children should work together according to the parts needed. If necessary, work with one of the groups to help them succeed.

4. Read the scripts, and watch the story come life.

Pantomiming

1. Choose stories with lots of characters and lots of dialogue.

2. Read the story and decide who the characters are and what they are saying and doing.

3. Make character cards, and let children choose the character they want to be.

4. Have the readers chorally read the story while the actors "pantomime" and ad-lib a few lines.

5. Do the book again so that all the children get to be characters.

CHAPTER 12

SMALL-GROUP DISCUSSIONS

Four of the thinking processes—connecting, predicting/anticipating, summarizing/concluding, and questioning/monitoring—lend themselves to being taught in specific guided reading lessons of various kinds (picture walks, Prove It!, KWL, etc.). However, two of the thinking processes—imaging/inferring and evaluating/applying—are so open-ended and broad that they are best taught through some kind of modeling. One way to use modeling to guide thinking while reading is with think-alouds (Chapter 7). Think-alouds are helpful for teaching all six of the thinking processes, but they are especially beneficial for teaching imaging/inferring and evaluating/applying. This chapter describes small-group discussions, another way of using modeling to teach these two kinds of thinking which are so important for reading.

The advantage of using small-group discussions to teach thinking is that they provide even more powerful modeling than think-alouds. Children experience the thinking being modeled during small-group discussions more directly. That is, students are actively involved in the thinking throughout a real dialogue, rather than witnessing your thinking, as helpful as that is. The disadvantage of small-group discussions for teaching thinking is that it is quite a challenge to guide children to think and talk using particular processes, especially open-ended and broad processes like imaging/inferring and evaluating/applying. It would be great if you could just put students into groups, ask them to discuss what they have read, and let them reap the benefits of good discussions. Unfortunately, that assumes students already know how to do what you need to teach them! From experience, many teachers know that such "unguided" discussions are often a waste of time. The worst of them are off-task, marked by arguments over procedures, or become monologues on the part of one or two "know-it-alls." The best of them have good student participation, and concentrate on restating the major events or points, summarizing or stating the main idea, and drawing conclusions. There is little evidence of imaging and inferring or evaluating and applying. (If a teacher wants to teach children to connect or summarize/conclude, graphic organizers and story maps are much more helpful than small-group discussions.)

Only with proper guidance can most students participate in small-group discussions that actually help them image/infer or evaluate/apply anything about the content of the texts they have read. This chapter describes two ways of structuring small-group discussions, "Talking Why and How" and "Me Purpose" conversations, that guide children to engage in higher-order thinking about what they have read. As Vygotsky (1978) has explained, the substantive dialogues children have with others gradually become internalized to change how their thinking operates.

Talking Why and How

Of the six thinking processes, imaging/inferring is one of the most difficult to teach. Why? Because readers only image and infer as they think about the situation behind or beyond the text. As long as they remain focused on the letters, words, punctuation marks, sentences, paragraphs, and sections of a text, readers image and infer very little. It is when they begin thinking about Dorothy and Toto, Alaskan winters, or supernovas that they image and infer. So, to teach students to image and infer while they read, we must somehow get them to think about the situation referred to in the text rather than the elements of the text itself. In Chapter 11, you learned how "doing the book" helps children move behind or beyond the text to image and infer what the book is about. In this section, you will see how one particular kind of small-group discussion—Talking Why and How—can also help children learn to image and infer when they read.

Imagine you are visiting a friend who lives a few miles away. It's getting late, and you have to teach tomorrow. Just as you're preparing to excuse yourself to leave, your friend tells you she has been worrying about what to do about her daughter's pet cat, who is old and in ill health. You find yourself asking for details, and before long, you and your friend have spent an hour talking about her daughter's level of emotional stability and maturity, whether the cat is likely to be suffering, and what actions might lead to what consequences. As you drive home, even though your friend did not make a decision about her daughter's cat, you have no regrets about having spent that extra hour, because you feel the conversation has helped you prepare for similar events that may occur in your life in the future. What has happened? The two of you have spent an hour imaging and inferring about a new situation. Your understanding (and your friend's understanding) of the situation has increased as a result.

Along with think-alouds and "doing the book," the best way to help students learn to image and infer when they read is to engage them in good small-group discussions so that they understand the situations referred to by the texts they have read. To realize what makes for a "good" discussion of this kind, consider the imaginary conversation you and your friend had about her daughter's cat. There were three features of that conversation which made it of interest and value to both participants. First, there was "openness" in the situation. In other words, there was a lot of room for imaging and inferring because there were many things to consider, and it was impossible to arrive at a certain understanding of the situation. Second, the conversation focused entirely on the situation of the daughter having an old, sick cat. There was no time or energy spent analyzing or evaluating the language of the conversation itself. Third, there was real dialogue, good listening as well as good talking. In other words, there was "give and take." Rather than just being an opportunity for two individuals to express what they already thought, the conversation actually went somewhere—taking both participants beyond their current understanding of the situation. Each participant imaged and inferred, and took the images and inferences of the other into consideration when doing so. Successful discussions to better understand a book or selection the children have read must also have the three features of openness, focus on the situation, and real dialogue.

Talking Why and How is a way of guiding discussions which increases the chance that students will image and infer about the situation to which the text refers, rather than focusing on the text itself, or worse, not focusing on anything relevant or productive. Talking Why and How uses "why" and "how" questions, constructed by the teacher and presented to the children before reading, to engage the students with the openness in the situation about which they have read and away from thinking about the text. These questions are used again after reading by each small-group discussion leader, along with impromptu follow-up questions from anyone in the group, to engage students in real dialogue on these questions. The discussion takes everyone in the group beyond where any individual could have gone alone. After small-group discussions end, the teacher has one person from each group share with the whole class something their group had discussed.

An Example of Talking Why and How

The students have recently read *Commander Toad in Space*, a fantasy by Jane Yolen, to fill out a story map. During today's Guided Reading Block, they will reread that story to discuss the following "why" and "how" questions in small-groups:

1. How did Jake Skyjumper feel when he was told he had to stay on board while the others went down to the planet?

2. Why did Deep Wader roar, "I am Deep Wader, and this planet belongs to me!"?

3. How did the landing crew of Commander Toad, Mr. Hop, and Lieutenant Lily feel when Deep Wader first appeared?

4. How did the landing crew feel when they lost their sky skimmer, and Deep Wader was getting closer and closer?

5. How did Deep Wader feel when the landing crew floated away?

6. How could the lily pad float all the way to the mother ship?

In preparation for small-group discussions, the teacher has assigned the students to mixed groups of four or five children. Every group has one member designated as the "group leader" for that day.

Before rereading the Yolen story, the students are given these six questions to guide their thinking while they read. The questions are written on the markerboard, presented on the overhead projector, or handed out to each child. Later, when the students move into their discussion groups, the teacher gives each group's discussion leader a copy of the "why" and "how" questions. (Do not allow children to write answers to the questions while they read. If you do, the discussion will consist more of sharing rather than of forming opinions!)

The children should know they are supposed to stay on task and move through the questions in order. They also should know that they probably won't have time to discuss all the questions, especially if the discussion prompted by a particular question is a good one. The teacher sets the timer for 10 minutes and tells everyone to begin. She moves around the room monitoring the group discussions and writing comments on the groups' interaction. She limits her interactions with individuals or groups to those she considers absolutely necessary. Otherwise, when a group tries to involve her in their discussion, she just smiles and moves on.

During the discussion of *Commander Toad in Space*, the teacher may make note of several positives and a few negatives. The most positive aspect of the discussion, she may decide, is how well the group leaders keep everyone on task. She expects to handle any discipline problems herself, but she may be pleased to see how well the group leaders handle children who mention personal experiences that could lead the discussion astray. For example, when a child in one group begins to talk about "how cool *The Phantom Menace* was," the group leader, Amanda, tactfully says, "Yes, I liked that movie, too," and then repeats the question they had started discussing before that comment. Other generally positive aspects that the teacher may note are the amount of participation most groups have, and most students' ability to understand the questions.

There may also be negatives she notes. She may become concerned that several children occasionally respond to another child's inference with an authoritative statement to the effect of "It doesn't say that." She may possibly come to feel that all the groups, including their leaders, seem to want to move through the questions too fast, failing to get the most out of each question. If so, she could decide to work on reducing those two negatives in future discussions.

Constructing the "Why" and "How" Discussion Questions for Talking Why and How

The best materials to use for Talking Why and How are stories, because fictional characters and plots require readers to make them come alive by relating them to real people and events about which the readers know. Hobbits, for example, may be unlike real people in many ways, but you still understand them in terms of goals and emotions real people have such as courage, love of home, and concern for others. Fantastic though they be, hobbits are still more like than unlike us. Tolkien left room in his characterization of Hobbits for us to image and infer human traits for them.

There are three aspects of a story where one is likely to find the openness needed for reader imaging/inferring:

- Causes of actions, events, and states—why something happened, or why something was the way it was

- Goals that motivate characters' actions—what a character was trying to accomplish by what he or she did

- Characters' emotional responses to actions, events, and states—how a character felt about something that happened, or felt about the way something was

Of course, when these causes, goals, or responses are stated in the text, they are not "open," but most stories leave some of these causes, goals, or responses unstated.

When reading a story or selection from a children's novel to construct "why" and "how" questions for group discussions, you may find the following question frames useful:

WHY DID [a character] [take a particular intentional action]?

WHY DID [an explicit action, event, or state occur]?

HOW COULD [an explicit action, event, or state occur]?

HOW DID [one or more characters] FEEL WHEN [an action, event, or state occurred]?

If you re-examine the six questions in the example with Jane Yolen's *Commander Toad in Space*, you will see that every question fits one of these four question frames. To construct those six questions, the teacher read through the story looking for any action, event, or state described by the author. When she found one, she tried to construct a question of each type that the author had not answered. She found at least the six questions she used to guide the group discussions of that story.

Preparing Children to Talk Why and How

Having good "why" and "how" questions to guide a small-group discussion of the situation referred to by a text is necessary, but not sufficient. Good "why" and "how" questions can be expected to focus the children's attention on the situation rather than the text, and on the unstated rather than stated aspects of that situation. However, even the best "why" and "how" questions cannot ensure that students will engage in real dialogue around those questions. Children also need guidance in how to discuss open-ended questions with no stated "right answer." You'll need even more patience than teaching usually requires because achieving real dialogue is difficult, even among adults!

It is best to introduce Talking Why and How with a whole-class lesson, during which you lead the students through a story pointing out that authors rarely tell us everything we want or need to know. In *Commander Toad in Space*, for example, Jane Yolen does not tell us how the landing party feels when the monster, Deep Wader, first appears, but she doesn't need to. In fact, our imagination does a much better job of giving us a feel for their probable sense of urgency to act than any words describing that sense would be likely to do. Taking students to several places in a familiar text where the situation suggested by the text has openness is a good way to introduce the concept of imaging/inferring to them. The greatest obstacle to overcome during this introductory lesson, and the subsequent small-group discussions, will be those children who resist "guessing" about things the author doesn't tell us. This resistance is natural, and is another main reason why think-alouds, "doing the book," and Talking Why and How are the ways to help children improve their imaging and inferring. All three methods motivate, rather than require, imaging and inferring on the part of the students.

After one or more whole-class introductory lessons where you lead the students through a story and show them "open" places their minds can and will naturally want to fill in, decide whether most students are beginning to accept the appropriateness of filling in some "open" places in the story with their imaginations. If not, it is probably a good idea to do the same thing with a few clips from a movie that is familiar to most of the students. The best clips to use are those which allow us to infer what a character is feeling from his or her actions or facial expressions, without the character or narrator telling us how the character is feeling. From these clips, most students get the idea that they are the ones deciding how the character probably feels in that situation.

After an introduction to the concept of openness and filling in some of that openness with the mind and imagination, it is important that you lead a sample small-group discussion about something the class has read. Have the children not involved in the small-group discussion to watch closely. Help the children in the small-group to role-play the kind of positive and negative behaviors of which you want everyone to be aware. Positive behaviors consist mainly of taking turns, not "hogging" the conversation, and listening carefully to what others are saying. Negative behaviors consist of the opposites of these positive behaviors, as well as making personal connections that are likely to take the discussion off track. Point out that you are also modeling how the group leaders should try to keep everyone talking, listening, and on track.

It can be especially helpful to teach the students some "listening" strategies. All of these strategies "show" that a child is listening carefully and respecting what others are saying. Teach children to say:

"I agree with [name of another child in the group] when [he or she] says . . . ."

"Let me put in my words what I think I heard you say . . . ."

"So, don't we agree that . . . ?"

"What did you mean when you said . . .?"

"I agree with the part about . . . , but I disagree with the part about . . . ."

Me Purpose Conversations

Evaluating/applying is also one of the most difficult thinking processes to teach. Why? Because it is really beyond comprehension in the ordinary sense. The other five thinking processes that are important for reading are used to understand the text—its sentences, paragraphs, sections, and what they all add up to mean—or to understand the situation on which the text is based. On the other hand, evaluating/applying is used to place the text or its content into a larger context. When you finish the latest novel by a favorite author, do you sometimes say to yourself, "I didn't enjoy this book as much as the last one he wrote."? If so, you are evaluating the entire novel, including all its elements and every aspect of the situation it portrays. The way you are evaluating it is by placing it into the context of another novel by the same author. Likewise, when you finish a non-fiction book about a subject, do you sometimes say to yourself, "Now, I know how to change my whole way of doing...." If so, you are applying what you learned from the entire book. You are applying it by placing it into the context of how you do something now. So, rather than increasing understanding of the text or situation, evaluating/applying is concerned with judging, or utilizing whatever was understood, by putting it into a larger context.

To teach readers to evaluate/apply, you can again rely on a particular kind of small-group discussion to provide powerful modeling of broad and open-ended thinking about reading. This time, however, you can use a question or task called a Me Purpose to focus readers' attention on a context for the text or the situation to which it refers. A Me Purpose conversation uses a Me Purpose that is constructed by the teacher and presented to the children before reading to engage the students in personally contextualizing the text or the situation to which it refers. This Me Purpose is used again after reading by each small-group discussion leader, along with impromptu follow-up questions from anyone in the group, to engage students in real dialogue on how they individually evaluated or applied the text or its content while reading. Think-alouds and Me Purpose conversations are the two best ways to teach elementary children to evaluate and apply while they read.

Me Purposes

Whenever you ask students to read or reread a text with a Me Purpose in mind, you are asking them to evaluate or apply the text or its content individually and personally. What makes a purpose for reading to evaluate/apply a Me Purpose is this individual, personal angle. It is remarkable how facilitative to good discussion it can be to personalize children's responses to a text or its content.

There are two kinds of Me Purposes: those asking students to evaluate, and those asking them to apply. Me Purposes to evaluate what was read or what was understood from the reading are usually best used with stories.

Here are some examples of this kind of purpose for reading or rereading:

Do you think *Charlotte's Web* by E.B. White ends as it should? If you had written it, would it have ended the same way?

Which of these two *Encyclopedia Brown* mysteries do you like better?

Imagine that you were a pilgrim boy or girl who lived where and when Sarah Morton did. What would you have liked about being a pilgrim boy or girl? What would you not have liked?

Me Purposes to apply what was read are best used with nonfiction. Here are some examples of this kind of purpose for reading or rereading:

How would you get a police officer to help you if you were in danger?

What would you do to stay warm if you lived in Antarctica?

If you could change any of the rules of soccer, what rules would you change?

Each of these Me Purposes assumes that the children have understood enough of the text or enough about the situation in the text to evaluate or apply. None of these Me Purposes asks a question that has a stated, or even unstated, "right answer" on which adult readers would all agree. Rather, Me Purposes ask children to place what they have understood from their reading into a larger context with a personal meaning for them.

An Example of a Me Purpose Conversation

This lesson is based on an article from *Weekly Reader* about the original Thanksgiving. The teacher chooses to have her students read the article with a Me Purpose, and to follow their reading by placing them in small-groups to have a Me Purpose conversation about it. This is the Me Purpose she uses: Imagine that you get to decide how you will celebrate Thanksgiving. How would you celebrate your Thanksgiving holiday to make it more like the first Thanksgiving?

In the before-reading part of the lesson, the teacher begins by reminding the children that Thanksgiving is only a week or so away. She also tells them that they will celebrate Thanksgiving in the classroom on Wednesday, the day before the Thanksgiving holiday from school. She then lets the students take brief turns sharing about Thanksgiving. Most children want to tell what they eat or do for Thanksgiving in their families, or that they like Thanksgiving because they don't have to go to school that day. After a few minutes, the teacher stops this sharing and writes the Me Purpose for reading on the board. She explains the purpose for reading and answers any of the children's questions about it that she can without giving anything away that is in the article. The children then read the *Weekly Reader* Thanksgiving article for the Me Purpose.

In preparation for small-group discussions across the curriculum, the teacher has previously assigned her students to mixed groups she is pretty sure can work together. On the day of this discussion, a few children are absent and she adjusts the groups so that every group has four to five children. She designates one child in each group as the "group leader" for that day. After the students finish reading, she directs them to move into their discussion groups. She gives each group's discussion leader a copy of the Me Purpose, even though it is still written on the board.

The students in this class have already had two Me Purpose conversations during the Guided Reading Block, so they are familiar with how they work. The students know they have to take turns speaking and listening carefully to what others say. They also know that they must respect other children's ideas, even when they don't agree with them.

The teacher walks around the room during the discussions, listening as well as she can to what is going on in the small-groups. She takes brief notes so she will know what to do next time to improve the children's comprehension, their discussion behaviors, and her own ability to construct a good Me Purpose. She finds that almost all the groups get off the subject. Some get back eventually, but two groups do not. There are a few children who are so busy trying to "get the floor" to say what they think that they aren't listening to what the others are saying. The teacher decides that she needs to lead a Me Purpose conversation with four children while the rest of the class watches and listens, and that she will do that one day the following week. (During that modeling of a Me Purpose conversation, she plans to give the children some "listening" strategies to improve their discussions.) The teacher is pleased, however, with the participation in all the groups, and with the turn-taking in most of them. She is also delighted with the enthusiasm for the Thanksgiving article she feels this lesson has engendered in most of her students.

Building Blocks Variations

Talking Why and How is not a teaching strategy you could use with kindergartners. Me Purpose conversations is also not a teaching strategy for use in kindergarten.

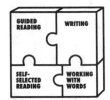

Big Blocks Variations

Talking Why and How becomes the premier strategy to help older children make imaging and inferring part of what they do naturally when reading. Talking Why and How can continue into the intermediate grades in the same way that it operates in grades 2-3, but there are two variations that may eventually prove to be useful extensions to the basic procedure. The first and most important variation is for the children in each small group to construct their own questions for discussion as they move through a story. The second important variation is for the children to discuss the why and how of the situations referred to in informational texts, beginning with biographies and moving to history and social studies.

Me Purpose conversations can also continue into the intermediate grades. A couple of variations become appropriate when these older children are comfortable having such discussions. Older students are often able to read for and to discuss two or three Mc Purposes rather than just one in the same lesson. They can also be guided to apply what they have understood from stories and to evaluate non-fiction texts and situations.

Small-Group Discussions

Two of the goals of the Guided Reading Block are to develop background knowledge, meaning vocabulary, and oral language, and to teach comprehension skills and strategies. Small-group discussions help students improve in their ability to communicate orally about topics of substance, while teaching them two of the most difficult comprehension strategies to learn.

How did you and other adults learn to image/infer and evaluate/apply about what you read? In several ways, no doubt, but you probably learned a lot from talking with others about books you and they had read. Over time, Talking Why and How and Me Purpose conversations will help your children learn to image/infer and evaluate/apply more and better while reading.

Talking Why and How

1. **Introduce Talking Why and How by leading the class through a book, a chapter in a novel, or a story they have read previously for another purpose. Show the students places where they naturally use their minds and imaginations to fill in some of the "why" and "how" questions the author has left open.**
2. **Model for the class how to lead and participate in a good small-group discussion of a book, a chapter in a novel, or a story they have read previously for another purpose.**

Talking Why and How (continued)

3. Group your students into mixed groups (four to five students per group) that you feel will work well together.

4. Read the book, chapter in a novel, or story you want your children to read or reread, and then do Talking Why and How. Decide if the selection has some "openness" in it so the children are free to infer and image how things happen, why things happen, how characters feel, and why characters do what they do.

5. If the selection does have some "openness," construct a maximum of six interesting "why" and "how" questions that your children would have to image or infer to answer. In your mind, a question may have a probable answer, but make sure it doesn't have a single "right" answer with which no good reader would argue.

6. Adjust the groups for absentees so every group has four to five children. Appoint a group leader to keep each group on-task. Set the timer for 10 minutes. Walk around, observing what you need to do to help the students improve their discussions next time.

Me Purpose Conversations

1. Model for the class how to lead and participate in a good small-group discussion of a book, a chapter in a book, or an article or story they have read previously for another purpose.

2. Group your students into mixed groups (four to five students per group) you feel will work well together.

3. Read the book, chapter, article, or story you want your children to read or reread, and about which you want them to have a Me Purpose conversation.

4. Construct a "Me Purpose" for the selection that either asks the children to evaluate (story) or to apply (informational text). Be sure there's no "right" answer to the Me Purpose question you construct.

5. Adjust the groups for absentees so every group has four to five children in it. Appoint a group leader to keep each group on-task. Set the timer for 8 minutes. Walk around, observing what you need to do to help the students learn to improve their Me Purpose conversations.

Guided Reading The Four-Blocks™ Way

CHAPTER 13

SENTENCE AND PARAGRAPH DETECTIVES

In Chapter 4, we explained that an important text strategy for readers is to follow sentence and paragraph structure. We also pointed out that, as a rule, very little Guided Reading instruction is devoted to teaching children this basic, but essential, strategy. Yet one of the differences between good and poor readers is the ability of the better readers to handle the structure of the sentences and paragraphs in texts that are challenging for them. While comprehending the sentences and paragraphs of a text is not as important or as interesting as understanding the text as a whole, or grasping the situation to which the whole text refers, it is just as necessary for reading. This chapter describes four types of lessons that will help you guide your students to attend to and make use of sentence and paragraph structural clues. These lesson types succeed with children by encouraging them to become "sentence and paragraph detectives."

All lessons that fit under the "sentence and paragraph detectives" label share three common instructional features. First, we always use the overhead projector to present the sentences or paragraph we are guiding the students to read. The students' books are closed. Second, we always take the sentences or paragraph for one of these lessons from the beginning of a book, story, or article. The first sentences or paragraph of a book chapter can also be used as long as it has a clear beginning, rather than just being a continuation from the previous chapter. Third, we always do each of these lessons as a group task. That is, we work with the group to achieve consensus, rather than having individual children give an answer and then telling them whether they are right or wrong. As usual, the children read the text on the overhead in whatever during-reading format you choose.

Each of these lessons always follows the before-and-after pattern because we always tell the children before they read the sentences or paragraph on the overhead what they are going to do after they read. What makes these lessons different from our other before-and-after reading activities is that these lessons are done with a small portion (the beginning few sentences or paragraphs) of a text the students have not read before. The children's reading of the entire text will be guided later using another before-and-after reading activity.

This chapter describes four lesson-types that fit under the "sentence and paragraph detectives" label, and gives you an example of each. In all four examples, the first several sentences or the first paragraph from a version of the story *The Bremen Town Musicians* by the Brothers Grimm is used. This way, you can see how each lesson focuses children's attention on different sentence and paragraph structural clues. Ordinarily, you wouldn't do more than one kind of "sentence and paragraph detectives" lesson with the beginning of the same book, chapter, story, or article.

Who Took Our Caps?

Capital letters at the beginning of sentences are very important clues to readers because—along with periods, question marks, and exclamation points—they help us divide the text up into sentences for meaningful processing. Moreover, knowing where to place beginning capitalization and ending punctuation when we write requires us to perceive the sentence as a meaningful structural unit. Even when readers attend to capitalization and punctuation, they must also have that sense that the sentence is a meaningful structural unit in order to comprehend the sentences in texts that are challenging for them. "Who Took Our Caps?" is a type of lesson that helps children learn to pay more attention to and make use of sentence structure when they read.

Before you teach a Who Took Our Caps? lesson to your class for the first time, it will help your children become interested in the activity if you will read them the book *Caps for Sale* by Esphyr Slobodkina. After reading the book to your children, you can tell them it will help them to remember that books, newspapers, magazines, and handwriting have "caps" that someone can "take." The "caps" in print and writing are the capital letters that start all the sentences. Someone can "take" those "caps" by retyping or rewriting the sentences without any capital letters, punctuation, or other indicators of where one sentence ends and the next one begins. Later, you can refer back to the book as a reminder to the children of what they do in a Who Took Our Caps? lesson.

A Sample Who Took Our Caps? Lesson

Turn on the overhead projector to reveal a transparency with the following sentences that begin the story *The Bremen Town Musicians*:

> once upon a time, a man owned a donkey the man had used him to carry sacks of grain to the mill for many years he was now old and worn out from all the hard work because the donkey was no longer strong enough to work, his owner was thinking about killing him he didn't want to have to feed and take care of him anymore

Tell the students that "someone took our caps, as well as our periods" and that "we need to try and put them back." Beginning with the first word, mark through the first letter and write a capital letter above it. Then, ask the students to try and figure out where the first period probably goes. (These sentences didn't have any question marks or exclamation points. If they had, then the children would have the additional challenge of deciding which ending punctuation marks to put where.) Tell the students that when the majority of them agree on where the "cap" and "period" should go in the sentence, you will put the capital and the period where they indicate. If there is a difference of opinion among the students as to where the first period goes, don't settle it for them. Rather, have students take turns reading the sentence aloud both (or however many) ways. Then, have students vote, and place the period where the majority say to put it. Start the next word after that period with a capital and repeat the process to determine where the next period goes. The majority of the students will probably be right about the location of the first period, but if they are not, it will become obvious to them as they try to place the second and third periods correctly. In that case, hopefully, they will figure out that they need to go back and redo the placement of the earlier period. If not, you will need to suggest it. The lesson ends with you asking the children to open their books and then leading them as a group to evaluate and correct their performance.

For this lesson type, you would never want to have more than six sentences in which the children are to find the beginnings and endings. Repeated use over time of Who Took Our Caps? lessons will help children learn to value and pay attention to beginning capitalization and ending punctuation as reading clues. It also will help sensitize them to seeing the sentence as a structural unit of meaning.

Link to Writing: Editor's Checklist

The best way to teach students to attend to beginning-sentence capitalization and ending-sentence punctuation when they read is to teach them to begin all their sentences with capital letters, and to end all their sentences with periods, questions marks, or exclamation points when they write. In the Writing Block, we teach children to use an Editor's Checklist to proofread and correct their own first drafts for the most important mechanics and usage rules.

Who Did What?

An often forgotten challenge of reading is keeping up with the referents for all the pronouns. One of the reasons texts can be challenging for students, even when they can identify almost all the words, is that texts use a lot of pronouns. Every pronoun requires the reader to infer to whom or to what the pronoun refers. As more and more pronouns are used in a paragraph, the more inferences the reader must make to understand the paragraph. "Who Did What?" is a lesson type that helps children learn to pay more attention to pronouns and be able to infer their referents better.

Obviously, the first paragraph you use for this lesson type must have several pronouns referring to different persons or things. Here is a list of pronouns to look for:

he, her, him, his, I, it, me, my, our, she, their, them, they, us, we, you, your

A Sample Who Did What? Lesson

Turn on the overhead projector to reveal a transparency with the following paragraph that begins *The Bremen Town Musicians*:

> Once upon a time, a man owned a donkey. The man had used [him] to carry sacks of grain to the mill for many years. [He] was now old and worn out from all the hard work. Because the donkey was no longer strong enough to work, [his] owner was thinking about killing [him]. [He] didn't want to have to feed and take care of [him] anymore. The donkey was smart, as donkeys go, and [he] figured out what was about to happen. So, [he] ran away and started on the road to Bremen. There [he] thought [he] could become one of the town musicians.

Tell the students that the words with boxes around them (or that are circled, underlined, etc.) are pronouns, and every pronoun stands for one or more persons or things. Also, tell the students that when they are reading, they have to figure out to whom or to what each pronoun refers, or they will be confused about "Who Did What."

Beginning with the first bordered pronoun, ask students to decide who or what the pronoun "stands for." Tell them that when they have decided the answer as a group, you will write what they think the answer is above the pronoun. If there is a difference of opinion among the students as to whom or to what the first pronoun refers, don't tell them who is right. Rather, have the students take turns reading the sentence aloud both (or however many) ways. Then, have them vote, and you write above the pronoun to whom or to what it refers, according to what the majority of students say. The majority of the students will probably be right about the first pronoun, but if they are not, it will probably become obvious as they try to determine the referent of the second and third pronouns. In that case, hopefully, they will figure out that they need to go back and redo the referent for the earlier pronoun. If not, you will have to suggest it. The lesson ends with you asking the children to open their books, and then leading them as a group to evaluate and correct their performance.

For this lesson type, you never want to have more than a paragraph or more than ten pronouns. Repeated use of Who Did What? lessons over time will help children learn to pay more attention to pronouns. It also will help them improve in their ability to infer the referents of pronouns.

What's the Missing Word?

The Cloze task has been used to assess reading comprehension for almost 40 years. The Cloze task is rarely used for assessment in Four-Blocks, but it has been found to be a valuable group task for a "sentence and paragraphs detectives" lesson type we call "What's the Missing Word?" These What's the Missing Word? lessons help children become more sensitive to the syntactic and semantic clues in a paragraph, and help them to pay more attention to the structural clues of the words when they are there for them to read.

While there are many variations, creating the standard Cloze task means deleting every fifth word from a text and replacing that word with a blank of uniform length. Using the standard deletion pattern, a Cloze passage is likely to have more structural words than content words deleted. That is helpful for this purpose because it is the structure words that most directly convey sentence and paragraph structure.

It is important to keep in mind, that not all the blanks in a standard Cloze passage can be filled in with the exact word that the author used. In fact, getting more than half of them exactly right is doing quite well. Therefore, an important part of any What's the Missing Word? lesson is to guide the students to decide whether the word they chose for a blank was the author's word, a different word that means the same as the author's word, or an incorrect word.

A Sample What's the Missing Word? Lesson

Turn on the overhead projector to reveal a transparency with the following paragraph that begins "The Bremen Town Musicians":

    Once upon a time, _____ man owned a donkey. _____ man had used him _____ carry sacks of grain _____ the mill for many _____. He was now old _____ worn out from all _____ hard work. Because the _____ was no longer strong _____ to work, his owner _____ thinking about killing him. _____ didn't want to have _____ feed and take care _____ him anymore. The donkey _____ smart, as donkeys go, _____ he figured out what _____ about to happen. So, _____ ran away and started _____ the road to Bremen. _____ he thought he could _____ one of the town musicians.

Beginning with the first blank, ask the students to decide what word the author probably put there. Tell them that when they decide as a group, you will write the word they choose in the blank. If there is a difference of opinion among the students as to what word goes in the first blank, don't tell them who is right. Rather, have them take turns reading the sentence aloud both (or however many) ways. Then, have them vote, and you write the word in the blank that the majority says goes there. The majority of the students will probably have put the right word or a synonym in the first blank, but if they did not, it will probably become obvious as they try to determine what word goes in the second and third blanks. In that case, hopefully, they will figure out that they need to go back and redo the word they put in the earlier blank. If they do not, and they have trouble because of a previously incorrect answer, you could suggest that they may need to redo an answer they did previously. The lesson ends with you asking the children to open their books, and then leading them as a group to evaluate and correct their performance.

Here is what one class of children agreed to put in the blanks left in the first paragraph of "The Bremen Town Musicians":

Once upon a time, ___a___ man owned a donkey. ___The___ man had used him ___to___ carry sacks of grain ___to___ the mill for many ___years___. He was now old ___and___ worn out from all ___*that*___ hard work. Because the ___donkey___ was no longer strong ___enough___ to work, his owner ___was___ thinking about killing him. ___He___ didn't want to have ___to___ feed and take care ___of___ him anymore. The donkey ___was___ smart, as donkeys go, ___*so*___ he figured out what ___was___ about to happen. So, ___he___ ran away and started ___*down*___ the road to Bremen. ___*So*___ he thought he could ___*be*___ one of the town musicians. [Words in the blanks that are different from the author's are in italics.]

This group of children chose the author's word for 15 of the 20 blanks. That is better than children can be expected to do ordinarily, and is probably due to the large number of structure words that happened to be deleted. Of the five blanks where they did not choose the author's word, the teacher had the children read and reread the sentence both ways to decide if their word meant the same, and was "a way we can say that." The children decided that four of the five meant about the same thing as the author's word and worked fine in the sentences. The children did decide that "So" in the next-to-last blank, rather than the author's "There," was incorrect. The teacher was very happy with this and did not feel the need to dispute the students' own evaluation of their performance.

For this lesson type, there should never be more than 20 blanks to be filled. At first, 10 is plenty. Repeated use of What's the Missing Word? lessons over time will help children learn to pay more attention to structure words. It also will help them improve in their ability to follow both meaning and syntactic structure through the sentences of a paragraph.

Who Mixed Up Our Sentences?

The order of the sentences is the most important aspect of paragraph structure. The linear logic of a paragraph is like a thread sewn through the sentences, one at a time, in sequence. Taking the sentences out of order destroys the logic of most paragraphs. By mixing up the sentences from the first paragraph of a book, chapter, story, or article, you can present students with a problem in paragraph logic. Presenting this problem to students as a group task helps them become more sensitive to the linear logic of paragraphs and the other meaning and structure clues that reflect that logic.

A Sample Who Mixed Up Our Sentences? Lesson

Turn on the overhead projector to reveal a transparency with the following five sentences that begin *The Bremen Town Musicians*:

1. Because the donkey was no longer strong enough to work, his owner was thinking about killing him.

2. He didn't want to have to feed and take care of him anymore.

3. He was now old and worn out from all the hard work.

4. Once upon a time, a man owned a donkey.

5. The man had used him to carry sacks of grain to the mill for many years.

Tell the children that these are all sentences from the first paragraph of the story and that all the sentences are correct. Then, tell them that "someone has mixed up our sentences" and it is "our job to put them back in the right order."

Begin by asking the students to decide which of the sentences is probably the first one. Tell them that when they decide as a group, you will mark through the number of that sentence and put a "1". If there is a difference of opinion among the students as to which sentence is first, don't tell them who is right. Rather, have them take turns reading both (or however many) sentences aloud. Then, have students vote and renumber the sentence with a "1" that the majority says should be the first sentence. The majority of the students will probably be right about the first sentence, but if they are not, it will become obvious as they try to determine which sentence is the second one. In that case, hopefully, they will figure out that they need to go back and redo the sentence they earlier thought was the first one. If not, you could suggest that they do so. The lesson ends with you having the children to open their books, and then leading them as a group to evaluate and correct their performance.

For this lesson type, you never want to have more than six sentences for the students to put in the correct order. Repeated use of Who Mixed Up Our Sentences? lessons over time will help children learn to follow the logic from one sentence to another when they read.

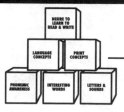

Building Blocks Variations

Lessons in becoming "sentence and paragraph detectives" are not teaching strategies you would use with kindergartners. Kindergarten children begin to follow sentence and paragraph structure during shared reading lessons when they learn that what they read should sound right and make sense.

Big Blocks Variations

There are more advanced lesson types than the four described here for encouraging older children to become "sentence and paragraph detectives." In the GIST Procedure, for example, you put the first paragraph of a text on the overhead projector, then cover all but the first sentence by maneuvering two pieces of thick paper. You also write fifteen blanks on the markerboard. You turn on the overhead, have the students read the first sentence to themselves, then turn off the overhead. Working as a group, the students restate the important information in that first sentence, and you write what they say in the blanks on the board. The students may remember and repeat the entire first sentence, but they don't have to, and using synonyms or alternate word orders is fine. Then, the two pieces of paper are moved to reveal both the first and second sentences. The overhead is turned on, the students read the first two sentences to themselves, then the overhead is turned off. Again working as a group, the students direct you to modify what they have in the blanks in order to include the important information from the second sentence. Under no circumstances would you write the sixteenth word on the board. If they have 16 or more words, they have to eliminate some words. This process continues until the entire paragraph has been summarized in a single sentence of 15 or fewer words. In "Old or New?", for another example, you place the first paragraph or two of a book, chapter, story, or article on the overhead projector and turn it on. Every content word or phrase is bordered or circled. For every bordered/circled word, you lead the students to decide whether that word or phrase refers back to the same or a synonymous word or phrase used earlier, or if that word is providing new information. You write "old" or "new" above each bordered/circled word as students reach a consensus.

Sentence and Paragraph Detectives

Two of the goals of the Guided Reading Block are to teach comprehension skills and strategies, and to teach children how to read all types of literature. Following sentence and paragraph structure is an important, but infrequently taught, comprehension strategy that is necessary for every kind of literature. Lessons that get children to become "sentence and paragraph detectives" help them learn to follow sentence and paragraph structure whenever they read. If you repeatedly begin your Guided Reading Block with one of the four "sentence and paragraph detectives" lesson types described in this chapter, your students will become more careful and capable readers of the sentences and paragraphs in whatever materials they read.

Who Took Our Caps?

1. Select the first six or fewer sentences from a book, book chapter, story, or article.

2. Print or write this selection on a transparency with no beginning-sentence capitalization, ending-sentence punctuation, or extra spaces between sentences.

3. Work to achieve consensus among the students as to where the first sentence ends and the second one begins. Add capitalization and punctuation to mark where the majority want the change of sentence to be.

4. Continue sentence-by-sentence until consensus is achieved as to where all the sentences begin and end.

Who Did What?

1. Select the first few sentences, or at most the first paragraph, from a book, book chapter, story, or article. Make sure there are several pronouns with different referents in these sentences.

2. Print or write this selection on a transparency with up to the first 10 pronouns bordered or circled.

3. Work to achieve consensus among the students as to whom or what the first bordered/circled pronoun refers. Write the referent on which the majority agree above that first pronoun.

4. Continue pronoun-by-pronoun until consensus is achieved as to whom or what each bordered/circled pronoun refers.

What's the Missing Word?

1. Select the first paragraph or two from a book, book chapter, story, or article.

2. Print or write this selection on a transparency with every fifth word deleted and replaced by a blank of standard length, up to a maximum of 20 blanks.

3. Work to achieve consensus among the students as to what word was probably deleted and replaced by the first blank. Write the word the majority want in the first blank.

4. Continue blank-by-blank until consensus is achieved as to what words go in all the blanks.

Who Mixed Up Our Sentences?

1. Select the first six or fewer sentences from a book, book chapter, story, or article.

2. Print or write those sentences on a transparency in random order in a numbered list.

3. Work to achieve consensus among the students as to what sentence should be first. Number the sentence with a "1" that the majority of students say is first.

4. Continue sentence-by-sentence until consensus is achieved as to the correct order of all the sentences.

CHAPTER 14

WRITING AND DRAWING BEFORE, DURING, AND AFTER READING

Writing and drawing are not only ways in which you show what you have learned and what you are thinking, they are also ways in which you can figure out what you know—or don't know—and clarify your own thinking. We use a variety of writing and drawing activities with children both before and after reading. Sometimes, everyone writes. Sometimes, everyone draws. Many times, children are given the choice of writing or drawing or are encouraged to do both. Before describing some of these writing and drawing activities, it is important to clarify what we mean by writing and drawing.

The writing we do before and after reading is, for the most part, short, first-draft writing. Children are often asked to write on an index card or bookmark. Some teachers have their students keep a reading response log, and the children write and draw in this log. We want the students to use writing to help clarify their own thinking and, generally, no one other than the student sees what is written in the log. Sometimes, children are asked to volunteer to share what they have written, but their writing is not displayed in any way. Also, this writing is not collected or corrected. We give children a limited amount of time to write (three–six minutes), and we emphasize that they are collecting and recording their ideas in order to remember them and be able to share them with others later.

The drawing we do is usually "sketching." It is usually done with pencils on a bookmark, index card, or in the response log. We encourage the children to use stick figures and sketch in other details. We give the students a limited amount of time to draw, and then we let them volunteer to tell about what they have drawn. The drawings are not displayed, and children soon learn that they can use drawing to clarify and record their thinking and ideas.

We use drawing and writing in all kinds of ways. The following are some examples for each of the thinking strategies.

Connecting

In Chapter Four, six thinking strategies that children need to do in order to comprehend were described. Connecting is one of these six strategies. As children read, they connect what they are reading to themselves, their world, and to other things they have read. There are numerous ways to use writing and/or drawing to help children make connections before and after reading.

Before children read, we want to help them both access and build prior knowledge. Teachers often lead children in a brainstorming session in which various children share what they know about the topic. This brainstorming can be much more effective and can include more children if you have the children write or draw things they know individually before gathering the group ideas. The easiest way to do this is to give children an index card—bigger cards for little children work best—and let them have three minutes to write and draw anything they know about the topic. This works well for any informational topic—bats, dinosaurs, Japan, the Pilgrims, Martin Luther King, Jr., etc. Giving children the "write or draw" option here is important because many children whose vocabularies are limited do know things and can depict what they know better with a sketch than with words.

When the three minutes are up, let children share by telling what they have written and/or showing what they have sketched. Accept all responses. If someone disagrees with a response, tell the children to be on the lookout for that piece of information as they read so that they may be able to resolve the disagreement.

Now, have the children read the text to find out some new things about the topic. Ask the students to draw or write what they learned on the backs of their index cards. Since they won't be able to write all the new things they have learned, tell the students to just pick two or three things they find most interesting. After reading, let children again share what they have written or drawn on the other side.

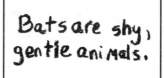

A similar activity can be used when you want children to connect what they are about to read with something else they have already read. You may want the children to compare two characters or to think about how the problem was solved in one story versus how the problem is solved in the story they are about to read. The children can write or draw what they remember about the story they have already read on one side of an index card, and then write or draw comparable things about the new story on the other side.

When children read, we help them access and build prior knowledge before reading, and we help them connect new knowledge gained from reading. Writing and drawing activities invite everyone's participation and give children a clear, concrete purpose for reading.

Predicting/Anticipating

Another thinking strategy important for comprehension is predicting/anticipating. Chapter Six described three activities to help children predict—Prove It!, Anticipation Guides and Rivet. Writing and drawing can also be used to help children predict and anticipate. Once children are used to doing Prove It! as a class, you can have them preview the selection and write down three of their own predictions. As they read, they determine if the predictions were true or not and change any predictions that were not true to make them true sentences. The same thing can be done with Rivet. After all the letters of the words are filled in, children can write down two or three sentences, using as many of the words as they can, and then read to see if the sentences reflect what actually happened in the story. Children enjoy making these personal predictions more if you ask them to keep their predictions secret before reading, and if you allow them to change their predictions so that they are all true after reading.

Shifting the focus from predicting (where you think you know what will happen) to anticipating (where you don't know what will happen, but are eager to find out), you can ask children to come up with some "I wonder questions." After previewing the pictures in *Aunt Flossie's Hats (and Crab Cakes Later)*, children came up with these "I wonder" questions:

I wonder who the two girls are?

I wonder why she's got all those hats?

I wonder what happened in the big fire?

I wonder why they were having that big parade?

I wonder how that dog got that hat out of the lake?

I wonder who those people are in the restaurant at the end?

The children brainstorm the "I wonder…" statements together, each child picks one or two and writes the statement(s) on an index card or in her response log, and then writes an answer after reading the text.

Once children learn how to generate "I wonder…" questions, they can be encouraged to generate some as they read. Some of the questions ("I wonder why . . ." and "I wonder how . . .") to which they don't find answers may be good initiators for "Talking Why and How" small-group discussions.

Summarizing/Concluding

As we read, we take the specific information we are reading and periodically summarize and draw conclusions from what we have read so far. As we continue reading, we expand our summaries to include the new information. We usually do this internally in our brains. As children write summaries and retellings, they learn how to summarize and draw conclusions.

The KWLs, graphic organizers, story maps, and Beach Ball questions described in Chapters 8, 9, and 10 all lend themselves to summary writing. Once the children have the information recorded somewhere, they can use that information to write summaries. Summary writing is not easy for young children, so we often give them a paragraph frame which they can use to organize the information. Here are some possible summary frames. All of them use the topic of frogs, but could be adapted to any informational text.

Frogs are very interesting animals. Frogs have _____.
Frogs eat _____. Frogs live in _____.
The most fascinating thing about frogs is _____.

Although I already knew that frogs _____, I learned many new things about frogs. I learned that _____.
I also learned that _____. Another fact I learned was _____. However, the most interesting thing I learned was _____.

Frogs and toads are alike in many ways. First, they both _____.
Second, they _____. They also both _____. Frogs and toads are also different in some ways.
Frogs _____. Toads _____. Frogs and toads are more alike than different.

Questioning/Monitoring

Connecting and Predicting lend themselves to writing and drawing activities children do before and after reading. Questioning and monitoring occur during reading. We model how our brains ask questions and express confusion during Think-Alouds as described in Chapter Seven. As children do their reading, they can occasionally be given one or two sticky notes and asked to use the notes to mark a place in the text that was hard for them to understand or a word they couldn't decode or for which they did not have an appropriate meaning. This is especially useful if the text they are going to read is a particularly complex text, or the topic is one that is unfamiliar to the children. Generally, children (and adults!) do not like to admit they don't understand what they are reading, but when they can mark the place with a sticky note and write the confusing part or word on that note, it becomes acceptable to be confused!

All good readers monitor their comprehension as they read. They know when they are comprehending and when they are not. When they become confused, they use "fix-up" strategies, such as rereading and rethinking. Children need to monitor their comprehension. They need to become aware of when they are comprehending and when they are not. In the after-reading discussion, guided by the sticky notes marking any areas that confused students, the teacher and the other children can help to clear up the confusion and answer any questions.

Imaging/Inferring

Both the "Doing the Book" activities from Chapter 11 and the small-group discussions described in Chapter 12 help children image and infer. Drawing is another activity you can use to help children image and infer. Children can draw sketches to show how they think different characters felt, what they think the settings looked like, what the characters might have done after the story ended, etc. They can write or draw their most probable answer to one of the "Why" or "How" questions from a "Talking Why and How" lesson. After reading for a Me Purpose, they can write or draw how they would have reacted or what they would have done if they were the character in the story. When you image or infer, you imagine yourself in a situation. Writing and drawing help children express their imaginations.

Evaluating/Applying

All children have opinions, and they love to tell you what they think. When we ask children to give us their opinions, we arc helping them learn to evaluate and apply as they read. Writing your opinion is probably the most commonly used writing connected to reading activity. Teachers often ask children to respond to questions such as:

My favorite part was when...

My favorite character was ...

I liked (did not like) this book because...

The funniest part was when...

The most interesting things I learned were...

All these questions ask children to evaluate and apply what they are reading to their own lives. When we want children to evaluate and apply, we should give them the option of drawing and/or writing. Here are some drawing and writing responses by some second-graders asked to respond to some of these prompts:

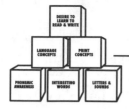

Building Blocks Variations

We often follow our shared reading of big books with shared writing in which the children come up with the ideas, and the teacher records these ideas on a chart. Kindergartners enjoy drawing something in response to what was read, and then telling about their drawing. Children who are more advanced can be encouraged to add some words to their drawings.

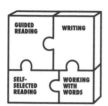

Big Blocks Variations

The writing and drawing activities described here are particularly helpful for older students as they respond to and make sense of what they have read. It is particularly important to include some drawing activities and, on occasion, to let students choose if they want to draw, write, or use a combination of both. Many older, struggling readers have some artistic talents and using drawing is one way to let them "shine" and invite their active participation in the lessons.

Writing and Drawing Before, During, and After Reading

Writing and drawing can be used before, during, and after reading to help children connect, predict/anticipate, summarize/conclude, question/monitor, image/infer, and evaluate/apply.

1. Have children do their writing and drawing on a sticky note, bookmark, index card, or in their reading response log. Make sure they know it is their ideas you want them to record—you are not expecting a finished writing piece or a work of art.

2. Give a limited amount of time for the drawing or writing. Some teachers call this activity a "quickwrite" or "quickdraw."

3. When feasible, let students choose if they want to draw or write, or both.

4. Use writing and drawing to provide another purpose for rereading and as follow-ups to predicting activities, KWLs, graphic organizers, story maps, the Beach Ball, and small-group discussions.

5. As you introduce each new writing/drawing activity, model how the students might do it. On different days, include drawing, writing, and a combination of both so that children see that you value all three.

Guided Reading The Four-Blocks™ Way

CHAPTER 15

SOUVENIRS

When you go on a special trip or have a special experience, do you collect souvenirs? Do you relive these experiences as you come across your rocks, shells, menus, soaps, postcards, and matchbooks? Do you think about throwing them away, but just can't bear to part with them? Concrete, tangible objects are wonderful reminders of experiences. They trigger memories and help us relive the experience. Providing children with a small, concrete souvenir of something they have read during Guided Reading is one way to help them remember and retell—to themselves and others—what they have read and what they have learned.

Some teachers call these souvenirs "story bits" because they are just a little "bit" of the story that help them to remember. Cheryl Sigmon describes the use of these story bits for books teachers have read aloud to children in Article 33 of her "4 Block Literacy Column" (*www.teachers.net*). She summarizes lots of Four-Blocks teachers' story bit suggestions in Article 34. We prefer to call them souvenirs because many of the texts we read are informational rather than stories, and we don't want to confuse the children by using the term "story" with informational text. We like the idea of using souvenirs after a teacher-read aloud book, but we also feel they can be valuable prompts for retelling after Guided Reading.

Regardless of what you call them (the most correct term is "artifacts"), giving children something concrete to help them remember and retell the story or information is a wonderful way to help children verbally practice the strategy of summarizing/concluding.

When we use souvenirs in connection with something read during the Guided Reading Block, we spend a few minutes with children "practicing" what they will say when they take their souvenir home. Here is an example based on any of the *Arthur* books by Marc Brown. The souvenir is a pair of brown "Arthur type" glasses made out of three pipe cleaners.   (See page 139 for instructions.)

If you keep your souvenirs simple, you will use them a lot more often. Remember, souvenirs are not meant to represent the whole story or informational piece—they are only to prompt the retelling and help the child remember. Some teachers include edibles—goldfish-shaped crackers after reading *Brown Bear, Brown Bear, What Do You See?* by Bill Martin, Jr., a cookie after reading *If You Give a Mouse a Cookie* by Laura Joffe Numeroff, teddy bear-shaped crackers after reading anything involving a bear, a candy heart after *Love You Forever* by Robert N. Munsch, etc. Other teachers want the children to make a collection of their souvenirs, so they give the students "fake" cookies or fish cut out of paper, foil, or felt. Stickers make wonderful souvenirs and are better given as a souvenir than as a reward. There are also wonderful souvenirs to be found in the different shaped pastas. A long piece of thick pasta will make a great wand or baton. Bow tie pasta would be a great souvenir for *Big Anthony* by Tomie de Paola. Shell pasta will help children retell ocean stories and books. Bean seeds and gold-wrapped chocolates would be wonderful souvenirs for *Jack and the Beanstalk*.

Giving students souvenirs is one of those ideas that most of us never thought of doing. When we first heard about them, we thought they would be hard (or expensive) to find. But once we started looking, we began to see how rocks, seeds, and pieces of pasta—things that are part of our everyday life—could become great souvenirs. Better yet, the children begin to make connections between the real world and what they have been reading. After being given several souvenirs by his teacher, one enterprising boy arrived early at school one morning and proudly handed his teacher a box of dog biscuits. To her amazed, "What's this for?" question, he explained, "It's the souvenir you can give everyone when we finish reading the *Clifford* book!"

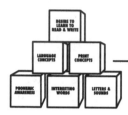

Building Blocks Variations

Use souvenirs to have children retell favorite books read during shared reading.

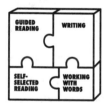

Big Blocks Variations

Intermediate-aged children love to collect things. A collection of reading souvenirs is a natural for older students. As children get older, parent-child communication about what they are learning at school decreases. When they take their souvenirs home, they have a "prop" and a reason to initiate conversations about what they have been reading.

Souvenirs

A souvenir is a reminder of a pleasant experience. Children like to collect things, and if you provide souvenirs regularly, they will begin to wonder as they are reading "What will he give us to remember this?" Those are the kind of pleasant and anticipatory associations we want to build for reading. Souvenirs are "little things" which mean a lot to children.

Arthur Glasses

Materials Needed:

4 brown pipe cleaners per child

Lots of patience as you go through the directions step-by-step with your students

Directions:

1. Create a loop in two of the pipe cleaners by bending and twisting them until they look like two balloons.

2. Cut about one inch off each of the two ends of the looped pipe cleaners.

3. Wind these two shortened ends together. This is the "frame" part of your glasses.

4. Take the two unused pipe cleaners and cut off approximately one fourth of the length.

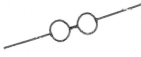

5. Take these two shortened pieces and wind one end around each side of the frame piece to create earpieces.

6. Bend the earpieces back at right angles.

7. Finally, put on the glasses and curl the ends around your ears to create a custom fit.

(Activity created by Regan McKay)

PART 3
FORMATS FOR "DURING" READING

You have gone a long way toward planning your Guided Reading time so that you are meeting the goals of this block. Comprehension skills and strategies are being taught and modeled. Prior knowledge, language, and meaning vocabulary are growing. You are using the largest variety of materials you can find, and teaching children how to read all types of text. You are integrating some of the reading with your science and social studies content and themes. The final decision you must make is how the children will read the materials. This part of the book will describe formats for reading which will help you achieve the goals of providing as much instructional-level reading as possible (and the instruction to go with it), while simultaneously maintaining the self-confidence and motivation of your struggling readers. If the material is not at the reading instructional level of some children in the class, you must decide what kind of support these students need so that they can successfully negotiate the text.

When you think about how the children will read materials, we want you want to consider shared reading, choral and echo reading, ERT…, partner reading, playschool groups, coaching groups, Three-Ring Circus, "You'se Choose" days, Book Club groups, Pick a Page, and once in a while—for fun and fluency—Musical Riddles!

CHAPTER 16

SHARED READING

Shared reading provides opportunities for you to model and interact with children, showing them how you think as you read. By using a big book in which all the children can see the print and the pictures, you can focus their attention on whatever strategy is being developed. Shared reading of big books should not be confined to kindergarten and early first grade. Rather, teachers should try to find and use big books that help them "think-aloud" and demonstrate any new comprehension strategies being introduced to students.

During shared reading, there are many different things that can be learned, depending on what children are ready to learn. Children who have had little experience with reading learn how print works, how to track print, and how the pictures and the words support each other. They also learn a few words, and they notice how the letters can help them tell which word is which. For children who are further along in reading, shared reading provides an opportunity to learn many words. All children enjoy shared reading, and participating in shared reading lessons helps them build concepts, vocabulary, and comprehension strategies. There is truly "something for everyone" in a good shared reading lesson, and consequently, we consider shared reading one of the most "multilevel" formats.

Shared Reading with Predictable Books

The best big books for beginning readers are those that are predictable by pictures or print. Two excellent examples of big books that are predictable by pictures are *Things I Like* by Anthony Browne and *Moonbear Likes Books* by Frank Ashe. In these books, children can "read the words" by looking at the pictures. The words are easily recognized because of the pictures. If children are taught to look at the pictures and stretch out the words they expect for each picture, then they can "cross-check" and see if they are right by looking for the letters that they expect to appear in these words.

In the book *Things I Like*, when the little monkey lists all the activities he likes, one on each page, the children can figure out the text by looking at the pictures and thinking about what the monkey is doing on each page. "What does it say on this page? Yes, it says 'riding my bike' because you see the monkey on a little red bike and know he is riding his bike." "Riding my bike" makes sense with the picture, sounds right, and makes sense with the sounds we hear, and the letters we expect to see. Predictable pictures allow young children to share the reading even before they are fluent at decoding many words. Thus, some books and stories are made easier for children because they are predictable by pictures.

Other books are predictable by print. In these books, words or phrases are repeated over and over again in the text. As soon as the children can hear this pattern, they begin to chime in and share the reading of the story. An example of this is *Brown Bear, Brown Bear, What Do You See?* by Bill Martin, Jr. and *Mrs. Wishy Washy* by Joy Cowley. Once the children have heard the story, they can pick up the pattern, and want to join in or "share" the reading of the book. The children enjoy chiming in, "Wishy, Washy, Wishy, Washy," every time Mrs. Wishy Washy puts an animal into the tub to wash him.

For our first example of shared reading, we will use the predictable big book, *The Doorbell Rang* by Pat Hutchins. In this big book, the repeated pattern is:

"Nobody makes cookies like Grandma," said Ma as the doorbell rang.

We recommend using this book for three days during Guided Reading and including some math and snack links. One day at snack time, before the first reading of *The Doorbell Rang*, we will tell the children that we have brought some cookies to share with them. As we say this, we will put 12 cookies in front of the students and ask them to estimate the number of cookies, and how many cookies each person can have. After estimating, we will count the number of cookies and the number of children present, and conclude that we don't have enough for everyone to have even one! At that point, we either divide the cookies in half (Let's hope they're big cookies!) or pull out some more cookies and count out enough for everyone to have at least one.

If you do this activity with your students, it will provide some concrete experience with the problem in *The Doorbell Rang*. Don't mention the book when you are sharing the cookies, and don't mention the cookies when you begin *reading The Doorbell Rang*. It is much more fun to let children discover the link as they are reading the book. Someone is sure to observe, "This is just like what happened to us when we only had 12 cookies!"

Shared Reading—Day One
The first thing the teacher does during Guided Reading when sharing a big book is to gather the students together where they all can see the book—both pictures and print. The teacher reads the title and author to them, and then asks them what they see in the picture on the cover. The children tell her that there is a woman, a cat, and a bunch of children. The "bunch of children" is counted, and there are 12 of them. The woman and all 12 children are peeking out the door, and they don't look happy.

The teacher turns the page, and this time, she asks the children to help her read the title and the author. There is a picture on this title page, too. The woman is in the picture and she is holding a cookie sheet full of cookies. The teacher leads the children in counting the cookies, and there are 12. The cat is sitting on the sink. There are no children in this picture, but both the cat and the woman are looking toward the door. The teacher gets the children to predict/anticipate by saying, "I wonder what is going to happen." Children make various comments:

"The doorbell just rang, and she is going to answer it when she puts the cookies down."

"There are 12 cookies, and 12 children are at the door."

"Hey, that's like we had 12 cookies at snack, but there are 22 of us!"

The teacher says, "Well, let's turn the page, and we will find out."

The teacher turns the page, and the teacher and children discuss the picture. Two children are sitting at the table and are about to grab some of the delicious-looking cookies. One child comments that those were two of the children on the cover looking out the door, and the teacher and children turn back and identify the two children on this page in the crowd of children on the cover. After discussing the picture, the teacher says, "Now, I am going to read the words to you. Watch and listen and then we will talk about what we learned from the words that we couldn't figure out from the picture." The teacher reads the page to the children, pointing to words as she reads them. After she reads, she asks the students what they learned. They tell her that the children are named Victoria and Sam, and the woman is their mother, who tells them to share the cookies because she made plenty.

Before turning the page, the teacher asks the students to make some more predictions. She uses the names—Victoria, Sam, Ma—to talk about the characters, and gets the children to use the names so that they will eventually be able to read them.

"What's going to happen?"

"Will Victoria and Sam get to eat all 12 cookies?"

"If they share them as Ma told them to, how many cookies will Victoria get? How many will Sam get?

The children conclude that if they share the cookies, Victoria and Sam will each get six. Some children think they should save some cookies for later. Someone suggests that, "All those other kids are going to come and want cookies."

The teacher turns the page again to show just Victoria, Sam, Ma, and the cat. The pictures are discussed, and the teacher then asks the children to watch, listen, and see what they can learn from the words that they couldn't learn from the pictures. The children watch, listen, and then tell what they learned:

"They are going to get six each, just like we figured out."

"They have a Grandma, and she makes cookies, too."

"The cookies look and smell as good as the ones their Grandma makes."

"The doorbell just rang."

"What do you think will happen next?" the teacher asks.

The teacher continues through the rest of the book, one page at a time, using the same procedure.

Each time the doorbell rings, more children arrive. Tom and Hannah arrive from next door—"That's three each." Peter and his little brother come by—"two each." As more children in the book arrive, the children in the class delight in going back to the cover and finding the children there. After Peter and his little brother arrive, the students begin to predict which children from the cover are coming next. When Joy, Simon, and four cousins arrive, there are 12 children and 12 cookies—"One each!" The children are just about to grab their one cookie, commenting that these cookies look and smell as good as Grandma's when the doorbell rings again. Everyone looks anxiously at the door, and Ma suggests that perhaps they should eat their cookies before opening the door. Sam decides everyone should wait, and he opens the door. Fortunately, it is Grandma with an enormous tray of cookies. The book ends:

"And no one makes cookies like Grandma," said Ma as the doorbell rang.

The teacher then takes a few minutes to let the children discuss what they liked about the story and to make connections to their own lives. Children talk about their Grandmas, making cookies, sharing, and how it's a good thing it was Grandma at their door and not more kids.

Next, the teacher tells the students that they will read the book again (Yeah!), and that this time, she wants them to read with her, joining in on the refrain and any other words they can read. Quickly, they look at the cover, reading the title and author again. The teacher asks them why they think the author, Pat Hutchins, named the book *The Doorbell Rang,* and the children delight in explaining why it is a good title. They count the children again, and some people begin to identify the children.

"That's Sam and his sister, Victoria"

"There's that kid and his little brother."

"Those are all the cousins."

The children don't remember all the names, and the teacher says that they will pay more attention to that when they read it this time. She asks the students if anyone remembers what they call the people in a story, and someone says, "They are the characters." The teacher then asks the students where the action in the story takes place, and they say it all happens in the kitchen. The teacher helps them remember that this is called the setting.

Once more they read the book, talking about the pictures and then joining the teacher as she reads some words, especially the refrain. This time, before turning each page, the teacher asks, "Does anyone remember what will happen on the next page?" The children enjoy sharing what they remember, and the second reading continues in this way.

They end the Shared Reading on this day by doing a group retelling. The teacher turns the pages again, and asks the children to tell the story based on the pictures. She leads them to use the names of the characters as they tell the story. By the end of the first day, the children all know the characters and can retell the action.

Shared Reading—Day Two

The teacher begins Day Two by displaying a laminated story map skeleton and having the children help her fill it in. The finished product looks like this:

Story Map

Title: *The Doorbell Rang*

Author: Pat Hutchins

Setting: in a kitchen

Characters: Victoria, Sam, Ma, Tom and Hannah, Peter and his brother, Joy, Simon and four cousins, and Grandma

Beginning: Ma made some cookies for Victoria and Sam to eat

Middle: The doorbell rang, and some friends came to see Victoria and Sam. They shared their cookies with their friends until there was just one cookie on each plate, and then the doorbell rang again.

End: Grandma was at the door with a big batch of cookies.

Conclusion: Everyone liked Grandma's cookies best. Now Victoria and Sam had a big batch of her cookies to share with her friends.

When the story map is completed, the teacher once again directs the children's attention back to the book. They reread the first page, and the teacher asks, "Who is talking on this page?" The children conclude that Ma, Victoria, and Sam are all talking, and they decide what each is saying. They do this for a few more pages. After looking at the first several pages, the children decide that most of the words on the pages are things people are saying. The teacher then announces that she thinks *The Doorbell Rang* would make a great play. If the students will help her, she will write down what everyone is saying, and tomorrow, the class will act out *The Doorbell Rang*. The children love acting out books, so they are eager to help her write this play.

The teacher hooks her computer up to the large monitor, sits down, and prepares to write. (If you don't have this technology in your classroom, you can write the script on a long sheet of paper or a transparency, but it is quicker and more dramatic to do it on the computer in front of the children. You can show them how you copy and paste to save time. You can also make copies for everyone to take home!) The teacher appoints one child to turn the pages of the big book, and everyone else to help her decide exactly who is saying what.

On the first page, they decide that Ma is talking to her children, Victoria and Sam. They notice that Ma is talking first, and she says, "I've made cookies for tea." Next, Victoria and Sam talk, "Good. We're starving." The page ends with Ma talking again. The beginning of the play looks like this:

Ma: *I've made some cookies for tea.*

Victoria and Sam: *Good. We're starving.*

Ma: *Share them between yourselves. I made plenty.*

As each page of dialogue is written, the teacher stops and has the children read it. For this page, she asks one girl to be Ma and asks the rest of the class to be Victoria and Sam. They read the first page of the play, and then the teacher and children continue through the book. For each page, they first read the page chorally, then decide who is talking and exactly what each character says. These lines get added:

Victoria and Sam: *That's six each.*

Victoria: *They look as good as Grandma's.*

When the children tell the teacher that she needs to write that Sam says, "*They smell as good as Grandma's,*" the teacher says she is going to show them a trick to do that line really fast. She then copies "*They look as good as Grandma's.*" from the script, pastes the sentence into the play script where it is needed, and highlights "look" and changes it to "smell." The page finishes with the refrain,

Ma: *No one makes cookies like Grandma.*

The children delight in telling her each time they come to the refrain to just "copy and paste it again."

The teacher and children continue reading each page in the book chorally and deciding what the play script should say. They copy and paste with abandon. As each page of the play script is written, the teacher appoints someone to read the new parts, while the rest of the class recites Ma's refrain, and the play script gets read as it is being created.

They conclude this day by doing the Beach Ball. The children are all fluent in telling about their favorite part, what happened, how it ended, and even naming all the characters.

Shared Reading—Day Three

The children can't wait for Guided Reading time, because they know that they are going to act out and read the play based on *The Doorbell Rang*. The teacher has written the character names on yarned cards for the children to wear. She has also made a card with a picture of a bell for the child who will make the doorbell sound. (She drew a bell at the right places in the script.)

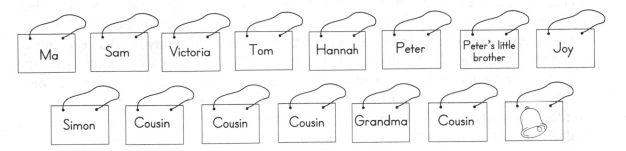

The teacher has the children choose parts as she always does by shuffling index cards with the children's names on them, pulling names from her set of cards, and letting the children choose who they want to be in the play. The first person whose card is chosen comes and puts the yarned card for Grandma around her neck. The next person chooses to be the doorbell. The choosing continues until the 15 yarned cards are around 15 necks. The teacher tells the six remaining children that she will join them as the audience, but that, as always, they will do the play again, and they will be the first six to choose parts for the second production.

The children are all given a copy of the script they helped the teacher to write on the previous day. For the most part, children read their lines and enter on cue because they are so familiar with the story by now. The "doorbell" enjoys going "ding, dong" when necessary and is the first "part" chosen for the next reading. The teacher decides that the four cousins should also get to choose a speaking part for the second reading since they didn't get to say anything the first time. The play is read and acted out the second time, and the children beg to do it a third time. The teacher tells them that they don't have time to do it again here, but that they can all take their scripts home. Perhaps they can recruit family, friends, and stuffed animals to play the parts and do the play at home.

For an after-reading activity, the teacher directs the students' attention to the last page in the book.

"And no one makes cookies like Grandma," said Ma as the doorbell rang.

The teacher asks the children to think about who is at the door now and what is going to happen next. "I don't want you to tell me aloud," she says, "I want you to tell me in writing." She gives everyone a piece a paper and asks them to write who they think is at the door and what will happen. She gives them just a few minutes to write, and then lets the children share with the class what they have written if they want.

Shared Reading with Informational Books

Many children in grades 2-6 have trouble reading content area textbooks. These books often have a table of contents, illustrations with quicktext, diagrams with labels, maps, charts, and sometimes a glossary or index. Using each of these parts requires a different skill, and children must be taught how to "read" each of these formats. Informational books or content area text require a different kind of reading than a story or novel (fiction). They require students to slow down their reading rate, and to pay attention to more than just the words if they expect to gain information from the selection. The following is an example of shared reading using a big book to teach these skills. The book we have chosen is from the Science Alive series entitled, *The Wonderful World of Plants* by Judith Hodge and Mary Atkinson. This book has a lot of information and will be read in a shared reading format over three days. In addition to learning more about plants, children will learn the various skills needed to successfully read informational text.

On the first day, the teacher gathers the students in an area of the classroom where they can see the big book. (When using a big book at any grade level, students need to be close enough to the book so that when the teacher points to the words, they can follow along and read the "quicktext" and the print on the pages, as well as some charts, graphs, and maps that are not large enough to be seen across the room.) The teacher begins the lesson by having the students preview the text using the What's For Reading? format. She tells the students that she is going to page through the text quickly, giving them just a peek at all the pages. Then, they are to think about two questions:

Is what we will read today probably a story or probably information?

What is it going to be mostly about?

She reminds the students that no one talks during the preview. Instead, they will use their eyes and brains to figure out the answers to the two questions. She then turns the pages of the book *The Wonderful World of Plants,* pausing for about 5–10 seconds on each page. As she gets to the last page, all the students' hands are up. The children agree it is not a story, but has lots of information about different kinds of plants. "How do you know?" the teacher asks. The students explain that they saw lots of pictures of plants, as well as diagrams of seeds and plant parts, and that everything looked real.

Next, the teacher reminds them that informational text often has special features you don't usually find in story text. She then pages through the book again asking, "What's this, and what does it tell us?" as she points to different items. The teacher identifies the table of contents and index, and explains how you use them to "find things." The teacher and children check out a few entries, and see that these two features are indeed ways of finding things. "Sometimes you don't want to read the whole book," the teacher explains, "and you can use the table of contents or the index to find quickly the pages that have the information you need. The glossary is identified, and the teacher leads the students to read a few of the definitions and explains how the glossary helps. "If you come to a big word you don't know, you can look and see if it is in the glossary and read the definition to figure out the word," one student explains. The children also notice many pictures and diagrams, and the "quicktext" labels that go with them. "How do they help?" asks the teacher. The children explain that you can learn a lot from studying the pictures and diagrams, and that the quicktext is easier to read because "it's not so long."

Having finished the What's For Reading? preview, the teacher and class begin a KWL chart. On a large piece of chart paper, the teacher writes all the responses to what children know about plants in the K column:

> They grow.
>
> Some have seeds
>
> Some have leaves.
>
> Some have flowers.
>
> They need sunshine, soil, and water.

The teacher then asks the students, "What do you want to learn?" and records some of their questions in the W column:

> Do plants grow everywhere?
>
> Why do leaves fall off the trees?
>
> How do seeds travel?
>
> How do plants reproduce?

Their questions are quite specific, and show that the preview has them thinking about what they would like to learn.

Next, the teacher turns to the table of contents on the first page of the book. She reads the different topics and the pages on which they are found. She asks the class a few questions:

> "Where will we find out about leaves?"
>
> "What pages would we go to if we were interested in health and plants?"

The children tell her the pages on which to look and she quickly turns to those pages to show the children that they are correct. She turns to pages 2 and 3 of the book, and they begin the shared reading of the text. On every page, they first talk about all the visuals and read the quicktext that accompanies them. On these pages, there are five different pictures, labeled "Desert Plants," "Alpine Plants," "Forest Plants," "Grassland Plants" and "Saltwater Plants." In bigger letters, there is another label called "Plant Habitats." The teacher leads the students to talk about the five pictures and the plants they recognize in each, and then asks them what the label "Plant Habitats" means. The children realize that the five pictures show five different kinds of habitats. Finally, the teacher and the students read the text. They talk about what they learned from the text that they hadn't learned from the pictures and quicktext, and decide that some of the information is the same but there is some additional information, too. One student explained that, "You have to read both, but it is easier to read the long text if you have learned some things from the pictures and quicktext first."

On the next pages (4 and 5) of the book, the teacher and class first read the title, "What is a Seed?" They look at the pictures of seeds and read the accompanying quicktext together, discussing what they know and what is new. Next, the teacher shows the students how to read the diagram "Parts of a Seed." They locate the part of the cut-in-half seed being pointed to by the arrows, and then read the quicktext underneath which describes the seed coat and embryo plant. Finally, they read the "long text" and again decide that some of the information from the pictures, diagrams, and quicktext is repeated, but there is also new information.

When they turn to pages 6 and 7 of the book, the teacher asks, "What should we read first?" The students are unanimous in their belief that they should start with the pictures and quicktext, and then read the long text to see what else it tells them.

They end the lesson by closing the book and writing down several new things they have learned about plants under the L (Learned) column on the KWL chart. They also decide that they have an answer to one of the questions in the W column: "How do seeds travel?"

The lessons on the next two days follow the same format. They begin the lesson by reviewing what they have on the KWL Chart, then follow the procedure of reading all visuals and accompanying quicktext on the pages of the book first, and then reading the other text. When they get to the "Parts of a Flower" diagram, the students notice that it works like the "Parts of a Seed" diagram. After looking back to make sure, they again identify the parts being pointed to by the arrows and then read the descriptions of the anther, filament, stamen, stigma, ovary, style, petal, and pollen.

They read the glossary definitions for some of the big words—horticulturist, photosynthesis, and respiration. Then, they use the index to find the pages where those words are mentioned, and they read those parts again.

At the end of each day's reading, they return to the KWL chart, adding new things to the L column and seeing if they have answers to any of their questions. When they finish, they have a very long list of things learned and are quite impressed by the length of the KWL chart. The teacher asks them if they also learned anything about reading information. They respond with a long list which she records and posts so that they can refer to it and add to it the next time they are preparing to read informational text.

Tips for Reading Information

1. **Preview the text first to see what it is all about and what special features it has.**
2. **If you are looking for something specific, use the table of contents and index.**
3. **See if the text has a glossary with meanings for the important big words.**
4. **Make a KWL chart in your brain or on paper, and think about what you already know and what you want to learn.**
5. **When you are reading informational pages, read the title first to see what the page is all about.**
6. **Next, read the pictures and all the quicktext.**
7. **Study the charts and diagrams, and figure out what they tell you.**
8. **Read the other text and see what it tells you that you didn't learn from the visuals.**
9. **Stop and add things you are learning to the KWL chart in your brain or on paper.**

Shared Reading with a Book That Has a Story and Information

Many stories contain true information. When children read *Wagon Wheels* by Barbara Brenner, a story of a family's trip across the country in a covered wagon, there is information to be learned about life 100 years ago. When children read a story about a boy and his horse, there is true information about horses. They are stories, however, and we read them as stories, paying attention to the characters, settings, problems, events, and solutions. After reading such a story, we might discuss the true things we learned, but the children understand that we have read a story.

Sometimes you come across a book that is primarily information, but is written in story form. A popular example of this is the *Magic School Bus* series by Joanna Cole. There are a number of books in this series, and each one contains lots of science information along with a story. Eight- and nine-year olds delight in the fantasy of going to the waterworks, a solar system, or inside the human body on an imaginary field trip. It can be very hard to figure out how to read one of these books. What do you read first, and how do you keep up with the story and learn new information simultaneously? Big books are made-to-order to help children learn how to read any kind of "different" text. This example of a shared reading is based on the big book version of *The Magic School Bus: Lost in the Solar System* by Joanna Cole.

The shared reading of this book begins with a What's For Reading? preview similar to the one done for the informational book on plants. Students are asked to decide whether the text they will be reading is a story or information, and what it is about. The teacher turns the pages of the book, pausing briefly on each two-page spread. The children use their brains and their eyes—not their mouths—to figure out the two questions. When they have looked at all the pages, the teacher asks the children again whether they think it is a story or information.

"It's a story," many respond.

"How do you know?" the teacher asks.

The children tell her it has characters (Ms. Frizzle and all the kids in the class), things happen, and it has a beginning, middle, and end.

"But it's all about the solar system, and it teaches us about it by taking us on a trip through it," someone else suggests. "I think it is information."

An argument ensues about what kind of text it is, and the teacher interrupts to suggest that maybe it is both. "Let's look at the special features of this text and see what we can figure out," she suggests.

The teacher then leads the students to look at several pages again, and they conclude that there are pictures, charts, and four different kinds of text on most pages.

"What Ms. Frizzle and the children in this story are saying is in rectangular speech balloons. There are also irregularly-shaped bubbles that show what people are thinking," the teacher explains. "The story is told in the long text on each page. The facts to be learned from each page are on the "notebook paper" on the side of many of the pages."

The teacher reminds the class that they had decided, when reading informational text, that it was best to read all the visuals and quicktext first, and then read the long text. "With a book like this," she says, "we need to decide which things on each page to read first, next, and last." The teacher then turns back to the first page and tells the children that she is going to read everything on the page, working from right to left and top to bottom, and they need to think about the best order in which to read a book like this.

Because it is all the way on the left side of the page, she reads the "notebook paper" text labeled, "What is the solar system?" This explains that the solar system is made up of the Sun, the nine planets, moons, asteroids, and comets. It also explains what asteroids and comets are.

Next, the teacher reads the "regular text" which explains that it is field trip day and Ms. Frizzle's class is preparing to go to the planetarium. She then reads the speech bubble in which Ms. Frizzle explains what an orbit is. The picture shows Ms. Frizzle pointing to a diagram of the solar system. There is also a picture showing a boy holding a ball orbiting a lamp labeled "the Sun."

After reading all the different text, the teacher asks, "What do you think we should read first on this page?" The children decide that it would be best to start by reading the visuals and any quicktext to see what they can learn. Next, they should read the regular text that tells the story. Then, they should read the speech and thinking bubbles. Finally, they will read the "notebook paper" text which gives facts about the solar system.

The teacher leads the students to try that order on two more pages. First, they read and talk about any pictures, diagrams, charts, or other visuals. Then, they read the regular text which tells the story. Next, they read the speech and thinking bubbles, and finally, they read the notes. This system seems to work well, so they return to the first page, and the teacher gives the children reading roles. She has the class count off by 3's, and then tells them that they are going to begin reading the book again. The teacher tells them that, for the first several pages, the 1's will discuss the pictures and read any quicktext, the 2's will read the story text chorally, the 3's will read the speech and thinking bubbles, and she will read the notes. The class reads about a third of the way through the book in this fashion. The teacher signals to the students that their reading time is up for the day. She assures them that they will finish reading the book over the next two days, and that each group will get to read the different texts.

As an after-reading activity, the teacher asks the students to get out their response logs and write two things they learned about the solar system. In addition, she asks them whether or not they liked this complicated book and why or why not. She puts on some "thinking music" and gives them five minutes to write. The children know that talking and moving around are not allowed when the thinking music is playing, so everyone sits quietly, thinks, and then writes something. She lets a few of the children tell something they learned and express their opinion about the book.

The reading on the next two days follows the same format, with the different groups of children getting to read the three kinds of text as the teacher reads the notes. Each day, they have five musical minutes to write in their response logs, and a few minutes to share what they learned and what they liked or disliked about the book. The children are almost unanimous in their enthusiasm about the book and the teacher promises to try to come up with some multiple copies of four more *Magic School Bus* books so that they can do book club groups with the books later in the year.

Science Link

Remember that one of the goals of Guided Reading is to build knowledge, meaning vocabulary, and oral language, and that linking what we read in Guided Reading to our science and social studies topics helps us meet this knowledge building goal. Both *The Wonderful World of Plants* and *The Magic School Bus: Lost in the Solar System* link to the science curriculum. There are other wonderful science big books in the Science Alive series, including *Nature's Shapes and Patterns*, *Work and Machines*, *All About Forces*, and *Adapt or Die*. There are also many other books in the *Magic School Bus* series (although not all come in big books). These include *The Magic School Bus at the Water Works*, *The Magic School Bus on the Ocean Floor*, *The Magic School Bus Inside the Earth*, *The Magic School Bus in the Time of the Dinosaurs*, *The Magic School Bus Inside the Human Body*, *The Magic School Bus in a Hurricane*, and *The Magic School Bus and the Electric Field Trip*.

Link to Writing

If you feel creative, make an imaginary trip the topic of your writing mini lesson over several days. The teacher is not Ms. Frizzle, but you, and the class and characters in this story would be the children in your class. You probably can't write like Joanna Cole, but the class will enjoy imagining with you as you take a fantasy trip together. Have fun!

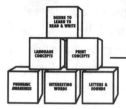

Building Blocks Variations

Shared reading is the format we use most for Guided Reading in our kindergarten classrooms.

Big Blocks Variations

Shared reading of big books can play an important role in teaching students how to read text—particularly informational text. Working with a big book, you can use a pointer to focus their attention on charts, maps, graphs and other visuals along with the accompanying quicktext. Many older children approach their science and social studies text the way they approach stories. Shared reading is the most efficient way to teach them strategies more appropriate for information.

Shared Reading

You can do any of the comprehension lessons described in Part 2 in a shared reading format. Shared reading is the most appropriate format when young children are just learning to track print and other print conventions. It is also the most efficient format for teaching any new strategy.

1. Be on the lookout for and select big books which help you teach the comprehension strategies you need to work on.

2. Decide how many days you will spend with the book and what you will do with children before and after reading.

3. Plan some rereadings of the book to help children develop fluency.

CHAPTER 17

CHORAL AND ECHO READING

Fluency is one of the strategies you work on during Guided Reading. Fluency is the ability to read at a good rate with appropriate phrasing and expression. You are working on fluency when you have children reread something two or three times for different purposes. Fluency is one of the major reasons to make sure that some of the reading we do each week is at the instructional level of our struggling readers. Children who read slowly, but with 95% word identification on the first reading of a piece, are usually able to read it almost perfectly, with more speed and expression, by the third reading.

Fluency Links to the Other Three Blocks

In Four-Blocks classrooms, fluency is being developed in all four blocks. In the Working With Words block, you have daily practice with your Word Wall words. These Word Wall words are primarily the high-frequency words that account for 50% of the words everyone reads and writes. We have a very ambitious goal for these high-frequency words. We expect every child to learn to recognize them immediately, without hesitating, when they are reading. We also expect every child to spell them correctly and automatically when writing. Being fast and automatic with every other word they read and write goes a long way toward helping children achieve fluent reading and writing. As children write daily during the Writing Block, they are developing fluency with these high-frequency words. Self-Selected Reading also helps build fluency. We conference with children each week and help them choose books on their level—or easier. Daily reading in easy materials builds fluency.

In addition to rereading and choosing appropriate materials, echo and choral reading help children develop fluency. In echo reading, the teacher reads first and the children become the echo, reading it back to her. As children echo read, they try to match the teacher's expression and phrasing. Choral reading is reading together "in chorus." Children are often assigned parts and practice their parts several times. Teachers often combine echo reading and choral reading. They do an echo reading of a selection the first time, and then assign parts for choral reading. In the remainder of this chapter, we will give you separate examples for echo and choral reading, but in the real world of classrooms they are often used together—especially if fluency is a major concern.

Echo Reading

A teacher had been doing echo reading for months in her classroom when a child suddenly asked, "What's an echo?" The teacher tried to explain it, and discovered that many children in her class had never heard an echo. After some "field research," the teacher located a spot

---

in the auditorium where sound would echo, and the class all got to hear their voices echoing back to them. Echo reading made a lot more sense to them after that, and they tried to "be the echo." It is sometimes easy to forget that your children don't know everything you know. If your children haven't heard an echo, you might try to find a place to take them where they can have firsthand experience with echoes.

Science Link

Do you study sound in science? Echoes are made as sound waves hit a large object and bounce back. The large object has to be at least 30 feet away. Sound travels about one mile in five seconds. So, if you shouted from one end of a canyon to the other and the echo came back ten seconds later, the canyon would be a mile wide - five seconds out and five seconds back!

Echo reading is usually done one sentence at a time. We often do echo reading with short easy text that has only one sentence on a page. Echo reading is fun to do when the text has different voices. *Brown Bear, Brown Bear, What Do You See?* by Bill Martin, Jr., *I Went Walking* by Sue Williams, and *Hattie and the Fox* by Mem Fox are favorites for echo reading. Echo reading also works well for stories such as *There's An Alligator Under My Bed* by Mercer Mayer, in which one boy is telling the story. These stories told in the first person format are called "I" stories. When we echo read "I" stories, we try to sound the way the character's voice would sound. When we read,

When it was time to go to sleep, I had to be very careful, because I knew he was there.

we read it in a careful, frightened way. When we read,

So, I'd call Mom and Dad.

we shout it! When we read,

I followed him down the stairs.

we whisper it.

Children love to use different voices and reading "I" stories aloud using an echo reading format is one of their favorite ways to read. You will be amazed how many "I" stories there are when you start looking for them. Some favorites are *One of Three* by Angela Johnson, *Enzo the Wonderfish* by Cathy Wilcox, and *My Friend* by Taro Gomi.

Echo reading is also appropriate for reading plays. We read the whole play in an echo reading format first, using different voices for the different characters. As we read, we ask the children to think about each character and which character they would like to be when we read the play again. We usually move from an echo reading format into a playschool group format, in which the children read their parts in small groups. Children love plays, and teachers tell us they would use more plays if they had multiple copies of easy plays. This is one of the few good uses of copying machines. You can easily take your students' favorite story and turn it into a play script. All of the fairy tales make good and easy plays. Children love reading and playing *The Little Red Hen*, *The Gingerbread Man*, *The Three Pigs*, and *The Three Billy Goats Gruff*. The nice thing about writing out and copying simple scripts for these classic stories is that you can let the children take them home. For their homework assignment, have them gather as many actors as they can and read the play at home. Parents love helping with this kind of homework, and often say they wish they'd had homework like that when they were in school.

Choral Reading

Choral reading works best for poetry, refrains, and books with lots of conversation. The whole class can read, or you can assign groups and parts. Teachers use old favorites for choral reading, such as *Itsy Bitsy Spider*, *Five Little Pumpkins*, *Rudolph the Red-Nosed Reindeer*, *Peter Cottontail*, and other nursery rhymes and finger plays. Choral reading is a wonderful way to reread materials such as *The Lion and the Mouse* and *Brown Bear, Brown Bear, What Do You See?* by Bill Martin, Jr., in which characters talk to each other. Choral reading should be used throughout the grades because rereading provides children with the practice needed to build fluency and self-confidence.

We are going to illustrate a variety of choral reading activities with nursery rhymes and traditional poems, chants, and songs. These are all in the public domain—which means that the author is unknown or that they are no longer copyrighted—and thus can be reproduced in this book. You could also use lots of contemporary poetry which can be found in poetry collections, reading texts, children's magazines, and at various Web sites. Most of these are copyrighted materials which could not be reproduced in this book. Take these ideas and apply them to the wealth of materials you have available to you.

Nursery and Other Rhymes

Begin by reading the rhyme to the children. You may want to echo read it with them once or twice. If you have the rhyme in a big book, use that. If not, reproduce the rhyme on a chart. After reading the rhymes together, children enjoy pantomiming them while other children read them aloud.

Humpty Dumpty

Humpty Dumpty sat on a wall.
Humpty Dumpty had a great fall.
All the king's horses, and all the king's men
Couldn't put Humpty together again!

For *Humpty Dumpty*, you might have your children simply count off—1-2-3-4-5—and then get together by numbers. Read the rhyme five times; each time, members from a different numbered group read a line or are the actors. Attach sticky notes to the lines and change the number each time. The first time, put the sticky notes in sequential order. Everyone reads the title. Then, the children in the "1" group read the first line, those in the "2" group read the second line, those in the "3" group read the third line, those in the "4" group read the fourth line, and students in the "5" group act out the rhyme. Move the sticky notes five times and everyone will get to read each line and act it out. This activity is quick, easy, fun, and fair! The same count-off procedure (with one group for each line plus the actors) will work nicely for *Jack and Jill*; *Hickory Dickory Doc; Little Jack Horner*; *Hey Diddle Diddle*; *Hop, Hop, Hop;* and many other short rhymes. The children build fluency as they read the lines of the poems several times. In addition, you can work with the students' sequencing skills and talk about what happened at the beginning, middle and end of each rhyme.

Jack and Jill

Jack and Jill went up the hill,

To fetch a pail of water.

Jack fell down and broke his crown,

And Jill came tumbling after.

Little Jack Horner

Little Jack Horner sat in a corner,

Eating his Christmas pie.

He put in a thumb, and pulled out a plum,

And said, "What a good boy am I."

Hickory Dickory Dock

Hickory, dickory, dock,

The mouse ran up the clock.

The clock struck one, and down he did run.

Hickory, dickory, dock.

Hey Diddle Diddle

Hey diddle diddle,

The cat and the fiddle,

The cow jumped over the moon.

The little dog laughed,

To see such sport,

And the dish ran away with the spoon.

Hop, Hop, Hop

Once I saw a little bird

Go hop, hop, hop.

And I cried, "Little bird,

Will you stop, stop, stop?"

I was going to the window

To say, "How do you do?"

When he shook his little tail,

And away he flew.

With longer rhymes and poems, you may want to assign children to verses rather than lines. We always begin by reading the poem to the students and then having them read it with us several times. Then, we assign reading parts and a pantomiming group. The process of counting off and letting each numbered group read every verse and be the actors works well with most rhymes that have actions you can pantomime. Count off by 5's to read and pantomime *The Squirrel*.

The Squirrel

Whisky, frisky,
Hippety hop,
Up he goes
To the tree top.

Whirly, twirly,
Round and round,
Down he scampers
To the ground.

Furly, curly
What a tail!
Tall as a feather
Broad as a sail!

Where's his supper?
In the shell,
Snappity, crackity,
Out it fell.

Once you get into "choreographing" your choral readings, you will find it easy to assign parts. To do the *Three Little Kittens*, have your children count off 1-2-3. For the first choral reading, let the 1's be narrators, the 2's be the kittens, and the 3's be the kittens' mother. Do the reading three times, giving everyone a chance to read all three parts.

Three Little Kittens

Three little kittens,
Lost their mittens,
And they began to cry,
"Oh, mother, dear,
We sadly fear,
Our mittens we have lost."

"What! Lost your mittens?
You naughty kittens!
Then you shall have no pie."

Three little kittens,
Found their mittens,
And they began to cry,
"Oh, mother, dear,
See here, see here,
Our mittens we have found."

"What, found your mittens?
You good little kittens,
Then you shall have some pie."

Three little kittens,
Put on their mittens,
And soon ate up the pie.

"Oh, mother, dear,
We sadly fear,
Our mittens we have soiled."

"What! Soiled your mittens?
You naughty kittens,"
And they began to sigh.

Three little kittens,
Washed their mittens,
And hung them out to dry.

"Oh, mother, dear,
Do you not hear?
Our mittens we have washed."

"What! Washed your mittens?
You good little kittens!
But I smell a rat close by."

"Meow, meow.
We smell a rat close by."

For *Five Little Monkeys*, put the children in groups of five. The first time you do the rhyme, call on one group of five to be the monkeys, assign another group to say the doctor's lines, and have the rest of the children read all the other lines. Continue until all the groups have gotten to be monkeys and doctors. You may need some "monkeys" from previous readings to be monkeys a second time to fill out your last group. You probably have lots of likely candidates!

Five Little Monkeys

Five little monkeys jumping on the bed.
One fell off and bumped his head.
Momma called the doctor and the doctor said,
"No more monkeys jumping on the bed!"

Four little monkeys jumping on the bed.
One fell off and bumped his head.
Momma called the doctor and the doctor said,
"No more monkeys jumping on the bed!"

Three little monkeys jumping on the bed.
One fell off and bumped his head.
Momma called the doctor and the doctor said,
"No more monkeys jumping on the bed!"

Two little monkeys jumping on the bed.
One fell off and bumped his head.
Momma called the doctor and the doctor said,
"No more monkeys jumping on the bed!"

One little monkey jumping on the bed.
He fell off and bumped his head.
Momma called the doctor and the doctor said,
"No more monkeys jumping on the bed!"

No little monkeys jumping on the bed.
None fell off and bumped his head.
Momma called the doctor and the doctor said,
"Put those monkeys back in bed!"

For *The Ants Go Marching*, you will need two sets of index cards numbered 1-10, with one set of numbers written very small and one set written normal size. The children with the small numbers will be the ones who do the action. So, the child with the small "1" will jump and run, the child with the small "2" will tie his shoe, and so on, and the child with the small "10" will shout "The End!" Everyone reads until it is their turn to join the march. As everyone reads, the two "ants" designated number one march in and the child with the small number does the appropriate action. Then, the two children designated by number two cards join them as everyone else reads. Then, the two "threes" join the others, and so on, until you have 20 marching ants. By now, you won't have very many readers! Have the children switch cards so that the other marching partner is now the one with the small number and do it again. If you are fortunate enough to have less than 20 children, designate a stuffed animal to be one of the numbers that does not have an action, and let the partner number march it in. If you have more than 20, do the whole thing again, letting those who didn't get numbers the first time pick their numbers and letting some children have parts again.

To save space and time in writing this, write the first verse on a chart and then write the parts that change—two by two, three by three, to jump and run, to tie his shoe, etc.—on sentence strips and cut them to fit on the chart. Have the readers stop after each verse and wait for you to insert the appropriate words.

The Ants Go Marching

The ants go marching one by one.
   Hurrah! Hurrah!
The ants go marching one by one.
   Hurrah! Hurrah!
The ants go marching one by one;
 The little one stops to jump and run,
And they all march down into the ground.
   Boom, boom, boom!

The ants go marching two by two.
   Hurrah! Hurrah!
The ants go marching two by two.
   Hurrah! Hurrah!
The ants go marching two by two;
 The little one stops to tie his shoe,
And they all march down into the ground.
   Boom, boom, boom!

The ants go marching three by three.
   Hurrah! Hurrah!
The ants go marching three by three.
   Hurrah! Hurrah!
The ants go marching three by three;
 The little one stops to catch a bee,
And they all march down into the ground.
   Boom, boom, boom!

The ants go marching four by four.
   Hurrah! Hurrah!
The ants go marching four by four.
   Hurrah! Hurrah!
The ants go marching four by four;
 The little one stops to jump and roar,
And they all march down into the ground.
   Boom, boom, boom!

The ants go marching five by five.
    Hurrah! Hurrah!
The ants go marching five by five.
    Hurrah! Hurrah!
The ants go marching five by five;
 The little one stops to jump and dive,
And they all march down into the ground.
    Boom, boom, boom!

The ants go marching six by six.
    Hurrah! Hurrah!
The ants go marching six by six.
    Hurrah! Hurrah!
The ants go marching six by six;
 The little one stops to pick up sticks,
And they all march down into the ground.
    Boom, boom, boom!

The ants go marching seven by seven.
    Hurrah! Hurrah!
The ants go marching seven by seven.
    Hurrah! Hurrah!
The ants go marching seven by seven;
 The little one stops to chase a hen,
And they all march down into the ground.
    Boom, boom, boom!

The ants go marching eight by eight.
    Hurrah! Hurrah!
The ants go marching eight by eight.
    Hurrah! Hurrah!
The ants go marching eight by eight;
 The little one stops to rollerskate,
And they all march down into the ground.
    Boom, boom, boom!

The ants go marching nine by nine.
    Hurrah! Hurrah!
The ants go marching nine by nine.
    Hurrah! Hurrah!
The ants go marching nine by nine;
 The little one stops to read a sign,
And they all march down into the ground.
    Boom, boom, boom!

The ants go marching ten by ten.
 Hurrah! Hurrah!
The ants go marching ten by ten.
    Hurrah! Hurrah!
The ants go marching ten by ten;
 The little one stops to shout
 "THE END!!"

Over in the Meadow can be choreographed in a similar way. Give children cards numbered 1-10 and a card that says, "Mother." The child with the "1" will be the turtle. The first verse has "Mother" and "1", who does the action. For the second verse, the child with "2" joins in, the "1" child is transformed from a turtle to a fish, and they both do the action. The "Mother" stays the whole time, but gets transformed into all the different mothers. When you get to the last verse, you will have all the children with numbers "1" to "10" and the "Mother." Unless you have 55 children in your class (Yegads!), transforming the animals is the only way to act this out and to have the right number of animals each time. You will need to do this a few times, letting the children with high numbers take the low numbers so that they can also be transformed and do all the actions!

Over in the Meadow

(A traditional counting rhyme adapted by Pat Cunningham and Dottie Hall)

Over in the meadow in the sand in the sun,
Lived an old mother turtle and her little turtle one.
"Dig," said the mother. "I dig," said the one.
So he dug all day in the sand in the sun.

Over in the meadow where the stream runs blue,
Lived an old mother fish and her little fish two.
"Swim," said the mother. "We swim," said the two.
So they swam all day where the stream runs blue.

Over in the meadow in a hole in a tree,
Lived an old mother squirrel and her little squirrels three.
"Jump," said the mother. "We jump," said the three.
So they jumped all day in a hole in a tree.

Over in the meadow by the big barn door,
Lived an old mother mouse and her little mice four.
"Squeak," said the mother. "We squeak," said the four.
So they squeaked all day by the big barn door.

Over in the meadow in a big beehive,
Lived an old mother bee and her little bees five.
"Buzz," said the mother. "We buzz," said the five.
So they buzzed all day in a big beehive.

Over in the meadow in a nest built of sticks,
Lived an old mother bird and her little birds six.
"Sing," said the mother. "We sing," said the six.
So they sang all day in a nest built of sticks.

Over in the meadow in the house built by Kevin,
Lived an old mother cat and her little kittens seven.
"Meow," said the mother. "We meow," said the seven.
So they meowed all day in the house built by Kevin.

Over in the meadow by an old wooden gate,
Lived an old mother rabbit and her little bunnies eight.
"Hop," said the mother. "We hop," said the eight.
So they hopped all day by an old wooden gate.

Over in the meadow by a tall green pine,
Lived an old mother pig and her little pigs nine.
"Oink," said the mother. "We oink," said the nine.
So they oinked all day by a tall green pine.

Over in the meadow in a cozy little den,
Lived an old mother fox and her little foxes ten.
"Play," said the mother. "We play," said the ten.
So they played all day in a cozy little den.

Math Link

We are sure you will think of it, but just in case, *Five Little Monkeys*, *The Ants Go Marching,* and *Over in the Meadow* make wonderful math links. You can subtract, add, skip count by twos, and demonstrate even and odd numbers. You may want to give students some concrete objects during math, and have them read the rhymes again as they act out the rhymes with their objects. Children also like doing these rhymes in centers.

Finally, we suggest you perk up your Guided Reading Block one day with *Little Bunny Foo Foo*. Divide your class into three groups—Bunny Foo Foos, Good Fairies, and Narrators. (It is prudent to let the field mice be imaginary rather than risk the heads of any of your precious children!) You may or may not want to include the "moral of the story" at the end, depending on whether you think your children will "get it," but we included it for your entertainment!

Little Bunny Foo Foo

Little Bunny Foo Foo, hopping through the forest,
Scooping up the field mice and bopping them on the head.

Down came the good fairy and she said:
"Little Bunny Foo Foo, I don't want to see you
Scooping up the field mice and bopping them on the head.
Now I'll give you three chances and if you keep it up, I'll turn you into a goon!"

Little Bunny Foo Foo hopping through the forest,
Scooping up the field mice and bopping them on the head.

Down came the good fairy and she said:
"Little Bunny Foo Foo, I don't want to see you
Scooping up the field mice and bopping them on the head.
I'll give you two more chances and if you keep it up, I'll turn you into a goon!"

Little Bunny Foo Foo hopping through the forest,
Scooping up the field mice and bopping them on the head.

Down came the good fairy and she said:
"Little Bunny Foo Foo, I don't want to see you
scooping up the field mice and bopping them on the head.
I'll give you one more chance and if you keep it up, I'll turn you into a goon!"

Little Bunny Foo Foo hopping through the forest,

Scooping up the field mice and bopping them on the head.

Down came the good fairy and she said:

"Little Bunny Foo Foo, I don't want to see you

Scooping up the field mice and bopping them on the head

You disobeyed me three times, so now I'm turning you into a GOON!"

And the moral of this story is: Always remember, "Hare today, Goon tomorrow!"

Link to Working With Words: Making Words

Here are some Making Words lessons linked to the rhymes:

Make: it, sit, set, met, men, ten, tent, sent, nest, test, stem, time, item, mints, mittens

Sort: rhyming words

Transfer: chest, then, pet, grit

Make: my, sky, yes, yen, Ken, key, keys, some, nose, nosey, money, smoke, smoky, monkeys

Sort: nose, nosey; smoke, smoky; rhyming words

Transfer: try, when, men, shy

Make: me, we, am, ad, Ed, mad, mow, meow, made, wade, mowed, meadow

Sort: rhyming words

Transfer: spade, glad, she, shade

Make: in, pin, nip, snip, spin, sing, sign, soon, goon, coop, scoop, snoop, spoon, poison, scooping

Sort: rhyming words

Transfer: troop, moon, chin, ship

Make: in, an, ran, man, main, rain, gain, grin, rich, hair, chair, march, charm, charming, marching

Sort: charm, charming; march, marching; rhyming words

Transfer: spin, Spain, pair, plan

Books with refrains make wonderful choral readings. Our favorite is *My Little Sister Ate One Hare* by Bill Grossman. Have your children count off 1-10. Have the 1's read the "one" part every time it repeats, the 2's read the "two" part, etc., and have everyone read the refrain, "*We thought she'd throw up then and there. But she didn't.*" Read the book several times and switch the numbers the children have, so that they read a different part. (By the way, we think the author of this book is aptly named!)

Math Link

Have the children add the total number of things she ate before the peas made her throw up!

1 hare; 2 snakes; 3 ants; 4 shrews; 5 bats;

6 mice; 7 polliwogs; 8 worms; 9 lizards; 10 peas

There is a very high correlation between the number of words children read and how well they read. More words = better readers! We need to maximize the amount of reading children do while they are with us and at home. One of the many reasons to avoid round-robin reading during Guided Reading is that children just don't read enough when they take turns! We want everyone reading as much as possible every day during Guided Reading, and we want to send them home with things they can read fluently and are motivated to read. Choral and Echo Reading help to create fluent, eager readers, and so does ERT, which is described in the next chapter.

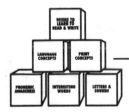

Building Blocks Variations

Choral and echo reading are wonderful Guided Reading formats for kindergartners. Many kindergarten teachers teach their children the traditional kindergarten songs, chants, and poems, and then write them in large class big books. The children enjoy reading these together during Guided Reading time, and by themselves during Self-Selected Reading.

Guided Reading The Four-Blocks™ Way

Big Blocks Variations

Including some choral and echo reading during guided reading is a nice change of pace for older students. They particularly like reading different parts and getting into the rhythm of reading which promotes reading fluency. If many of your students read well below grade-level, poems about animals, sports, scary things and other appealing topics are a readily available source of appropriate and "not babyish" material.

Choral and Echo Reading

Choral and echo reading are most appropriate for plays, predictable text, text with refrains, and texts with lots of dialogue. Children enjoy reading this way, and it helps build the confidence of struggling readers.

1. **Choose poems, plays, songs, predictable books, and other text your children will enjoy.**

2. **Choreograph the reading in some simple way so that children are reading different parts.**

3. **Reread the selection several times, letting different groups read different parts.**

4. **If possible, provide copies for children to take home or to store in their personal reading binder.**

CHAPTER 18

EVERYONE READ TO... (ERT)

Everyone Read To...(ERT) is a way of guiding the whole class (or a small group) through the reading of a selection. Use ERT when you want the students to do the initial reading on their own, but you want to keep them together to provide a lot of guidance and support for that initial reading. With ERT, you tell students how much to read. They read that segment, and then you follow up on whatever purpose was set by asking questions like:

"What is the author telling us?"

"What new things did you learn?"

"What seems to be the problem in this story?"

"What did you find out was making the sky so dark?"

When the information the children are reading for is stated directly on the page, we ask them to read to find out. When they have to make inferences, we ask the children to read to figure out.

Children tell in their own words what they read, and then everyone goes on to the next segment. For older children, Everyone Read To... is usually silent reading. Because children must develop some reading fluency before they can "read it in their minds," this ERT time with young children is often not silent, but is called "whisper" reading. In ERT, everyone is reading the text for themselves in whatever way is appropriate to find out specific things they will then share with the class. Here is an ERT example for the book, *Arthur's Pet Business* by Marc Brown.

The teacher and children have already read the title, author, and illustrator and have taken a picture walk through the book. They are now going to do the first reading of the book, and the teacher is going to guide them through each two-page spread using ERT to help the students set purposes.

For the first page, the teacher reminds the students that during their picture walk, they decided that pets were a big part of the story and that Arthur eventually had lots of pets.

"Everybody read this page to figure out what Arthur is going to ask his mom and dad."

The children read the page to themselves, some silently and others whisper-reading it. As they figure out the answer to the question, they raise their hands, and the teacher calls on students to tell what Arthur was going to ask.

The children explain that even though it doesn't "exactly say it," they have figured out that Arthur wants a puppy and is waiting for just the right moment to ask.

The teacher turns the page and reminds students that during their picture walk, they decided that Arthur and his family are having dinner.

"Everybody read to find out what Arthur's father and mother say about Arthur getting a puppy."

The teacher reminds them that this is a "two-hander." They are reading to find two things, and they should raise one hand as soon as they find each thing. Again, the children read silently or quietly, and quickly raise both hands. It is clear that they enjoy "two-handers."

The teacher turns the page again and reminds the children that Arthur and his sister are listening at the door, and that the expressions on their faces must mean the news is good. The children read to find out what Arthur has to do before he can have the puppy. The teacher leads the class through each two-page spread. For each spread, she reminds students what they learned from the pictures, and then sets a purpose for that page that seems to be "the natural thing" you would want to read to find out after having pondered the pictures.

"Everybody read to find out what Arthur's friends suggested he could do to earn the puppy."

"Everybody read to figure out what the phone call is about."

"Everybody read to figure out who the first customer was and what Arthur's family thought about this pet."

"Everybody read to find out what is written on the long list that Perky's owner brings."

"Everybody read to figure out what Arthur did to take care of Perky, and how he felt."

This takes the class almost to the halfway point and is a good stopping point for the first day. For their after-reading activity, the children work on summarizing/concluding. The teacher has them talk to a partner sitting next to them, and try to retell the important events that have happened so far in the story. She encourages them to use the pictures as reminders and not to read this time, but to tell what they learned on each page. The teacher listens in on their retellings, and then leads the whole group in a quick retelling, using the pictures as prompts.

The next day, the teacher continues the ERT, leading the class through each two-page spread and having them read to find out, or figure out, the important events. Children raise their hands as soon as they figure out the answer—two hands for questions with two parts—and then finish reading the pages. As each question is answered, the teacher calls on someone to read aloud the sentences with the important information. Unless the answer is obviously stated, the teacher leads the students to explain how they figured it out.

The children explain that it doesn't say why Arthur is under the table, but it does say that Perky is lost. Since Arthur is looking for her, he must be under the table looking for Perky. Children read to find out if Arthur found Perky. They say that he did, and then someone reads the sentences that say,

Suddenly they heard a bark. "Everybody come quick," called Arthur.

The children explain that the bark and Arthur's calling must mean he found Perky.

When the story is finished the second day, the teacher again asks the students to partner up and, using the pictures in the book, retell the second part of the story.

This ends the ERT two-day lesson, but rereading is important for fluency. So, on the following day, the teacher forms playschool groups of five or six students. She gives each group a set of index cards with the names of the characters written on them—main characters on white cards,

Arthur   D. W.   Mother   Father

minor characters on another color,

Mrs. Wood   Muffy   Binky Barnes   Francine B.

and a Narrator on a third color.

She gives the Narrator and Arthur cards to the two best readers in each group. She gives the main character cards to the others in the group and also gives them one of the minor characters. The children read the story together, with the narrator reading everything except the things in quotes which the characters read. She asks the children to find their favorite quotation from any character and be ready to read this quotation to the whole group. If the group finishes reading before the time is up, they should practice reading the favorite lines of everyone in the group. Here are some of their favorites:

"Isn't that the dog the mailman calls 'JAWS'?"
"Any dog I get will be easier than Perky!"
"Wow! Ten dollars and my very own puppy! I can't believe it!"

The teacher then gives each student a pair of pipe cleaner Arthur glasses as a souvenir. (See page 139 for directions.) Their homework assignment is to retell the story of *Arthur's Pet Business* to someone at home and have the person to whom they retell the story write a note to the class telling what their favorite part was.

Link to Self-Selected Reading

Read aloud another *Arthur* book and then make lots of *Arthur* books available for Self-Selected Reading, if students would like to read them (and many will!) .

ERT can also be done with informational and content area books. The procedure is the same. Children are asked to preview and predict before they read. During reading, the children can be asked to read each page to find the answer to a question (raise one hand) or two (raise two hands). As you ask the students to read, use the phrase, "Everyone read to...." Here is an example based on a short section on communities in a social studies textbook.

Page 275 "Everyone read to find out what goods and services are."
(two-hand answer)

Page 276 "Everyone read to find out why people work." (one-hand answer)

Page 277 "Everyone read to find out what a consumer is."

Page 278 "Everyone read to find out what we mean by 'our economy.'"

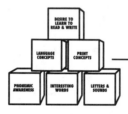

Building Blocks Variations

Everyone Read To... is not a strategy we would use with kindergartners.

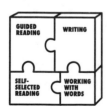

Big Blocks Variations

Everyone Read To... is a wonderful strategy for older children. They love raising their hands as soon as they find the answer, and they like explaining how they figured things out. It engages their attention much better than the more common round-robin reading format. Even children who do not read well can often find answers when they know exactly what they are looking for. Students learn comprehension skills as their classmates "think-aloud" and explain how they figured out ideas the book didn't' exactly tell them.

Everyone Read To... (ERT)

ERT is a format used to guide children through text, a page or two at a time, and to help them understand the important information on each page. This format can be used with a small group or with the whole class. Even children who struggle with reading can often read better if they have something specific for which to read. Their success motivates them to continue to try.

1. Choose text for which you think children need page-by-page guidance.

2. Plan a before-and-after reading activity which will develop comprehension strategies.

3. Lead the children though the text a page or two at a time. Have students read to find or figure out important events or information.

4. Include questions to which the answers are not literally stated, but which can be inferred. For example, you may say, "Read to figure out how Charlie is feeling." The text may say it has been a bad day, and Charlie is stomping down the street. The children have to infer his feeling and explain how they knew. Ask the children to "find out" when the answer is literal and "figure out" when it is inferential.

5. Have children raise their hands when they read the part that helps them to figure out the answer and continue reading. Warn them when you are asking a "two-hander" (which they love!).

6. When most hands are up, ask a volunteer to give you the answer. Ask someone else to read the parts aloud that helped them figure out the answer.

7. When the answers are not literally stated, ask children to explain how they figured it out. You might say, "Yes, he is feeling bad and unhappy. It didn't say that in the text but you figured it out. What did it say that let you figure it out?"

CHAPTER 19

PARTNER READING AND PLAYSCHOOL GROUPS

So far, this book has described three different formats for the during-reading part of the Guided Reading Block. We use shared reading, echo and choral reading, and Everyone Read To… as ways to guide children through text, maximizing the amount of support and the amount of reading for every child. Most of the time, these formats are used with the entire class. Most teachers begin the year with these "everyone-together" formats and use them to teach children how to do picture walks, make predictions, do KWL's, graphic organizers, Beach Balls, and all the other before-and-after reading activities described in Part Two. Then, they teach children how to read in partners and playschool groups. By the time we put them in partners or playschool groups to read and to come up with things to add to a web or prepare to answer the Beach Ball questions, webs and Beach Ball are familiar activities which have been done together many times. Now, the children can focus on a new thing—how to teach and help each other.

Partner reading and playschool groups are wonderful formats when they work correctly, but we have to warn you, that doesn't just happen. In the first section, you will discover some of the "tricks of the trade" and caveats for partner reading. Most of these tricks and caveats also apply to playschool groups, but there are times when playschool groups work better than partner reading and we will describe these in the final section.

Partner Reading

1. Arrange the "marriages" carefully!

Think about who you will partner up with whom—and who you won't! Children whose families have been feuding for generations probably won't make good partners. The best reader in the class is probably not the best partner for the worst reader. If students are at the "can't stand the girls" and "boys are yucky" stage, it is probably best to do same gender partnerships. Think about your struggling readers first and who would be the best partners for them. Ask yourself, "Who will be patient, and not just tell them all the words?" "Who will be insightful and able to coach them and get them to talk about their reading?" In most classrooms, there are a couple of very nurturing children who would love to help some of their struggling classmates. These are the children to try out as partners for your most struggling readers.

2. Think about how often to change partners.

Partner reading seems to work better when the partners can work together long enough to establish a working relationship. There doesn't seem to be any real advantage to assigning new partners every time. You may want to change the reading partners more frequently as you begin partner reading, so that you can find the right matches. Once you have partnerships that work well, it is probably best to leave them together for awhile.

3. Decide where the partners will read.

Some teachers have partners reading at their desks, but unless you have just the right people sitting next to each other, your partnerships may be determined by proximity rather than by your deciding who will work best with whom. Partners seem to work best when they can sit in corners or sprawl out on rugs. They need some space, and they stay focused better if they can't easily hear other pairs of partners reading. Some teachers designate partner reading spaces by a number—10 reading spaces if you have 20 children; 13 reading spaces if you have 26. They label these spots with the number, and then put the initials of the partners who will read in that spot on that day. A laminated poster works well for this display. Some spots are perceived as better than others, so do rotate where the partners will read and try to keep it fair. If you keep your partnerships together, they can simply rotate through the ten spots each day the class partner reads, and will eventually get to read in all 10 spots.

Partner Reading Spots for Today	
Where?	Who?
1. Back corner	HR, JB
2. Reading table	JW, MM
3. By the sink	EH, MW
4. Teacher's desk	AB, CM
5. Beanbag chair	PC, RL
6. On the carpet	LP, PT
7. In the rocking chair	JW, MD
8. By the gerbil cage	WH, TM
9. Near the bookshelf	JR, BNF
10. You choose!	DL, BPF

4. Decide how you will handle absent partners.

This sounds trivial, but a lot of teachers spend a lot of time "negotiating" with kids when a partner is absent. Some teachers have an "absent partners with absent partners" rule. If three partners are absent, you have a trio. Other teachers let children whose partners are absent join any other partnership—forming a trio. Some teachers let partnerless children decide if they want to read by themselves,with another partnerless child, or form a trio. It doesn't really seem to matter as long as there is some clear policy in effect, and time is not wasted "negotiating."

5. Always make sure partners know how they will read the selection.

Depending on the age of the children, we teach them a variety of different partner reading strategies, including:

- **Take Turns** One partner reads the first page, the other partner reads the second page, and so on. This is the most common way of partner reading—but not necessarily the most productive.

- **Read and Point** One partner points to the words on the page while the other partner reads. Then, they switch reader/pointer roles on the next page. This is particularly helpful in the beginning when print tracking is a big issue with some children. You will be surprised at how quickly some of your children pick up print tracking when a nurturing, helpful student is pointing to their words, and then making sure that their partners point to the words correctly when it is their turn. We would not recommend this once children become more fluent, however, because it does slow children down and can take their focus away from the meaning.

- **Ask Questions** Both children read each page—silently if they can, or chorally if they need help. They then ask each other a "good question" about what they have read.

- **Say Something** Say Something is also a good partner working strategy. The simple notion is that after you read a page, you "say something." If you don't have anything to say, you may have been concentrating too much on the words, and not enough on the meaning. You may need to reread the page, thinking about what you might say about it. Some teachers have partners taking turns—one partner reads a page, the other partner says something, and then they reverse roles. On other days, partners can be told to read the page together, or silently, and then each say something.

- **Echo Reading** Once they know how to echo read, they will enjoy echo reading some sections. Give the child who is the echo in each partnership something to designate their status or have them read the selection twice, switching first reading and echo reading roles. For struggling readers, make sure they are the echo on the first reading.

- **Choral Whispering** Choral whispering is a variation of choral reading. Children whisper with their partner. Children use "whisper" voices so that their reading will not distract partners seated nearby.

- **Everyone Read To...** Children love doing ERT with each other. It is particularly effective as a rereading strategy when they know what the selection is about and need a good purpose for rereading. Even children who are not very fluent readers can usually find the answer to a question and pose a good question for their partner when they have already read the selection.

- **You Decide** Once the children have learned the different partner reading formats you want them to use, you may occasionally want to declare a "you decide" day when the partners can decide to read together in any way they wish. Be stingy with your "you decide" days, however, because you may want to decide on the partner reading format according to the type and difficulty of the selection, whether this is the first, second or third time they have read it, and who is making up the partnerships.

6. Always have partners read for a purpose.

The purpose for reading is not the same thing as the format—format is how the partners will read it. Purpose is what they are getting out of the reading, and what they should be ready to contribute to the after-reading activity. If students are going to "do the Beach Ball" after reading, the partners should be reading and talking about their answers to the Beach Ball questions. If students are going to add things to the KWL chart, they should be reading to find things to add to the L column. If the students are going to be "talking how and why" in discussions groups, they should be reading to answer the "How?" and Why?" questions. Remember that the Guided Reading Block is where you teach the children how to think about text—the comprehension skills and strategies. Having a clear comprehension-oriented purpose for reading helps children become good thinkers and comprehenders.

7. Set a time limit for reading.

Before children begin reading, tell them exactly how long they have to read the selection. Make it a reasonable time, but don't give them longer than most of them will really need. Most behavior problems during partner reading happen when children have extra time to "goof off." Don't give students the same amount of time each day because some selections are longer, and some rereading of selections can be done in less time. But, set a time and write it on the board and/or set a timer. Children seem to pay more attention to "odd numbers," so tell them they have 11 minutes, not 10, or 14 minutes, not 15. When the time is up, tell students that you are sorry if they didn't finish, but you need them to join the group—or tell them if they haven't finished, they can finish and then join the group. It doesn't matter which way you do it, but be consistent and enforce your time limits. You will be amazed how much more students can read and how much better they behave when the "clock is ticking."

8. Make sure they have something to do if they finish before the time is up.

Always give students a "filler" activity—what they should do if they finish before reading time is up. Make this related to the purpose if possible. Some suggestions include:

- Take turns asking each other all the questions on the Beach Ball and come up with some "awesome" answers.
- Write down things you would like added to the KWL chart.
- Decide which character you would like to be when we "do the book," and practice what you will say and how you will act.
- Write down some "Why?" and "How?" questions.
- Practice reading your favorite page aloud until you can read it perfectly with terrific expression. If you still have time, practice reading your second favorite page aloud.

Having something they are to do is absolutely essential for successful partner reading. If you don't, some of the partners will rush through and then create problems because they're "all done!" Children are not in such a rush to finish first when they have to think and prepare.

Don't make this a requirement for everyone, have them turn it in, or give them time to finish it – it will put you right back in the same old "they don't all finish at the same time" bind. The message you give to your children as they go to read in partners should be perfectly clear:

> "Your job in these 13 minutes is to echo read the selection with your partner, so that you are ready to prove which of our predictions are true and which are not. If you finish before the 13 minutes is up, write down the numbers of the true predictions and the page number on which you can read to prove it. If you still have time (very doubtful), rewrite the predictions that weren't true so that they are."

9. Before beginning partner reading, model and role-play the behaviors you want.

Call on a child to be your partner, and model how to get quickly to your reading spot. Then, model whatever kind of partner reading you have decided the students should do. For the first month or two, before the beginning of every partner reading session, model how partners coach each other to figure out words, and how partners explain things to each other to make sure they understand what they read. This will take some time, but this time investment will pay off as the year goes on and your children really do begin, not only to "read it together," but to teach each other as well. Once the Guided Reading Block is up and running, we always focus on a comprehension skill or strategy before the children read each time, and follow it up after reading. Until children learn how to partner read, we use our before-reading time to model and our after-reading time to discuss how the partner reading went and to comment on the good strategies we saw partners using.

10. Circulate, "spy on", and coach the partners.

When you are just beginning partner reading in your class, circulate as the partners read and comment or make notes about the good strategies you see partners using. When the group reassembles, point out the examples of how partners coached each other (use students' names!) with the words and helped each other understand what they were reading. Be specific about who you saw doing what, and ask those partners to go back to that page and demonstrate for the group. Comment on how you knew certain partnerships were focused on the purpose you gave them, and how you noticed certain partners using their time wisely when they finished reading to be ready to contribute to the after-reading activity. Accentuate the positive by only pointing out good things.

Once the children know how to partner read, shift your focus from how the partners are working to how individual children are reading. We stop for a minute and listen to each partner read, and we model individually how to coach partners to figure out words and how to explain what "it means." We make anecdotal notes about students' reading fluency, their discussion, how they are figuring out words, and how they are helping each other. By stopping for just one minute and listening to each set of partners, teachers can monitor all the children's reading in a 12-15 minute period.

Playschool Groups *Teams and coaches for older kids*

The guidelines just discussed also apply to playschool groups. Think about who to assign to which groups, how long to leave the groups together, where they will meet, and all the other logistical variables. Playschool groups know what format they will use, and they can use all the formats described for partnerships—and a few others. They know what their purpose is, how long they have, and what they should do if they finish before the time is up. In the beginning, the teacher circulates, commenting and making notes on how their groups are functioning. Once the children know how to work in playschool groups, the teacher's focus shifts to noticing how individual children are doing.

Playschool groups, because they have more children, is the format we would use when we were doing any of the "doing the book" activities. We would also do small-group discussions in playschool groups. After we have done a graphic organizer or KWL activity several times as a whole class activity, we would turn the activity over to the playschool groups. The children would contribute ideas, and one child could do the writing on the chart. Finally, all charts would be compared and displayed.

Playschool groups always have a "teacher," and one problem that must be solved is letting all the children have a chance to be the teacher. We don't necessarily give everyone the same number of times to be the teacher, but the same "bossy girls" cannot be the teachers every time!

To get around this problem, consider which playschool formats do not require a super reader. Imagine the class has read a story and done an appropriate activity with it the preceding day. Today, they are going to reread the story to decide what the characters are saying and doing on each page in preparation for pantomiming the book. Divide your struggling readers up, and make them the "teacher" in each group. The rest of the group will take turns reading the pages. Since you read it the day before and the struggling readers are not reading aloud, the other children should be able to fluently read their pages aloud. The "teacher" tells everyone whose turn it is and then asks, "Who was talking, and how would they act?"

Struggling readers can also be the "teacher" when the format being used by the playschool group is choral reading. For echo reading, on the other hand, you need one of your best readers to be the "teacher." If the groups are doing a "talking why and how" discussion, your strugglers might be the "teacher," because the "teacher" is leading the discussion while the others read the questions and talk about what they think are the answers. When groups do Everyone Read To…, they need a good reader to formulate the purposes for reading each page.

Playschool groups are one of the children's favorite formats for reading and rereading selections. With some clever thinking, you can allow all your children to be "teachers" on various days. As the children read, you can circulate and coach them as they need help with words or with the thinking required to fulfill their purpose for reading. In addition to coaching students as they circulate the room, some teachers like to appoint a word coach in each group. This is the person—and the only person—who can help someone figure out a word. The word coach and the "teacher" are not the same person, so this gives you more opportunities to let children who are not the best readers be the "teachers."

Building Blocks Variations

Kindergartners enjoy rereading favorite big books in partners or playschool groups.

Big Blocks Variations

Partner reading and playschool groups can work in upper grades, but you really have to follow the guidelines and make sure everyone knows what their role is and exactly what they are supposed to do. You also have to be even more aware of the "social" realities in your classroom, and partner struggling readers with someone they like and who likes them. Older students are happier if they can choose their partners, and you may want to see if this will work in your classroom.

Partner Reading and Playschool Groups

Children accept the fact that some of their friends are better ball players and better artists. In real life, friends help each other and learn from each other. Partner reading and playschool groups allow friends to help each other read, just as they help each other with numerous other activities. To make partner reading and playschool groups most effective, follow these guidelines:

1. Arrange the partnerships and playschool groups carefully!

2. Think about how often to change partners and playschool groups.

3. Decide where the partners or playschool groups will read.

4. Decide how you will handle absent partners.

5. Always make sure partners or playschool groups know how they will read the selection.

6. Always have partners or playschool groups read for a purpose.

7. Set a time limit for reading.

8. Make sure students have something to do if they finish before time is up.

9. Before beginning partner or playschool reading, model and role-play the behaviors you want.

10. Circulate and coach the children as they read.

CHAPTER 20

THREE-RING CIRCUS AND YOU'SE CHOOSE

On some days during Guided Reading, certain children read the selection on their own, others read it with partners, and the teacher meets with a small "coaching" group to guide their reading. Most of the time, the teacher decides who will read with whom. We call these days a "Three-Ring Circus" because there are three formats being used simultaneously. Once children understand how Three-Ring Circus days work, you can sometimes let them choose how they would like to read the selection. We call these days "You'se Choose" days.

Three-Ring Circus

Once partner reading is working well, most teachers use the Three-Ring Circus format on some days. You may want to begin by explaining to students that there are advantages to all three types of reading. When they are reading by themselves, they can read at their own pace and focus on just their own ideas. When they are partner reading, they have the advantage of getting help when they need it, and they have someone with whom to share ideas. Explain that you, the teacher, like to read with a small group so that you can see how they are progressing, and can coach them to apply the strategies they are learning. Make sure children already know how to read with their partners and have practiced the partner format you want them to use on this particular day. Most teachers use some kind of an organizational chart so that children can quickly see how they will read the selection that day and not waste time waiting for the teacher to get everyone in the right place. Here is a Three-Ring Circus chart one teacher uses to let students know how they will be reading. On days when the teacher wants to have a Three-Ring Circus organization, the teacher places the children's names in the appropriate ring.

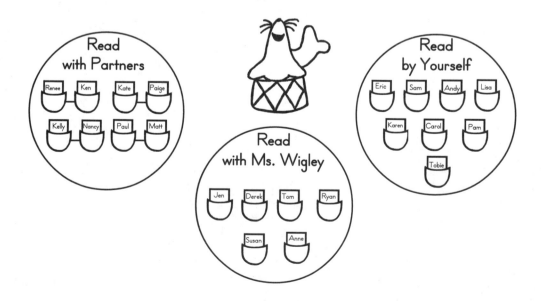

Guided Reading The Four-Blocks™ Way   © Carson-Dellosa CD-2407

When planning a Three-Ring Circus, consider both the levels of your children and the selection in deciding who should read in which format. You may want to have your accelerated readers read the selection individually or with a partner of similar ability. Children who need support are paired with supportive partners or assigned to the coaching group. We do not assign children to read in partnerships who do not work well together, and we never assign a child to read individually unless we believe he can successfully complete the reading on his own.

In deciding who should read with you in the coaching group, again look at the selection and think about your children. One of the ways we make Guided Reading multilevel is to include easier and average selections. While it might seem logical to include the struggling readers in your coaching group for the "grade level" selections, this is usually not the case. These selections are probably above the instructional level of your struggling readers, who would profit more from being coached through the easier selections. We would make sure our struggling readers have nurturing partners for that day, and include more "grade-level" readers in the coaching group who could profit most from being coached through a selection that is apt to be at their instructional level. We try to include struggling readers in the coaching group when we are reading an easier selection.

It is important to include all children in coaching groups, but we don't try to give them "equal time." Accelerated readers don't need a lot of coaching and should be included occasionally, but not as often as struggling readers. This might seem unfair to your advanced readers, unless you remember that Guided Reading is one block and is only getting about one fourth of our teaching time and energy. Accelerated readers profit greatly from the multilevel activities in our Working With Words Block and from the mini-lessons and individual conferences during Writing and Self-Selected Reading. Accelerated readers also profit from Guided Reading as they learn a variety of comprehension strategies for all types of text. Their background knowledge, understanding of concepts, and oral language skills increase as they participate in the before-and-after reading activities. But, accelerated readers are fast learners and don't need a lot of coaching and reteaching. They are generally happier reading a selection on their own or with partners.

While deciding which children could most benefit from some coaching on a particular selection, keep in mind that your coaching groups are not "fixed" ability groups. You may want to include different children for different reasons on different days. Imagine, for example, that you had done the first reading of a selection on the previous day with the whole class using an Everyone Read To… format. The next day, you plan to reread the selection for a different purpose using the Three-Ring Circus format. Two children who were absent the day before might be included along with the others in your coaching group, so that you can support them in their first reading of the selection. There are also usually one or two children in every classroom who need help, but just don't work well with partners—particularly when the teacher is working with a coaching group and the partners are expected to function without the teacher circulating around the room. These children are often included in coaching groups so that the Three-Ring Circus format can run smoothly.

Of all the blocks, Guided Reading is the hardest one to make multilevel. Any selection is going to be too hard for some, too easy for others, and just right for some. For that reason, many teachers who have help coming to their classrooms schedule Guided Reading at that time. In those classrooms, the Three-Ring Circus becomes a "Four-Ring Circus" and two coaching groups go on simultaneously.

You'se Choose

If you were to enter a Four-Blocks classroom and see some children reading with the teacher while others were reading individually or in partners, you would probably assume the format for reading that day was a Three-Ring Circus. Maybe, maybe not! Another format that looks the same and works the same is one in which the children decide with whom they want to read a selection. We call this format You'se Choose. (In some Southern classrooms, it is referred to as "Y'all's Call"!)

Once you have the Three-Ring Circus format established, it is easy to tell children that on some days, they will get to choose how they want to read the selection. We always establish the rule, however, that they must make a good choice. As part of our before-reading activity, we clearly establish the purpose for reading by making it clear to children what they will be doing in the after-reading activity. Then, we tell them that they must be ready to contribute to the reading activity, and ask them to preview the selection and decide how best to read it so that they can contribute. We tell the students that they can read the selection with a friend, if both of them want to read it together, and together, they can be prepared for the after-reading activity. Explain that students can choose to read all by themselves, with the same caveat—they must be able to "handle it on their own." Finally, tell students you would like some of them to "come and read it with me," and you all will read the selection together and get ready to contribute to the after-reading activity.

Just as with partner reading and playschool groups, make sure the children know what they are preparing to do, and give them some filler task to do if they finish before the time is up. We always relate that task to what we will do after reading (writing down things to add to the timeline, deciding which character they would like to be, and practicing reading the parts that character would say in the way they think that character would say them, etc.). We give students the same amount of time to read that we want to use to work with the children who choose to read with us. The rest of the class will work individually or with their partner to begin the filler activity if they have time. Be sure not to make this something anyone has to complete or turn in because then you have still not solved the problem of children taking differing amounts of time to do things. But, when you have a good and clearly established filler activity, no one gets done before the allotted time is up! Having a filler activity solves some of the management problems which often occur when the children are working in different configurations.

When you decide to do You'se Choose, it is important to really let everyone make the choice for themselves. This is easier said than done. The first time you do the activity, you may see some children who you know can't read the selection on their own or who have partners who won't be any help at all! You might casually ask the ones who haven't chosen well, "Are you sure you don't want to come and read with my group? I'd love to have you!" But, if they decline your kind invitation, let them do it the way they chose. When the class reassembles for the after-reading activity, call on these children for their contributions. Don't embarrass them, but make it clear that you expect them to be able to contribute. If they are unable to, take them aside privately and tell them that the next time, you are going to have to approve their choices! Be resolute with this a few times, and you will find your children making better choices. Don't be surprised if some of your more able readers choose to read with you. You said they could choose any way that would get them ready to contribute, and they have! Children have preferences about how they want to do things. Like adults, some are more social than others. You'se Choose lets children express those preferences, and it is a favorite format in many classrooms.

In the next chapter, we will discuss some ways that teachers coach children when meeting with a small group during the Three-Ring Circus and You'se Choose formats.

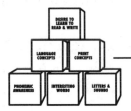

Building Blocks Variations

Three-Ring Circus and You'se Choose are not formats we would normally use with kindergartners. We would work with coaching groups as needed while the other children are working in centers.

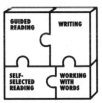

Big Blocks Variations

You'se Choose is a favorite format among older children who like to decide things for themselves and love to do things with their friends. Be sure that they have a purpose for reading and that they understand they must make a responsible choice. Children who choose to read on their own or with a partner but who are unable to contribute to the after-reading activity should be chosen by you for your group the next time. Then, give them the choice again the following time. Be resolute and most children will learn to make good choices.

Three-Ring Circus And You'se Choose (Y'all's Call)

Both Three-Ring Circus and You'se Choose give you a lot of flexibility in how you support children during Guided Reading. When you do You'se Choose, you lose the advantage of being able to decide how much support children need, but you gain a lot of cooperation as everyone likes to be in control! These formats should be used only after children know how to partner read and are familiar with the after-reading activity for which they are preparing. Most teachers would begin with the Three-Ring Circus format and expand that to include You'se Choose when their children are used to the idea that some children read by themselves, others with partners, and others with the teacher.

1. If you are doing a Three-Ring Circus, decide who will read by themselves, with a partner, or with you, by thinking about how much support the students will need to read, based on the purpose you set. When you do You'se Choose, make sure the children understand that they must make a responsible choice, or they will lose the privilege of making that choice the next time.

2. Set time limits just as you would for partner reading or playschool groups.

3. Children who cannot handle the freedom to read on their own or with a partner while you work with a group may need to be included in your group more often.

4. If you have help coming during Guided Reading, you might have two or more coaching groups and thus a "Four or Five-Ring Circus!"

CHAPTER 21

COACHING GROUPS

In Four-Blocks classrooms, decoding skills are taught and practiced each day during the Working With Words Block. Children learn to read and spell high-frequency words during the daily Word Wall practice. They also learn how some of the Word Wall words—the ones with regular spelling patterns—help you decode and spell other words. They learn how our complex vowel system works during Making Words when they change the vowel to change *tan* to *ten* and add a vowel to change *tap* to *tape*. All the activities in the Working With Words Block stress transferring this knowledge to reading and writing. In the transfer step in a Making Words lesson, children use rhyming words they have made to decode and spell other rhyming words. Using Words You Know lessons help children see how the words they can already read and spell help them read and spell hundreds of other words. Guess the Covered Word lessons help children learn to decode a new word based on all the beginning letters and the sense of the sentence.

We think of the Working With Words Block as the time when all the skills needed to quickly and accurately identify words are taught and practiced. Some children have little difficulty actually applying these word identification strategies as they read. Other children need to be "coached" to use what they know as they are actually reading. Coaching groups are how we provide that coaching to children as they read text on their level. Once children know how to read with partners, call together small groups of children and coach them to use their word identification strategies in text at their reading instructional level. Include different children on different days, but try to include children who are at just the right level with the text. With a little coaching, they probably will be able to successfully read the text. We explain coaching groups to the children by making analogies to sports teams. Children understand that you practice various soccer moves and then, in a game format, the coach watches you play and stops you from time to time to coach you to use the skills you have practiced. We include some more advanced readers in coaching groups and once they understand how to coach, we let them play the role of word coach. Before long, the children learn how to coach and begin to use their coaching skills when reading with a partner.

When reading with the whole class, we use formats such as choral and echo reading and Everyone Read To... to avoid "turn taking," round-robin reading. In coaching groups, have children read to themselves first, and then ask a child to read that page aloud. We tell the children that we hope they will come to at least one word they need help with so that they can all learn how to be word coaches.

Coaching Steps

Before the children start to read, remind them of the strategies they can use to figure out an unfamiliar word. You may want to post a chart of these steps, which you can review each time before children begin reading.

How To Figure Out a Hard Word

1. **Put your finger on the word and say all the letters.**

2. **Use the letters and the picture clues.**

3. **Look for a rhyme you know.**

4. **Keep your finger on the word and finish the sentence and pretend it's the covered word.**

These are the steps to use if children stop on a word. If, they misread a word instead of stopping, let them finish the sentence and then bring them back to the word they have misread. Imagine, for example that the child read "There was not a cold in the sky." When the sentence said: *There was not a cloud in the sky.*

When they misread *cold* for *cloud*, *cold* did make sense. But, by the end of the sentence, they should realize that the sentence didn't make sense and go back and try to fix something. Let them finish the sentence, so that they will develop their own self-monitoring system. If, however, they don't notice and just continue reading, stop them and say something like,

"That didn't make sense. Let's look at this word again. Say all the letters in this word."

Then, take them through steps two – four as needed to help them decode the word.

Here is how you coach each step and why each step is important. (Depending on their age, share as much of this explanation with children as you think they can understand. With older, struggling readers, explain it all. They love to know how their brains work!)

1. Put your finger on the word and say all the letters.

When a child comes to a word he does not know, have him put his finger on the word and say all the letters. It is very important here that the child says the letters. Saying the letters is not sounding out the word by saying individual sounds. English is not a sound-it-out-letter-by-letter language, and the worst readers are the ones who try to do it letter by letter. You want students to say all the letters so that you know they have indeed looked at them all in the right order, and having the students say the letters is the only way to know for sure. You also want students to say the letters because there is strong evidence that retrieval from the brain's memory store is auditory. If they just look at letters and search in their brains for that word or a rhyming word, it is apt to be harder to find than if they say the letters which go through the brain's auditory channel.

In our experience, if children are reading at the right level and say the letters of an unfamiliar word aloud, they will sometimes correctly identify that word immediately. Proof positive that they needed the auditory channel for retrieval! When they say all the letters and then successfully pronounce the word, cheer! They have scored a goal. "See, it was in there. You just had to say it so that your brain could find it!" If, after they say all the letters, they still don't know the word, remind them of step two. (The exception here is strange names. If the word they are trying to decode is Timbuktu, Claribel, or Houdini, we just pronounce it for them and let them continue reading. The decoding strategies in the remaining steps don't help with names.)

2. Use the letters and the picture clues

For this to work, you must be doing some pictures walks prior to reading in which you preview the pictures with the whole class and have children find a few words by asking them to stretch out a word and think about the letters they would expect to see. Children should know that just guessing based on pictures or on letters won't get them very far, but the two together are a powerful team. The child who sees the word *raccoon*, and says all the letters, and then glances at the picture may indeed see a picture of a raccoon. The picture, along with the letters you know he has looked at because he just said them, will often allow him to decode the word. So, once the child has said all the letters aloud, cue him by saying something like, "Will the picture help?" "What is that animal called?" If the child gets the word correct now, cheer! If not, proceed to step three.

3. Look for a rhyme you know.

Like the previous step, this will only be helpful if, each day during Working With Words, you have been stressing that you can often figure out a word you know by looking at the pattern. *Raccoon*, for example, rhymes with *moon* and *soon*. If the child does not see this, the coach can say, "That word rhymes with moon and soon!" If the child still doesn't get it, proceed to the final step.

4. Keep your finger on the word, finish the sentence and, pretend the word is the covered word.

Guess The Covered Word is the activity you use during Working With Words to help children use beginning letters and context to figure out words. Children become very good at this during the Words block, but they often need to be coached to use it as they read. We have them keep their finger on the word so that when they have read the sentence, they can quickly look back at the letters. Most of the time, if children in your coaching group are reading at the right level, they will be able to figure out the word by using these four steps.

Everyone should cheer and talk about how they did it! If they can't figure it out, it is often a word they don't have in their listening vocabularies. For example, an ostrich may be in the picture. The word *ostrich* rhymes with *rich* and makes sense, but if a child doesn't have the word *ostrich* in her listening vocabulary, she won't be able to decode it. When this happens, just tell her the word and say, "Good try! That was a really tough word," and move on to the next page!

When To Do Coaching Groups

Coaching groups are most commonly done when using the Three-Ring Circus and You'se Choose formats. Children not in the coaching group are reading with partners or by themselves. Usually, we read the selection that everyone else is reading and for which we are teaching comprehension strategies through our before-and-after reading activities. In our coaching group, we may occasionally read something different from what the other children are reading. Imagine that you read a selection the previous day with the whole class using a Choral or Echo Reading or Everyone Read To… format. The children in the coaching group have read this selection once. The other children are rereading it for a different purpose. You might wish to use a different, easier text with your coaching group since they have already read the main selection and could benefit more from being coached in a new text, rather than rereading the main text.

Some teachers find time in their weekly schedule to meet with coaching groups outside the Guided Reading time. In some classrooms, the teacher meets daily with an After Lunch Bunch and does coaching at that time. We include all children in the After Lunch Bunch activities across the week, but we include the struggling readers almost every day and the others less frequently. In some classrooms, teachers have "center time" each day and do a coaching group which they call a "Fun Reading Club" during that time. Coaching groups only last 10-15 minutes. We don't do before-and-after activities to teach comprehension with coaching groups since that is our focus during Guided Reading. We also don't introduce high-frequency words or teach decoding strategies since this is our focus during Working With Words. We simply choose some material at the instructional level of most of the children we intend to include and begin reading it. With this activity, you really want to simulate what children must do during Self-Selected Reading when they tackle text on their own without any preteaching. As they read and encounter problems, we coach them to apply what they have learned when they actually need to use it.

In some classrooms, special teachers or assistants do coaching groups with children. If you have help coming and have many children that need coaching, you might schedule Self-Selected Reading at that time and have the helper coach children in their self-selected books. Many teachers like to schedule Guided Reading when they have help coming. The helping teacher can coach children through the selection if it is close to their instructional level, or he can read that selection to them and then coach them in material at their level.

Finding the time, people, and reading materials to do coaching groups is not easy. But when you add some regular coaching in instructional-level material on top of all the good instruction struggling readers receive throughout the Four-Blocks each day, you will be amazed at the rapid progress struggling readers can make.

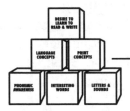

Building Blocks Variations

Use coaching groups with kindergartners who need help with print tracking and other early reading skills.

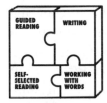

Big Blocks Variations

Coaching groups are important for older children, particularly those who haven't developed useful decoding skills. We change the composition of the groups regularly and include some average readers for reading models. We teach the children to be word coaches and when a child is about to read a page aloud, we let that child choose his own word coach! Even struggling readers can coach, because they don't necessarily need to know the word, only how to give the right prompts.

Coaching Groups

Coaching groups help children learn how to apply all that you have been teaching at the point they need it. Try to choose material at the appropriate level for children who need coaching and include a few other more able readers in the groups. Once children know how to coach, let them be word coaches, and occasionally let each reader choose her own word coach. The "coaching" steps to use are:

1. Put your finger on the word and say all the letters.

2. Use the letters and the picture clues.

3. Look for a rhyme you know.

4. Keep your finger on the word, finish the sentence, and pretend the word is the covered word.

CHAPTER 22

BOOK CLUB GROUPS AND LITERATURE CIRCLES

So far in this book, you have learned about formats for organizing children to read and reread text when they are all reading the same text. As your students become better and more independent readers, you can use Book Club groups or Literature Circles and let them have some choice about what they read. In this chapter, you will find some Book Club examples first, and then learn about some of the special features of Literature Circles.

Book Club Groups

For Book Club groups, the teacher usually selects four books, tied together by author, genre, topic, or theme. Reading aloud the first chapter or several pages of each book to the children, or previewing the pictures or books with them, have the children indicate their first, second, and third choices for the book they would like to read. Whenever possible, in choosing the three or four books, try to include one that is easier and one that is harder. If children who are struggling choose the easier book as one of their choices, they are put in the group that will read this book. If the more advanced readers choose the harder book for any of their choices, they are put in that group. (We don't tell the children that some books are harder or easier!) Each time we do Book Club groups, the groups change and while we consider the reading levels and choices of children when assigning them, the groups all have a range of readers and are not ability groups.

Once Book Club groups are formed, they meet regularly to read and discuss the book. The teacher rotates through the groups giving guidance, support, and encouragement. Each day the groups report to the class what has happened or what they have learned in their book so far.

Dr. Seuss Book Club Groups

Here is an example using four Dr. Seuss books. Many teachers find this a "fun" activity as March draws near and schools all over the country are celebrating Dr. Seuss's birthday. Teachers often build up to this activity by reading Dr. Seuss books during the teacher-read-aloud portion of the Self-Selected Reading Block. Then, teachers encourage children to bring in copies of their favorite Dr. Seuss books. When children bring their favorite Dr. Seuss books to school, the teacher will often notice that there are many copies each of several books. The teacher may be able to "borrow" these books from the children, combine them with library and classroom copies, and use them for Book Club groups.

The Dr. Seuss books chosen for this example are: *Hop on Pop*, *The Foot Book*, *Ten Apples Up On Top*, and *One Fish, Two Fish, Red Fish, Blue Fish*. There are many others you could chose. *Hop on Pop* is the "easy" selection because most of the pages have just two words with the same spelling pattern, and then a simple sentence using those two words. (Example: *UP PUP Pup is up.*) The pictures support the text and can be used by the children to "cross-check" their reading. *The Foot Book* and *Ten Apples Up on Top* are a little more difficult than *Hop on Pop,* but can easily be read by primary-grade children. The hardest of the four books is *One Fish, Two Fish, Red Fish, Blue Fish.* This book is harder because there are more words in this book and more text on each page. Once again, the pictures support the text, and the children can "cross-check" as they read. When you do Book Club groups, you want a book that is also a little more challenging than "grade level" for those who need the challenge. *One Fish, Two Fish, Red Fish, Blue Fish* is a little harder than *The Foot Book* and *Ten Apples Up on Top.* Thus, you have books with a range of reading levels for your Book Club groups. (But, we do not put the children in groups based solely on their reading ability.)

Book Club groups usually last for several days. The teacher decides that the Dr. Seuss Book Clubs will last three days.

Day One

She begins the Guided Reading Block the first day by telling the children that she has found four wonderful Dr. Seuss books for them to read in "Book Club groups". If this is the first time using this format, the teacher may talk about how grown-ups often read the same book and get together with friends to talk about it. She might use Oprah Winfrey's book club as an example, or tell about her own experience with a book club. The teacher then explains that the children are such good readers they are now ready for Book Club groups with their friends!

The teacher shows the cover of each book, one at a time, and lets the children tell what they know about the books and some of their personal experiences with these books. Using only the cover, she gets children thinking about what they know about these books and about what they might read. She then tells the children that they only have three days to spend on these books, and they don't have enough time or copies of the books for each child to read all four books. Each Book Club group will read one book and hear about the other three books from the other groups.

Next, she gives each child an index card and asks the children to write their names and the numbers 1, 2, and 3 on the cards. She then explains that she is going to give them 20 minutes to preview the books—five minutes for each book. At the end of the 20 minutes, they will return to their seats and write down their first, second, and third choices. She places all the copies of each book in the four corners of the room. She then divides the class into four random groups, and sends a group to each corner. She sets her timer for five minutes and tells the children that when the timer sounds, they must move to the next corner and the next group of books.

For the next 20 minutes, the children are busily trying to read as much as they can and look at as many pages as they can. Each time the timer sounds and they have to move, some children groan. When the 20 minutes are up, the children return to their seats to make their choices. It isn't easy! Most protest that they want to read them all! They have trouble deciding which is their first choice and which is their second choice. The teacher tells them not to worry too much about the order of choices because she can't guarantee they will get their first choice—or even their second choice. "I want the groups to be about the same size, and I need to put groups together that will work well together. I promise I will give you one of your choices. I will try to give you your first choice, but I can't promise it!"

After school, she looks at all the cards. First, she looks at the cards of the struggling readers. Four of her five struggling readers have chosen *Hop on Pop* as one of their choices, so she puts them in the *Hop on Pop* group along with two more able readers who have also chosen *Hop on Pop* (Why would a more able reader choose this book? As one excellent reader said, "*Hop on Pop* is a really funny book. It has always been my favorite Dr. Seuss book!") One struggling reader chose *Ten Apples Up on Top* as his first choice, and the teacher puts him in the *Ten Apples Up on Top* group. Next, she looks at the choices of her most able readers. Four of these have chosen *One Fish, Two Fish, Red Fish, Blue Fish* and she puts them in this group along with two fairly able readers. She puts the other eleven children in the remaining two groups, five in the *Ten Apples Up on Top* group and six in *The Foot Book* group.

Day Two
The second day, the children read the whole book with their Book Club group. Before passing out the books, the teacher tells them how they will read it and their purpose for reading. The teacher explains that during reading today they will echo read the book and "read and point." The children know that this means the leader will read each page first while the others point to the words. Then, the rest will try to be the echo—reading exactly the way the leader did. ("Read and point" is used in the early reading stages to help children stay focused and track print.)

Their purpose is to read the book with good expression, emphasizing the funny words and the rhyming words, and to think about what they like best about the book. What pictures do they like best? What words? What is really funny? Really silly? The teacher explains that they are going to think more about this tomorrow, but if they finish before the time is up, they should go back through the book and begin to talk about what they like best.

The teacher passes out the books. As she is handing each group their books she says, "The person who gets the book with the index card in it is the leader today." She makes sure that a fluent reader and a responsible person is given that book.

As the children read, the teacher circulates, "drops an ear" and listens, coaches if needed, and moves on. She monitors most closely the *Hop on Pop* group; visiting them at the beginning and making sure they know what to do and how to do it. After she monitors the other Book Club groups, the teacher returns to the *Hop on Pop* group and coaches them some more, if needed.

As the groups finish reading, they begin to discuss what they liked about the book. They like the funny pictures, the rhyming words, and the silly things that Dr. Seuss writes about in his books. The leader will share these things with the whole class in the after-reading phase of this lesson.

Day Three

On the third day, the children reread the book with their Book Club group. This time, they read it chorally. Their purpose is to find their favorite page to read to the group. Each child is given a bookmark. As they chorally read the pages, the children can put their bookmarks in to mark a favorite page. As they continue and come to an even "more favorite" page, they can move their bookmark. Once the whole book is read chorally, each child will practice reading his favorite page. The leader in each group makes sure each child can read the page fluently and can explain why it was chosen. If several children in a group have chosen the same page, they practice reading that page chorally.

The Guided Reading Block ends with all the children reading aloud and explaining their choices. They talk about the pictures, what the author is saying on the page, and how the text is illustratec. The teacher hears members of other Book Club groups saying, "I liked those funny fur feet, too!" or "The house on the mouse was the best illustration in that book, but a mouse can't really carry a real house!" It is apparent from their faces and their comments that they want to read or reread these books.

Link to Self-Selected Reading

The teacher ends the lesson by telling the class that although the Book Club groups are over, she wants to "borrow" these books a little longer. If the owners will let her, she will put one book from each group in each of the book baskets so that everyone has a chance to read or reread their favorite Dr. Seuss books at Self-Selected Reading time if they choose.

Biography Book Clubs

You learned in Chapter Three that it is important for children to learn to read all the different kinds of text. Biographies are interesting to almost all children. The children who like information enjoy them because they "really happened." The children who like stories like them because they are stories—true stories of a person's life.

For this Book Club group, the teacher has chosen four biographies by David Adler. Each book has 25 pages and ends with a page of important dates and events (like a time line). The easiest biography is *A Picture Book of Abraham Lincoln*. It follows the life of the popular president from his childhood on the frontier to his assassination after the Civil War. Most pages have two to four lines of text and illustrations. Some pages have only illustrations. Most children who have been in school for a year or more know something about Abraham Lincoln. Children's prior knowledge about Lincoln, combined with shorter text and more illustrations, make this biography easier than the others.

Two biographies that are a little harder than the one about Abraham Lincoln are *A Picture Book of Martin Luther King, Jr.* and *A Picture Book of Jackie Robinson.* Each of these books has more text on the pages than the biography of Abraham Lincoln. Also, most children are not as familiar with these two people as they are with Lincoln. The hardest biography is *A Picture Book of Rosa Parks.* The vocabulary is the most difficult of the four by far (*boycott, protest, humiliated, segregated, discrimination,* etc.). There is more text on each page, and there are several pages with just text and no illustrations.

The Biography Book Clubs will last for four days. They will preview and make their choices on the first day, read the book over the next two days, and do a summary writing activity on the fourth day.

Day One

The first day of a Book Club cycle is always the previewing and choosing day. The teacher gathers all the children and tells them that they are going to focus on biographies this week, and she has four great biographies from which they can choose. She shows them the covers of the four biographies, and lets them tell what they know about each person. She then proceeds to read aloud the first six or seven pages of each of the four biographies. The children take an index card and indicate their first, second, and third choices. The teacher reminds them that she may not be able to give them their first choice, or even their second choice, but she will give everyone one of their choices.

After school, the teacher looks at the children's choices. She looks first at the choices of her struggling readers. *Abraham Lincoln* was chosen by three and *Jackie Robinson* was the choice of the other three. She gives all of these children their first choice. Next, she looks at the choices her advanced readers made. Four of the advanced readers were girls, and they all chose the *Rosa Parks* book! The boys who were excelling readers chose *Jackie Robinson* or *Martin Luther King, Jr.* The remainder of the class was given their first, second, or sometimes third choice, so that all four groups had either five or six members.

When the children come to school the next day, they immediately check the posted list of Book Club groups. Some are disappointed that they didn't get their first choice. The teacher sympathizes, but points out that she was able to give them one of their choices. She also tells the students that she will be able to keep the books in the room for the next week, and they can read the others during Self-Selected Reading if they choose.

Day Two

On the second day of Book Club groups, the children once again gather in the front of the room and huddle around the teacher. There are four sheets of chart paper taped to the board behind her. She takes one of the four sheets of chart paper and shows that each piece of paper has the name of one of the books and the names of the children in that group. She explains that she wrote the name of the person they will read about in the oval in the center of the chart paper. She has four lines that come from the center with circles at the ends of these lines. There are "spokes," or lines coming from each circle. In the circles she has written birth/early years, family, work, later years/death.

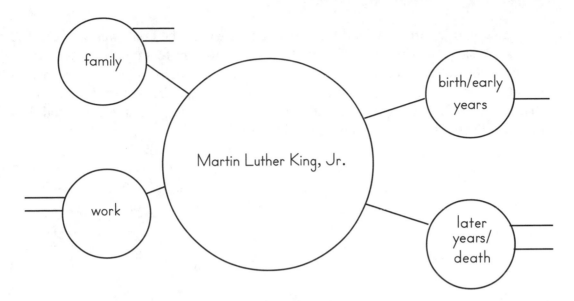

The children have helped complete webs before, so they understand that their purpose for reading will be to find important facts related to each subtopic and write it on the appropriate "spoke." The teacher points out that she has starred the name of a child in each group whom she has chosen to do the writing on the web and be the group leader. In each group, the teacher has appointed one of the more able readers and writers for this task. She gives markers to the member of each group whom she has chosen to do the writing, and tells the children that the writer will also be the "teacher" and lead the group, just as she does when the class does webs together.

In preparation for this activity, the teacher has placed the books in the four corners of the room. She used large paperclips to clip together the pages in the last half of each book, so that students will not read beyond that point on the first day. The groups go to their corners after the teacher orients them as to how they will be working for the next two days. She explains that they will have 20 minutes to read the pages in the first half of the book and add information to the spokes on their web.

As the groups work, the teacher goes around and listens to them reading. She stops and coaches individuals that need help with reading, and just "drops an ear" to monitor the reading of many others. At the end of 15 minutes, one group has not gotten to writing any information on their web, so the teacher signals to them that there is only 5 minutes left and they should be discussing and writing things on their web. She adds that some groups will have to "move a little faster." The last ten minutes of Guided Reading are spent with each group sharing their webs with the other three groups and telling what they have learned so far.

Day Three
On the next day, the teacher meets with the class and makes sure that they know what they will do. "Review what you have learned so far, and read the remaining pages of your biographies." Each group must have its web completed by the end of twenty minutes and be

ready to share details from the life of the person about whom the book was written. The teacher uses the same procedure as she used the previous day to support their reading, giving a little extra time to coach those who need it. (She remembers one of her teacher-friend's motto, "Being fair isn't giving everyone the same thing, being fair is giving each child what he needs!") At the end of the allotted time, she reassembles the class, and they share the new information on their finished webs.

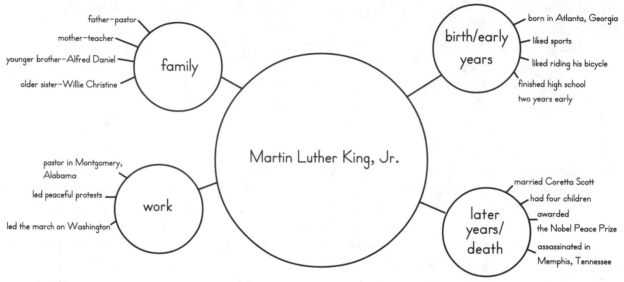

Day Four

On the final day, the teacher tells the students that they are all going to write a paragraph summarizing some of the important things they learned about their person. She shows them a paragraph frame that she has written on the board and they read and discuss each sentence.

> I learned a lot about _____. I learned that (s)he was born _____. I learned _____. (S)he is remembered for _____. The most important thing I learned was _____.

She then gives the children four sticky notes and shows them how they can use these to mark the places to which they want to refer as they complete the sentences in their paragraph. They can read it by themselves or with a friend, and they can write their own summary or write one with a friend, if they can agree on what they want to say.

As the children read, the teacher goes around to each child or pair of children and asks them to read a page aloud to her. She makes notes about their fluency and word identification and is pleased to see that all the children are able to read their biographies with good fluency and adequate word identification. As they begin writing, they use both the book and the web to help them. Because they know so much about their topic, have the web and book for support, and have the frame to help structure their writing, each child writes a good paragraph to share with the class.

> I learned a lot about Rosa Parks. I learned that she was born in Tuskegee, Alabama in 1913. I learned that growing up she lived and worked on her grandparents' farm. She is remembered for being the Mother of the Civil Rights Movement. The most important thing I learned was that it is against the law to discriminate against people because of their race or color.

> I learned a lot about Martin Luther King, Jr. I learned that he was born in Atlanta, Georgia in 1929. I learned that he won the Nobel Peace Prize. He is remembered for leading the famous march on Washington. The most important thing I learned was that he helped to end the unfair treatment of African-Americans.

Social Studies Link

Biographies make history come alive, and thus, are natural social studies links. The biographies listed here are appropriate for children from late second grade and beyond. There are many biographies written for older children, including "The Childhood of Famous Americans Series." Children also enjoy reading about living people and Sports Stars by Children's Press has a long list of books about athletes including *Mark McGwire: Home Run King; Lisa Leslie: Queen of the Court; Grant Hill: Smooth As Silk; and Mia Hamm: Good As Gold.*

Book Club Groups with Plays

Most children love to be in plays. Rigby has made it easy to do plays and have children reading on their own levels by adding some *Tales and Plays* to their PM collection. For our example, we have chosen four books from their collection of *Tales and Plays* to do in Book Club groups. Each book has 20 pages for the story and an 11 or 12 page play. *Goldilocks and the Three Bears* and *Town Mouse and Country Mouse* are the "average" difficulty books. *The Three Billy Goats Gruff* is easier. *Robin Hood and the Silver Trophy* is more challenging. This round of Book Club groups will take five days, with the children previewing and choosing on the first day, reading the story and play for three days, and reading the plays for the other groups on the final day.

Day One

The teacher begins these Book Club groups by sharing the covers of the books and explaining that they contain both a story and a play! Most children have smiles on their faces because they know what comes next – "doing the books"! The teacher explains that on this first day, they will get to look at all the books. He asks the students to think about which character they would like to be as they look at the books, and then read a few lines to see if they sound like a good match for a character. After previewing the four books, the students will get to write down which books they want to read. Eight copies of each title have been placed in four gathering places in different corners of the room. Students will have six minutes per book, and then six minutes to decide and write their choices after previewing the books.

As the children are previewing the books, the teacher circulates and spends a few minutes in each corner. He gives some attention to the most struggling readers, who are mixed in with the other readers in all four corners. He reads a page or two with them and helps them to think about which books they like best and which characters they want to be.

When the children have previewed all the books, they write their three choices. Most children like all the books and want to do all the plays. A few children have a particular book and character they really want to be, and write pleading notes to the teacher on their choice sheets!

The teacher looks at their choices and divides the children into groups. Given that they are going to do the play, he also decides who will be which character, although the children are not told this until they have read the book. He puts six children in the *Goldilocks* group, which will need five actors and a narrator; and five students in the *Billy Goats* group, which has four characters and a narrator. He assigns students to the *Mouse* group to play all the characters and the narrator. He puts all the other students in the *Robin Hood* group, which has lots of characters – including several with very few lines. He assigns two children several small parts to round out this cast.

Day Two

The teacher has put the names of the children in each group on an index card and hands the card to the leader of the group and narrator/director of the play. The leader calls out the names on her list and leads the children to the appointed area. Each group is to read a two-page spread (pp. 2-3, 4-5, 6-7, 8-9) and then discuss what has happened on the pages. The children begin to read these familiar tales two pages at a time. They follow the procedure set up by the teacher—read and discuss, read and discuss, etc. When the class gets together at the end of the lesson, someone in each group reports on what has happened in their book so far.

Day Three

The whole class is gathered together before the lesson, and someone from each group retells what has happened in each story so far. The teacher congratulates each student for their accurate retelling, and praises them for telling the events in the correct sequence. They follow the same procedure to finish reading and discussing the book. Someone in each group finishes retelling the tale when the class is reassembled again at the end of this reading lesson.

Day Four

On the fourth day, each Book Club group reads the play in the back of the book. The teacher gives the leader a list of the parts and who will read which part. The groups begin reading the play with each child reading her appropriate part. (Depending on your class, you may let each group decide who will play each part if this can be done amicably and quickly.) The teacher circulates as the children read and coaches them to read with appropriate expression. The children enjoy the reading and compete to see who can be the "hammiest." The teacher lets students take the books home overnight to practice reading their parts, so that they can read them fluently the next day. Many children tell of their plans to read the whole play at home, giving everyone they can corral some parts to read!

Day Five

The fifth and final day begins with the teacher clearing some space in the front of the room and declaring it their "stage." The leader/director/narrator in each group draws a straw on which the numbers 1, 2, 3, or 4 have been written. The numbered straw tells which of the groups will be first, second, third, and fourth to do their plays. The first group comes forward, and the rest of the class becomes the eager audience. The students begin reading and "acting" out their parts. After the applause, someone in each of the other three groups is allowed to tell something they liked. "I like the way each of the goat's voices sounded different." "The troll walked just like a big troll would—very slowly!"

Each group takes its turn reading and doing their play. When all the plays have been done, the children get out their reading response logs and write about which play—other than their own—they liked best and why. The children demand to keep the books in the room for awhile, and several children ask to check books out so that they can read all the plays at home with their family and friends!

Literature Circles

Literature Circles are similar to Book Club groups in that children choose books and meet in small groups to discuss them. Unlike in Book Clubs, children in Literature Circles usually do the reading on their own rather than with the group. For this reason, you should only do Literature Circles when you are sure children can read their books without help, or you may want to modify the literature circle format to allow children who have picked a certain book to partner read. Another major difference is that rather than give the whole group the same purpose for reading, children in Literature Circles have different roles and can choose the role they want. These roles determine their purpose for reading. There are a variety of roles, but the most commonly used ones are Character Sketcher, Author Authority, Plot Person, Conflict Connector, and Solution Suggester. A student who likes drawing can become the Character Sketcher and sketch the characters in the story his group is reading. Another child in each group who knows a lot about the author can become the Author Authority. The Plot Person makes sure that everyone in the group understands what has happened in the story so far. To carry out this task, the Plot Person must keep track of who (somebody), what they wanted (to happen), what happened (but), and how the problem was solved (so). The Conflict Connectors helps the groups understand the conflicts that exist (character versus character, character versus nature, character versus society, etc.) in their books, and how the characters in their books work through the conflicts. These roles help the children discuss the books they are reading and share what is happening in the stories with the whole class.

Another way of assigning roles is to give students a role sheet. Here is an example of the role sheet one teacher used:

Discussion Director: Your job is to develop a list of questions that your group might want to discuss about today's reading. Try to determine what is important about today's text. Focus your questions on big ideas.

Passage Master: Your job is to locate a few special sections of the reading on which the group should look back. You should help your group notice the most interesting, funny, puzzling, or important parts.

Vocabulary Enricher: Your job is to be on the lookout for a few especially important words that your group needs to remember or understand. You should look for new, interesting, strange, important, or puzzling words.

Connector: Your job is to find connections between the material you are reading and yourself and other students. Also, look for connections to the world and to other books we have read.

Illustrator: Your job is to draw some kind of picture related to the reading. It can be a sketch, diagram, flow chart, or stick figure scene.

You will find more roles and their descriptions in the books *Literature Circles* by Harvey Daniels (1996) and *Literature Circle Role Sheets* by Christine Boardman Moan (1998).

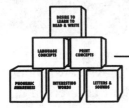

Building Blocks Variations

We would not do Literature Circles or Book Club groups with kindergartners.

Big Blocks Variations

Older children love Book Club groups and Literature Circles because they get to choose their own books. If you offer groups of books that include an easier and a harder book, this is a very multilevel Guided Reading format.

Book Club Groups and Literature Circles

Book Club groups and Literature Circles are one of our favorite ways to organize Guided Reading once the children read well enough that you can find multiple books tied together in some way. Most teachers find that the children participate eagerly in these groups and that the books they didn't get to read are the most popular selections during Self-Selected Reading the following week. It is not unusual for children to read all three books their group didn't read. Students' knowledge of each book is greatly increased by each group sharing information with the class. Students are often able to read books at a higher level because of their increased knowledge of the topic and writing style.

1. Select four books tied together by author, topic, genre, or theme. Try to include one easier and one more challenging book.
2. Let children preview books and indicate their choices.
3. Form groups considering the choices made by the children and the difficulty of the books.
4. For Book Club groups, have children read for the purpose you determine and the amount you determine each day. For Literature Circles, let groups decide how much to read each day and gather to discuss it and use role sheets that fit the age and sophistication of your children.
5. Have each group share with the other groups what they have learned.
6. Make the books available for Self-Selected Reading so that children who want to read the other books can.

CHAPTER 23

PICK A PAGE

Pick a Page is a fluency building activity in which children are given one or two pages in a story to read and practice. They practice this in a group of "same pagers." Next, new groups are formed which contain one reader for each page. Pick a Page can be done as a rereading activity but it is more fun to do it as a first reading. Part of the intrigue as you are practicing your page is not knowing what happened before or how it all turns out in the end. You can do Pick a Page with any story. If you can use selections from old reading textbooks or inexpensive paperback books that you can actually cut apart, it is more dramatic because everyone really has to wait until the reading group gathers to find out the rest of the story (no one can peek ahead). If children are reading their pages and the rest of the story is available, make a firm "no peeking" rule and deal swiftly and severely with anyone who does! Take a "No peeking or else!" stance, and have an appropriate "or else" in mind.

For the Pick a Page example, are using Vera Williams' *A Chair for My Mother*. Our copy comes from an old reading textbook so it has been cut apart. The selection has 15 pages, and the teacher decides to distribute the pages so that each child is actually reading two pages, printed front and back on one sheet. The last page only has words on one side so she groups it with the preceding two pages, which don't have much text on them. There are 23 children in the class, so the teacher decides to create two reading pairs who will chorally read their pages.

Before beginning, the teacher explains to the children how Pick a Page works. She tells the students that they are going to read a story, but that each reader is only going to know a small part of the story. First, they will practice reading their page with the others who have the same page until they can read it well. Next, they will form three groups to read the whole story and find out how their part fits into the whole.

The teacher then distributes the pages to the children. The pages have page numbers on them, and the teacher has written an A, B, or C on each. Once the children have their pages, she asks them to raise their hands if they have pages 17/18. Three children raise their hands, and she explains that they are the practice group for those pages. She then quickly asks the students who have pages 19/20, 21/22, 23/24, 25/26, 27/28, 29/30, and 30/31/32 to raise their hands.

> "Now, I am going to give you seven minutes to practice reading your page and to think of a good question to ask everyone once the whole story is read. First, I want all the A's to raise your hands—all the B's, and finally all the C's. When the time is up the A's will gather at the back table, the B's will gather on the rug, and the C's will gather in the computer area to read your story. First, I want you to practice your page using good partner-reading strategies so that you can read it well and with expression. You can read it chorally or echo read it, taking turns until you can all read it well. When you can all read it, think of a good question or two."

The children get into their practice groups. The teacher goes quickly over to the groups that have an extra child and explains that the numbers didn't work out exactly. She tells them that the two children with the same letter will join that group and read their page chorally. She then circulates around and makes sure that the students are practicing the page several times and that they are coaching and helping each other.

Next, the A, B, and C groups assemble. The teacher tells them to get in the proper order, according to page numbers, and to listen as each person reads his pages aloud. "When you finish, ask each other the good questions you thought of. You may not have time to ask them all, but ask as many as you can." As the children read, the teacher circulates and notices that all the children are paying unusually good attention. She realizes that no one knows how the story really goes, so they are all genuinely interested in listening to each other read!

Pick a Page is a nice change of pace variation for Guided Reading. It can be combined with many different before-and-after reading activities. Like all stories, children can do the Beach Ball or complete a story map. *A Chair for My Mother* has lots of characters, and children would enjoy pantomiming the book and adlibbing some of the lines as described in Chapter 11. Children often have strong feelings about the mother, the grandmother, and the fire in this story, and you may want them to write a response in their response journals comparing the lives of the people in the story to their own lives.

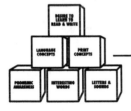

Building Blocks Variations

Pick a Page is not a strategy we would use with kindergartners.

Big Blocks Variations

Pick a Page is very popular with older children. They like having just one or two pages to practice, and they like the drama of reading their part to their classmates. Everyone usually listens well because they really want to know what happens on the pages they didn't read.

Pick a Page

Pick a Page is a fluency building activity. It is most successful if it is the first reading of a story—particularly a story with some interesting twists.

1. Choose a selection that your children will enjoy and that has enough pages.

2. Divide it into pages. If you can cut the story apart, children can read the page on the front and back. If not, it works best if they can read the two-page spread.

3. Let children know which page/pages they will read. If you are using a cut-apart story, write A, B, C, D. etc., on the page so they will know to which group they will read their page. If you are using an intact book, give children a strip with the page number and letter designation on it.

4. Have the children gather by page number and practice reading their pages. Enforce the "no peeking" rule!

5. Have the children gather by the letter of their group and let each child read his page(s) aloud.

CHAPTER 24

MUSICAL RIDDLES

Children love riddles. Musical Riddles is a way of involving the whole class in reading and solving riddles. By rereading their riddles to the other children and to find their partners, students are building fluency. Riddles help children learn to infer, and because many riddles are based on similar-sounding words, they help build meaning vocabulary.

To prepare for a Musical Riddles activity, find some riddles you think your children will enjoy and understand, and type them on one sheet of paper—answers first, then questions. Number the answers, but not the question. Include as many riddles as you have children. Cut the sheet apart into strips with one question or answer per strip. Then, give each of the children a strip and ask them to come join you if they have an "answer." (Talk about how they can tell if they are an answer or a question by looking at the punctuation.) The "answers" join hands to form a circle facing inside. Next, ask all the "questions" to stand back- to-back with someone in the inner circle, forming an outer circle that is facing out.

Next, play some music and have the circles march around in opposite directions. When the music stops, the children turn around and stand directly across from the nearest person in the other circle. When the children are clearly paired, the teacher signals a "question" person to read his question aloud and the "answer" person with whom he is paired to read the answer. The class decides if they are a match or not. If they are a match, the question and answer pair leave the circle and go somewhere to write and draw their riddle. Each person writes the question or the answer and then illustrates it. The music starts again and the children march around until the music stops, then turn around and find the nearest person in the other circle. The questions and answers are read, and more pairs should go off. The activity continues until all the children have found their mates and have had a few minutes to write and illustrate their riddles. Children who finish before the time is up are given a copy of the whole list of answers and questions and try to read and match them all. They write the number of the answer next to the matching question. Not everyone has time to match the questions and answers because this is the filler, but everyone gets a sheet with all the answers and questions. Their homework is to ask someone the riddles and find out what their family and friends thought were the best (and worst!) riddles. This is homework that is sure to get home! Here are 13 riddles—enough for a class of 26 children. If you have fewer children, pick your favorites. If you are unfortunate enough to have more than 26, you will have to hunt some more riddles.

Musical Riddles

1. A hot dog.
2. Any kind because a house can't jump.
3. Because he had too many problems.
4. Because he pulls off its ears.
5. Because he wanted to go to high school.
6. Because he wanted to grow mashed potatoes.
7. Because her students were so bright.
8. Because it is too far to walk.
9. Because they bring their own sheets.
10. Because they can catch flies.
11. Because they have so many fans.
12. Lunch and dinner.
13. Stop picking on me.

What did the apple tree say to the farmer?

What dog has no tail?

What kind of frog can jump higher than a house?

What two things can't you have for breakfast?

Why are rock musicians so cool?

Why are spiders good baseball players?

Why did the farmer stomp on his garden?

Why did the silly boy take a ladder to school?

Why did the teacher wear sunglasses in school?

Why do birds fly south in the winter?

Why doesn't the corn plant like the farmer?

Why is it easy to have ghosts spend the night?

Why was the boy crying when he was doing his math?

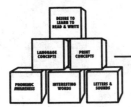

Building Blocks Variations

Musical Riddles is not a strategy we would use with kindergartners.

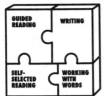

Big Blocks Variations

Intermediate-aged children love riddles—particularly the ones with plays on words. Do Musical Riddles with them once or twice and then send them on a riddle hunt—in newspapers, books and magazines. Choose some of their riddles for your next musical riddle day and credit the person who found the riddle by including his or her initials with each riddle. Be sure to send a riddle sheet home. This is homework that will get done!

Musical Riddles

Riddles help children infer and become sensitive to language. Rereading riddles builds fluency.

1. **Find some riddles your children will enjoy and type them on one sheet of paper—answers first, then questions. Number the answers, but not the questions.**

2. **Cut the sheet into strips and distribute one strip to each child.**

3. **Have students form two circles with "questions" as the outer circle and "answers" as the inner circle.**

4. **Play music and have the children move around, with the two circles going in opposite directions.**

5. **When the music stops, have the children closest to each other read their questions and answers.**

6. **When the children find their match, have them leave the circle and begin to write and illustrate their question or answer.**

7. **Continue the music until all riddles are matched.**

8. **Give the children a sheet of riddle questions and answers to match and take home.**

CHAPTER 25

BOOKMARKS, STICKY NOTES, AND HIGHLIGHTERS

When adults read, they often make notes on what they are reading. Some people write notes in the margins. Others turn down the corners of pages, and use pens or highlighters to mark what they found interesting. Some people fill their books with sticky notes, even using different colors to mark different kinds of things. Because "No writing in the book!" is a cardinal rule in schools, children are deprived of and don't learn how to use this valuable and natural comprehension strategy. Utilize bookmarks, sticky notes, and highlighters for reproduced text so that children can learn to mark what they want to remember, what they find interesting, or what is confusing to them. Children love bookmarks, sticky notes, and highlighters, and read their texts with more enthusiasm and purpose when they have one of these ways of marking text.

Bookmarks

When children are reading during Guided Reading, they always have a purpose for reading—something to find and think about and bring back to the after-reading activity. Bookmarks help them stay focused on this purpose and give them a "non-threatening" place to record their thoughts. There are as many different ways to use bookmarks as there are creative teachers to think of them. Here are just a few of the ways teachers use bookmarks. Once you start using them, you will think of lots more.

Some teachers make bookmarks to go with each of the before-and-after reading activities they use frequently. If they are going to do a story map or Beach Ball, children get a sheet of bookmarks to cut on the dotted lines. These bookmarks have abbreviated story maps or Beach Ball prompts. Children put them in the appropriate places in their book, and write a few words to remind them of what they want to say.

Main Characters	What happened?	Setting?	Favorite Part?

A similar sheet could be used when children are going to help complete a graphic organizer– web, data chart, time line, Venn diagram, or causal chain. Children write the spoke label, category, date, or other information along with a few words.

Bookmarks can be used to help children prepare for small-group discussions. When children are preparing for a Talking How and Why discussion, they might be given two bookmarks and asked to find places in the text which relate to two of the "how" or "why" questions. Children can write the one or two questions they choose on the bookmarks before they begin their reading. They use the bookmark to mark places in the text and to make a few notes.

Some artistic teachers give children bookmarks cut in the shape of what they are reading about or with a small picture related to what is being read. Other teachers use index cards, sometimes using different colors of cards to designate different things.

Regardless of how you use bookmarks, it is best to give children a limited number. Some teachers give students the number they think is appropriate and let the students come and get more if they have more ideas. Other teachers limit how many bookmarks students can have so that the children will have to be choosy about what they mark. Limiting the number of bookmarks in some way is an example of "reverse psychology." If students have too many, they will feel overwhelmed and not want to do the bookmarks. If you limit what they can have, they will ask for more!

Sticky Notes

Sticky notes serve the same function as bookmarks. They have the advantage of being able to be placed at the spot where children need them. Like bookmarks, sticky notes can be used by children reading alone, with partners, in a small group, or a whole class. Children use sticky notes to mark what they find interesting, important, or confusing. Sticky notes work particularly well when children have made predictions or begun a KWL or graphic organizer before reading. As children are reading and come to something that proves or disproves a prediction, or needs to be added to the KWL or graphic organizer, they write a word or phrase on the note and stick it next to where they found the information. During the follow-up, children can refer to their notes and sometimes read aloud the part that related to the prediction or gave them a particular piece of information.

Some teachers also use sticky notes to help children focus on their successful decoding. One teacher gives children two sticky notes as they get ready to read the selection. A blue sticky note is to be used for a word that was hard but that the child was able to figure out. The pink sticky note is to designate a hard word they couldn't figure out or for which they didn't know the meaning. The child writes the "successful" word or the "stumper" word on the appropriately-colored note and puts it next to the word. At the beginning of the after-reading activity, before beginning the comprehension purpose, the children quickly share their "successful" word and their "stumper." Successful decoding is applauded. The teacher agrees that they found some real "stumpers," and helps them figure out these words.

Just as with bookmarks, limit the number of sticky notes children have and don't give them sticky notes every day. "Do we get sticky notes today?" or "Can we have blue and pink sticky notes today to mark our successes and stumpers?" are pleas you love to hear, but don't give into their pleas every day!

Highlighters

When the selections the children are going to read are from a reproducible book or some text you have written and copied for them, give highlighters to the students. Highlighters, like sticky notes, can be used both for marking ideas for the comprehension discussion, and for marking "successful" words or "stumper" words. If you are going to use highlighters for all three purposes, introduce only one purpose at a time and designate a color system. You might begin with children having only yellow highlighters to mark information they want to share. When they are good at this, add a pink highlighter for a "successful" word and a blue highlighter for a "stumper." Partners can work together with one set of highlighters or each partner can have his own.

Another way to use highlighters is to give the children something to read—perhaps something they have already read for a comprehension purpose—and let them highlight all the Word Wall words they can find. Children love looking for these words, and since Word Wall words are high-frequency words, they will find lots of them! Some teachers give children a duplicated Word Wall with some reproduced text and a highlighter, and make the Word Wall search the homework assignment one night each week! The children delight in finding the words, and some children count how many they found and come back with their tally. Looking for these words in real text improves students' fluency with these words and reinforces the notion that Word Wall words are important because they are everywhere!

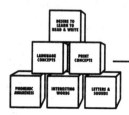

Building Blocks Variations

We would not use bookmarks, sticky notes, or highlighters with kindergartners.

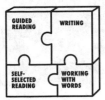

Big Blocks Variations

Big kids love bookmarks, sticky notes, and highlighters!

Bookmarks, Sticky Notes, and Highlighters

When adults read, they often mark things they want to go back to with bookmarks, sticky notes, or highlighters. Children read more purposefully when they use one of these marking methods.

1. Decide if students would read more purposefully if they could mark the text with a bookmark, sticky note, or highlighter.

2. Give them the bookmarks, sticky notes, or highlighters and make sure they know what they are going to mark with them.

3. Limit the number of bookmarks or sticky notes each child can have. It is better for them to use what they have and wish they had more than for them to wonder how they will ever use them all!

4. Use the bookmarks, sticky notes, or highlighted text to guide the after-reading activity.

5. Once children know how to use sticky notes and highlighters to note things they want to contribute to the after-reading activity, consider having the students occasionally use them for words they successfully decoded or any "stumpers."

PART FOUR
WHY DO GUIDED READING
THE FOUR-BLOCKS™ WAY?

This section gives a brief history of reading instruction over the past several decades and explains the reasons behind the development of the Four-Blocks™ Literacy Model. In this final chapter, we also discuss why we believe Guided Reading the Four-Blocks way can be used to provide effective reading instruction for all students.

CHAPTER 26

SUPPORT FOR GUIDED READING THE FOUR-BLOCKS™ WAY

Since the late 1930s when whole-class, phonics-oriented reading instruction was generally replaced with reading groups and basal readers, Guided Reading has been the mainstay of American reading instruction. Basal reading programs from the late '30s through the mid '80s were designed to be taught in small reading groups—three or four per classroom. The teaching plan followed a DRA—Directed Reading Activity (Betts, 1946) or DRTA—Directed Reading Thinking Activity (Stauffer, 1970) format. Most reading series provided Informal Reading Inventories to help teachers place children in the appropriate level of materials. They also provided worksheets and other independent activities and suggestions for managing the different groups in the classrooms. The instructional plan included prereading activities, silent and oral reading, and postreading activities. While the teacher carried out instruction with one group of children, the other children worked on independent activities at their seats or in centers. From the late '30s to the mid '80s, reading instruction in America generally consisted of Guided Reading in leveled reading groups using a basal reading series.

There were always, however, dissenting voices—researchers and teachers who adamantly believed that ability-grouped Guided Reading was not the best approach to reading. Competing approaches came and went—gaining popularity for awhile, but never replacing Guided Reading as the dominant approach. In the late '50s, for example, language experience, individualized reading, and various phonics approaches were relatively popular.

Language experience (Stauffer, 1970; Roach Van Allen,1966) was a "writing" approach to reading, done using dictation because we had not yet learned how to teach young children to write. In language experience classrooms, teacher spent their time taking dictation from individual children and helping them learn to read what they dictated. Language experience advocates believed children would be able to read their dictations since it was their own language, and they would understand it since it was their experience. Reading instruction in language experience classrooms looked very different from reading instruction in guided reading-basal reader classrooms. Teachers spent most of their time working with individual children. The children were not in leveled groups, and their reading material was their own writing.

Individualized reading (Veatch, 1959) advocates believed that the most successful way to teach children to read was to let them choose books they wanted to read and help them learn to read those books. Classrooms that used individualized reading as their approach to reading had huge classroom libraries and made good use of school and public libraries. If you visited a classroom using an individualized approach to reading, you would see children reading all different types of books and doing various response activities related to those books. Just as in language experience classrooms, the teacher would spend most of her time working with individual children rather than with groups. Teachers conferenced with children and taught skills as needed. Sometimes groups were formed if many children needed to work on a specific skill, but the majority of the teacher's time and energy was spent on individual instruction, and there were no "reading groups."

Both language experience and individualized reading were based on beliefs about the primacy of children's choice, experience, and engagement as motivating factors in learning to read. They were considered "child centered" approaches in contrast to basal readers, which were considered "materials and teacher centered."

Also in the "materials and teacher centered" approaches camp were the various phonics programs competing for the "best approach to reading" prize. There were many of these and the most widely used were probably the Spaulding Approach (Spaulding,1966), Economy's Phonetic Keys to Reading (1983) and ITA—Initial Teaching Alphabet (1964). In phonics classrooms, teachers spent most of their time not in leveled groups or with individual children, but teaching the whole class. Children were taught various sounds and letters, involved in numerous segmenting and blending drills, and then required to practice reading "decodable" texts containing the letter-sounds taught. Writing was also included, but children were writing not to express their ideas, but to use the sounds they were being taught by learning to spell specific words.

So, by the late '50s, we had in America a dominant approach—Guided Reading in leveled reading groups in basal readers—and three less common, but very vocal, approaches—language experience, individualized reading, and various phonics approaches. Guided Reading in leveled basal readers had the most advocates, but dissatisfaction with the results of this dominant method kept the search for alternatives going. All of these programs claimed to be best, but there was little data to back these claims.

In the early '60s, the federal government decided it was time to end the debate and determine the best approach to beginning reading. Studies were designed which compared the competing approaches, and researchers all over the country collaborated to collect data. Teachers and children in first and second grades around the country using various approaches to beginning reading were included in the research. Some teachers used basal readers and the different basals were compared. Some teachers used various phonics programs and these were compared. There were also classrooms using language experience and others using individualized reading programs—which the research called "literature" classrooms.

The results of this study were inconclusive. Some approaches did better in certain schools, but other approaches did better elsewhere. Virtually every approach had good results in one place and poor results in another. How well a teacher carried out the approach seemed to be the major determinant of how well an approach worked.

The finding that "the teacher—not the program—makes the difference" was the major finding of the first-grade studies. There was, however, another finding which was equally significant. When the researchers began to identify which approach was being used by which teacher, they discovered that some teachers were using more than one approach. They might be doing a basal program and language experience, or a phonics program and literature (individualized reading), or a phonics program and a basal. The researchers labeled these classrooms "combination approaches" and concluded that in general, combination approaches worked better than any single approach (Bond & Dykstra, 1967). Adams (1990) also concluded that children—especially at-risk children—need a rich variety of reading and writing experiences, as well as direct instruction in letter-sound patterns. This finding was confirmed in studies of exemplary primary-grade teachers (Wharton-McDonald, et al, 1997). The International Reading Association has recently issued a position statement in which it affirms the widespread support for multiple methods (IRA, 1999).

This quick history of beginning reading instruction in the last century has a lot to do with why we do Guided Reading the Four-Blocks™ way. Having watched hundreds of teachers and children, and having read the research, we became convinced that with so many smart, caring people holding so passionately to their competing views, there must be some truth in all the views. Our belief that there was no one best approach and that more children would learn to read if we provided them with daily instruction in all four competing approaches propelled us to devise Four-Blocks instruction as the '80s were ending. Our data from Four-Blocks schools around the country (Cunningham, Hall & Sigmon, 1999) and the data we are currently collecting have confirmed this belief.

Four-Blocks is a multimethod framework. The children receive instruction each day in the four competing approaches. Four-Blocks is also a multilevel framework. The teacher's role in making each block multilevel is critical.

The Working with Words Block is our phonics approach. The teacher works with the whole class to learn how to practice decoding and spelling words. During the Working with Words Block, teachers guide the daily activities to include both warm-ups and challenges.

The Self-Selected Reading Block is our individualized reading approach. The Writing Block is our Language Experience approach. (We have modified this so that the children do their own writing—rather than dictating to the teacher—by providing spelling support through our Word Wall and strategies for spelling unknown words. In doing so, we have merged the Language Experience approach with what we have learned about teaching writing over the past quarter century.) In both Self-Selected Reading and Writing, the teacher's role is to provide modeling through the daily teacher read-aloud and writing minilesson, and to conference with individual children. During these conferences, teachers make sure children are reading books on their level and provide tailored instruction to each child in the context of writing.

In the Guided Reading Block, the teacher teaches the comprehension skills and strategies by using a variety of before- and after-reading activities. During reading, the teacher works with children in a variety of formats—whole class, small groups, partners, individuals—depending on what is being read and how much support children need.

Our history of reading instruction took us to the mid '80s when "whole language" swept the country. Whole language is a philosophy of instruction, not an approach to reading, but during the whole language era, the approaches which were promoted were writing and individualized reading. Although whole language advocates insisted you couldn't put whole language in a basal, publishers of reading textbooks claimed to have done so. The leveled books of prior years became literature anthologies, filled with rich literature too hard for most children to read. Reading groups were replaced with whole class reading instruction which often meant that the teacher was the one doing the reading since the children couldn't. There was little phonics instruction, and teachers were told not to put children in reading groups. Basically, children were exposed to two approaches to reading during the whole language era. Many children successfully learned to read during this era, but many children didn't.

As we write this book, phonics and Guided Reading in leveled books are back! Many teachers do phonics instruction with the whole class, and then spend the rest of their time meeting with leveled groups while the other children spend their time doing independent reading and writing in centers. Other teachers spend all their time meeting with leveled groups, so that even phonics is being self-taught by the children.

When children do reading and writing independently in centers or at their desks, they are practicing reading, but they are not being taught through an individualized reading or writing approach. To be instructional approaches, the teacher must be interacting with the children, teaching them through modeling and conferencing. The writing and individualized reading approaches which consumed most of the teacher's time and energy in the previous decade have been replaced with phonics and reading groups. To the extent that phonics is being taught by workbooks, worksheets, and learning center activities, we also predict that many children will fail to learn how to decode unfamiliar words. We won't have the data for several years yet, but our predictions are that, just like in the last decade, many children will learn to read, but many others won't.

So, we do Guided Reading the Four-Blocks way because we believe that Guided Reading is only one approach to learning to read, and we want the teacher to devote equal time and energy to the other three approaches. We make our Guided Reading as multilevel as we can, but children are not always on the appropriate instructional level during Guided Reading. The teacher works with children during Self-Selected Reading and Writing, however, providing instruction that is "right on the mark" for all children. We stretch our Working with Words Block in both directions so that all children can profit from that approach.

Why do Guided Reading the Four-Blocks way? We do Guided Reading the Four-Blocks way because:

1. We can meet the goals of the Guided Reading Block in 40 minutes and still have time and energy to carry out instruction in the other three approaches.

2. We can focus on comprehension and include well-planned before- and after-reading activities each day because we are only planning one Guided Reading lesson, not three or four lessons for three or four groups.

3. We can select materials for children to read that tie-in with science and social studies themes and topics, and have a more integrated curriculum.

4. We can eliminate the "seatwork," worksheets, or center activities whose major function is to keep children "meaningfully occupied" while we work with groups.

5. We can coach children to use what we have taught them during Working With Words as we circulate during partner reading, playschool groups, and Book Club groups, and when working with coaching groups.

6. We can model and demonstrate how children can "coach" each other and increase the amount of coaching our struggling readers receive.

7. We can include all four instructional approaches every day in 120-135 minutes and still have time in our day for quality math, science, and social studies instruction, and even a little P. E., art, and music.

8. We can live up to our "mission statement" and provide reading instruction that honors the truth that "all children are individuals and do not learn in the same way."

9. We can avoid having the struggling readers seen by others and (unfortunately) themselves as the "dumb group."

10. We can make sure our advanced readers are not just "treading water" as we meet with them individually in reading and writing conferences.

CHILDREN'S BOOKS CITED

Amazing Fish by Mary Ling (Alfred A. Knopf, 1991, an Eyewitness Juniors book).

Amazing Frogs and Toads by Barry Clarke (Alfred A. Knopf, 1990).

Are You My Mother? By P. D. Eastman (Random House, 1988).

Arthur's Pet Business by Marc Brown (Little Brown, 1990).

Arturo's Baton by Syd Hoff (Clarion, 1995).

Aunt Flossie's Hats (and Crab Cakes Later) by Elizabeth Fitzgerald Howard (Clarion, 1991).

Bats by Gail Gibbons (Holiday House, 1999).

Beauty and the Beast by Annette Smith (Rigby, 1999).

Big Anthony: His Story by Tomie de Paola (Putnam Publishing Group, 1998).

The Boy Who Cried Wolf by Alan Trussell-Cullen (Dominie Press).

Brown Bear, Brown Bear, What Do You See? by Bill Martin, Jr. (Holt, Rinehart and Winston, 1970).

Cam Jansen and the Chocolate Fudge Mystery by David A. Adler (Puffin, 1993).

Caps for Sale: A Tale of a Peddler, Some Monkeys, and Their Monkey Business by Esphyr Slobodkina (HarperCollins Children's Books, 1975).

Caterpillar Diary by David Drew (Rigby, 1994).

Cats by Gail Gibbons (Holiday House, 1996).

A Chair for My Mother by Vera Williams (Greenwillow, 1984).

The Childhood of Famous Americans Series by various authors (Aladdin paperbacks by Simon & Shuster; publication dates vary).

China by Henry Pluckrose (Franklin Watts, 1999).

Clouds by Gail Saunders-Smith (Grolier Publishing, 1998).

Commander Toad in Space by Jane Yolen (Paper Star, 1993).

Danny and the Dinosaur by Syd Hoff (HarperCollins Children's Books,1993).

Days with Frog and Toad by Arnold Lobel (Harper, 1972).

Dogs by Gail Gibbons (Holiday House, 1996).

The Doorbell Rang by Pat Hutchins (Scholastic, 1986).

Ed Emberley's Drawing Book of Animals by Ed Emberley (Little, Brown & Co., 1994).

Egypt by Henry Pluckrose (Franklin Watts, 1999).

Enzo the Wonderfish by Cathy Wilcox (Ticknor and Fields Books, 1993).

The Foolish Fisherman by Beverley Randell (Rigby).

The Foot Book by Dr. Seuss (Random House, 1988).

France by Henry Pluckrose (Franklin Watts, 1998).

Frog and Toad Are Friends by Arnold Lobel (Harper, 1970).

Frog and Toad Together by Arnold Lobel (Harper, 1972).

Frogs by Kevin J. Holmes (Bridgestone Books, 1998).

Germany by Henry Pluckrose (Franklin Watts, 1998).

The Gingerbread Man by Eric A. Kimmel (Holiday House, 1994).

Goldilocks and the Three Bears retold by Jenny Giles (Rigby, 1999).

Grant Hill: Smooth As Silk by Mark Stewart (Children's Press, 1999).

Gulls by Gail Gibbons (Holiday House, 1997).

Harry Potter books by J.K. Rowling (Scholastic, Inc.; publication dates vary).

Hattie and the Fox by Mem Fox (Simon and Schuster, 1988).

Hop on Pop by Dr. Seuss (Random House, 1963).

How Spiders Got Eight Legs by Katherine Mead (Raintree Steck-Vaughn Publishers, 1998).

I Went Walking by Sue Williams (Harcourt Brace, 1990).

If You Give a Mouse a Cookie by Laura Joffe Numeroff (HarperCollins Children's Books, 1985).

India by Henry Pluckrose (Franklin Watts, 1999).

Is Your Mama a Llama? by Deborah Guarino (Scholastic, 1989).

Jamaica by Henry Pluckrose (Franklin Watts, 1999).

Japan by Henry Pluckrose (Franklin Watts, 1998).

Laura Ingalls Wilder: An Author's Story by Sarah Glasscock (Raintree Steck-Vaughn Publishers, 1998).

Lightning by Gail Saunders-Smith (Grolier Publishing, 1998).

The Lion and the Mouse by Alan Trussell-Cullen (Dominie Press).

Lisa Leslie: Queen of the Court by Mark Stewart (Children's Press, 1998).

The Little Red Hen by Paul Galdone (Houghton Mifflin, 1991)

A Look at Spiders by Jerald Halpern (Raintree Steck-Vaughn Publishers, 1998).

Love You Forever by Robert N. Munsch (Firefly Books Ltd., 1989).

The Magic School Bus and the Electric Field Trip by Joanna Cole (Scholastic, 1998).

The Magic School Bus at the Waterworks by Joanna Cole (Scholastic, 1990).

The Magic School Bus in the Time of the Dinosaurs by Joanna Cole (Scholastic, 1995).

The Magic School Bus on the Ocean Floor by Joanna Cole (Scholastic, 1994).

The Magic School Bus Inside a Hurricane by Joanna Cole (Scholastic, 1996).

The Magic School Bus Inside the Earth by Joanna Cole (Scholastic, 1989).

The Magic School Bus Inside the Human Body by Joanna Cole (Scholastic, 1990).

The Magic School Bus: Lost in the Solar System by Joanna Cole (Scholastic, 1990).

Mark McGwire: Home Run King by Mark Stewart (Children's Press, 1999).

Mia Hamm: Good As Gold by Mark Stewart (Children's Press, 1999).

The Miller Who Tried to Please Everyone by Alan Trussell-Cullen (Dominie Press).

Moonbear Likes Books by Frank Ashe (Houghton Mifflin, 1996).

Mrs. Wishy Washy by Joy Cowley (Wright Group, 1989).

Multicultural Plays by Judy Truesdell Mecca (Incentive Publications, 1999).

My Friend by Taro Gomi (Chronicle Books, 1990).

My Little Sister Ate One Hare by Bill Grossman (Crown, 1996).

My Prairie Summer by Sarah Glasscock (Raintree Steck-Vaughn Publishers, 1997).

One Fish, Two Fish, Red Fish, Blue Fish by Dr. Seuss (Random House, 1981).

One of Three by Angela Johnson (Orchard Books, 1991).

A Picture Book of Abraham Lincoln by David Adler (Holiday House, 1990).

A Picture Book of Jackie Robinson by David Adler (Holiday House, 1997).

A Picture Book of Martin Luther King, Jr. by David Adler (Holiday House, 1989).

A Picture Book of Rosa Parks by David Adler (Holiday House, 1993).

Rain by Gail Saunders-Smith (Grolier Publishing, 1998).

Robin Hood and the Silver Trophy retold by Jenny Giles (Rigby, 1999).

Rudolph the Red-Nosed Reindeer by Robert Lewis May (Applewood Books, 1994).

Sarah Morton's Day by Kate Walters (Scholastic, 1989).

Sea Turtles by Gail Gibbons (Holiday House, 1995).

Spain by Henry Pluckrose (Franklin Watts, 1999).

Stellaluna by Janell Cannon (Scholastic, 1993).

Sunshine by Gail Saunders-Smith (Grolier Publishing, 1998).

Ten Apples Up On Top by Dr. Seuss (Random House, 1961).

There's An Alligator Under My Bed by Mercer Mayer (E. P. Dutton, 1987).

Things I Like by Anthony Browne (Houghton Mifflin, 1996).

The Three Billy Goats Gruff retold by Annette Smith (Rigby, 1999).

Tornado Alert by Franklyn M. Branley (Harper Collins, 1988).

Town Mouse and Country Mouse retold by Annette Smith (Rigby, 1999).

The Very Greedy Dog by Alan Trussell-Cullen (Domine Press).

Wagon Wheels by Barbara Brenner (Harper, 1993).

Wolves by Gail Gibbons (Holiday House, 1994).

The Wonderful World of Plants by Judith Hodge and Mary Atkinson (Shortland, 1993).

REFERENCES

Adams, M. J. (1990). *Beginning to Read: Thinking and Learning About Print*. Cambridge, MA: M. I. T. Press.

Betts, E. A. (1946). *Foundations of Reading Instruction*. New York: American Book Co.

Bond, G. L., & Dykstra, R. (1967). "The Cooperative Research Program in First-Grade Reading Instruction." *Reading Research Quarterly*, 2, 5–142.

Calkins, L. M. (1994). *The Art of Teaching Writing*. Portsmouth, NH: Heinemann.

Carr, E. & Ogle, D. (1987). "KWL Plus: A Strategy for Comprehension and Summarization." *Journal of Reading*, 30, 626–631.

Cunningham, P. M & Allington, R. L (1999). *Classrooms That Work, 2nd ed.* New York: Addison, Wesley Longman.

Cunningham, P. M. & Hall, D. P. (1996). *Building Blocks: A Framework for Reading and Writing in Kindergartens That Work.* (Video) Clemmons, NC: Windward Productions.

Cunningham, P. M. & Hall, D. P. (1997) *Month-by-Month Phonics for First Grade*. Greensboro, NC: Carson-Dellosa.

Cunningham, P. M. & Hall, D. P. (1998). *Month-by-Month Phonics for Third Grade*. Greensboro, NC: Carson-Dellosa.

Cunningham, P. M. & Hall, D. P. (1999). *The Four Blocks: A Framework for Reading and Writing in Classrooms That Work.* (Video) Clemmons, NC: Windward Productions.

Cunningham, P. M., Hall, D. P. & Sigmon, C. M. (1999). *The Teacher's Guide to the Four-Blocks™.* Greensboro, NC: Carson-Dellosa.

Cunningham, P. M., Hall, D. P. & Defee, M. (1991). "Nonability Grouped, Multilevel Instruction: A Year in a First Grade Classroom." *Reading Teacher*, 44, 566–571.

Cunningham, P. M., Hall, D. P. & Defee, M. (1998). "Nonability Grouped, Multilevel Instruction: Eight Years Later." *Reading Teacher*, 51.

Cunningham, P. M., Moore, S. A., Cunningham, J. W. & Moore, D. W. (2000) *Teachers in Action*. New York: Addison, Wesley Longman.

Daniels, H. (1996) *Literature Circles*. Portsmouth, NH: Heinemann.

Fountas, I. & Pinnell, G. S. (1999) *Matching Books to Readers*. Portsmouth, NH: Heinemann.

Graves, D. H. (1995). *A Fresh Look at Writing*. Portsmouth, NH. Heinemann.

Hall, D. P. & Cunningham, P. M. (1997) *Month-by-Month Reading and Writing for Kindergarten*. Greensboro, NC: Carson-Dellosa.

Hall, D. P. & Cunningham, P. M. (1998) *Month-by-Month Phonics for Second Grade*. Greensboro, NC: Carson-Dellosa.

Hall, D. P. & Williams, E. (currently in production) *The Teacher's Guide to the Building Blocks*. Greensboro, NC: Carson-Dellosa.

Hall, D. P., Prevatte, C. & Cunningham, P. M. (1995) "Eliminating Ability Grouping and Reducing Failure in the Primary Grades." In Allington, R. L and Walmsley, S. (Eds.) *No Quick Fix*. Teachers College Press, 137–158.

International Reading Association (1999). *Using Multiple Methods of Beginning Reading Instruction: A Position Statement of the International Reading Association.* Newark, DE: International Reading Association.

Keene, E. O. & Zimmermann, S. (1997) *Mosaic of Thought.* Portsmouth, NH: Heinemann.

Moan, C. B. (1998) *Literature Circle Role Sheets.* Teaching and Learning Company.

Ogle, D. (1986). "KWL: A Teaching Model That Develops Active Reading of Expository Text." *The Reading Teacher*, 39, 564–570.

Pugliano-Martin, Carol. (1998). *25 Just Right Plays for Emergent Readers.* New York: Scholastic.

Pugliano-Martin, Carol. (1997). *Easy-to-Read Folk and Fairy Tale Plays.* New York: Scholastic.

Routman, R. (1995) *Transitions, 2nd ed.* Portsmouth, NH: Heinemann.

Sigmon, Cheryl. "Four Blocks Column" at *www.teachers.net*

Spaulding, Romalda Bishop (1966). *Spaulding Method* (a Teacher's Book). New York: Wm. Morrow & Co.

Stauffer. R. G. (1970) *The Language-Experience Approach to the Teaching of Reading.* New York: Harper Row.

Van Allen, R. V. & Allen, C. (1966). *Language Experiences in Reading: Teachers' Resource Book.* Chicago: Encyclopedia Brittanica Press.

Veatch, J. (1959). *Individualizing Your Reading Program.* NY: Putnam.

Vygotsky, L. S. (1978). *Mind in Society.* Cambridge, MA: Harvard University Press.

Wharton-McDonald, R.,Pressley, M.,Rankin, J.,Mistretta, J.,Yokoi, L., & Ettenberger, S. (1997). "Effective Primary-Grades Literacy Instruction–Balanced Literacy Instruction." *Reading Teacher*, 50, 518–521.

Additional References:

fourblocks mailrings at *teachers.net* and *www.readinglady.com*

ITA—Initial Teaching Alphabet (1964). Attributed to Dr. Albert Mazurkiewicz. New York: Initial Teaching Alphabet Foundation.

Phonetic Keys to Reading. (1983) The Economy Company. Oklahoma City, OK